D0385925

Mark Driscoll is one of the best thinkers and Bible teachers in the church today. He is also deeply spiritual and understands the work of the Holy Spirit from his own personal experience. Mark is a dear friend of mine, and there is no one I respect more than him as a theologian, pastor, Bible teacher, and true man of God. *Spirit-Filled Jesus* is a great book that will enlighten your understanding of Christ and enrich your spiritual life.

—JIMMY EVANS
FOUNDER AND CEO, MARRIAGETODAY
LEAD APOSTOLIC SENIOR PASTOR, GATEWAY CHURCH

When we think about what being Spirit-filled looks like, we probably think about the Book of Acts and the amazing work God did through the first Christians. But Mark reminds us that the perfect example of living by the power of the Holy Spirit was Jesus Himself. Whether he is teaching or writing, Mark has a gift for making the Bible understandable and accessible. I'm so glad he's written this book, and you need to check it out!

—GREG SURRATT
FOUNDING PASTOR, SEACOAST CHURCH
PRESIDENT, ASSOCIATION OF RELATED CHURCHES (ARC)

Sometimes we mistakenly rely on our own strength rather than realizing we have access to a power greater than our own, the same power that raised Jesus from the grave. In his book *Spirit-Filled Jesus*, Pastor Mark Driscoll challenges us to lean into the Holy Spirit when making decisions, resisting temptation, and overcoming the obstacles that are holding us back. This book will change the way you relate to people, endure suffering, and grow your faith.

—CRAIG GROESCHEL
PASTOR, LIFE.CHURCH
NEW YORK TIMES BEST-SELLING AUTHOR

The essential for living an abundant life is the ministry of the Holy Spirit within every believer. This life is the living presence and power of Jesus alive in us. Mark Driscoll describes this life in *Spirit-Filled Jesus* in a way that will enlighten your mind, energize your walk, and strengthen your witness. May this extraordinary book encourage and equip you to experience the fullness and freshness of the Jesus-filled life in your life every day.

—Jack Graham
Pastor, Prestonwood Baptist Church; Author; Two-Time
President, Southern Baptist Convention

Spirit-Filled Jesus is one of the most practical books on the power of the Holy Spirit at work in the life of a believer I've ever read. Mark Driscoll is truly a gifted communicator. Mark makes the complex simple. I would recommend this book to anyone, and I was blessed and touched reading it.

—Greg Laurie
Senior Pastor, Harvest Christian Fellowship; Author;
Harvest Crusades

If we want to know what God is like, we need to look at Jesus. If we want to know what a genuinely Spirit-filled life looks like, we also need to look at Jesus. His entire life and ministry were guided and empowered by the Spirit. He fulfilled His Father's will as led by the Spirit. He performed His miracles by the power of the Spirit. And He spoke truth as informed and prompted by the Spirit. In *Spirit-Filled Jesus*, Mark Driscoll cuts through the theological grids, personal speculations, and unfounded notions that so often cloud our understanding of the Spirit's work. You'll find this book to be theologically accurate, culturally relevant, personally challenging, and at times laugh-out-loud funny. I highly recommend it.

—Larry Osborne
Author and Pastor, North Coast Church

If you picked up this book in hopes of finding more, something wonderful has begun for you. More strength, more wisdom, more grace to endure and conquer—more of Jesus Christ! Not just *what* Jesus did but *how*! Thank God for giving my friend Mark Driscoll such a wonderful way with the Scriptures. Life-changing truth is at your fingertips in this incredible new book, *Spirit-Filled Jesus*.

—DR. JAMES MACDONALD
SENIOR PASTOR, HARVEST BIBLE CHAPEL; WALK IN THE WORD
MINISTRIES; AUTHOR, *ACT LIKE MEN* AND *VERTICAL CHURCH*

If you're not living by the power of the Holy Spirit, you're not living at all! Spirit-filled living is the only way God wants us to live. In Mark Driscoll's superb and accessible book you'll get a definitive primer on the most important subject there is.

—ERIC METAXAS
NEW YORK TIMES BEST-SELLING AUTHOR, *BONHOEFFER*,
MIRACLES, AND *IF YOU CAN KEEP IT*

This is classic Driscoll—deep and solid evangelical Bible teaching. Mark shows us not only how the Spirit empowered Jesus, in no-nonsense language, but also how the Spirit empowers our lives today as Christians. In fact, the Holy Spirit is so central—so essential—to our daily walk, I can't imagine a believer not benefiting from this compelling message.

—LES PARROTT, PHD
NEW YORK TIMES BEST-SELLING AUTHOR, *LOVE LIKE THAT: 5
RELATIONSHIP SECRETS FROM JESUS*

As a mental health expert, I am particularly interested in resources that build up the whole person and equip individuals to walk in strength and healing during extreme hardships and to find redemption in challenged relationships. You will find that *hope* in these pages, and encouragement for living a life of victory.

—GREGORY L. JANTZ, PHD, CEDS
FOUNDER, THE CENTER: A PLACE OF HOPE; THERAPIST; AUTHOR

From a biblical basis and out of his personal life-changing journey, Mark Driscoll has given us a readable, thoughtful, practical, and helpful book for any believer who seriously desires to be more like Jesus. His insights into the ministry of the Holy Spirit in the life of Jesus and every believer encourages and challenges us. You will want to dive into this work!

—Claude Thomas
President, C3 Global Network

Spirit-Filled Jesus comes from the pen of one of today's great Bible expositors. Mark's insights come from careful study of the Scriptures as well as a careful eye on our evolving culture. The next generation of believers will have to be of a different flavor with faith that will be contended for as well as courage lived out with no compromise. And yet the purpose of all truth is love, and that will come from the Spirit of God within us. If the light of the gospel is going to light up a new generation of faith, it will come from Christians who have a good handle on what it means to follow Jesus Christ. Mark has given a gift to the church in sharing how the power of Christ can permeate our lives.

—Darryl DelHousaye
President, Phoenix Seminary

Jesus didn't live, learn, love, and lead from self-help. He did it by the Spirit's help. Mark's book *Spirit-Filled Jesus* not only will increase your theological understanding but will also help you walk in the Spirit's power in every area of your life.

—John Lindell
Lead Pastor, James River Church

I have known Mark Driscoll from afar for years, but since he and his family moved to the Arizona desert, we have become friends. Mark has a great mind, a deep love for Jesus, and a passion for the Word of God. In *Spirit-Filled Jesus*, Mark weaves personal stories, insights from Scripture, quotes from authors, and practical wisdom into a tapestry of truth that is both compelling and enlightening. In this book Mark stays focused on life-giving truth. He avoids nonessential issues because of his commitment to producing healthy disciples of Jesus. I admire Mark's writing because it is inspired by the Holy Spirit and full of truth, which will be helpful to both experienced believers as well as those just starting to follow Jesus.

—Mark Buckley
Living Streams Church
Grace Association
Mark Buckley Ministries

In *Spirit-Filled Jesus*, Mark reminds us that the best way to understand the power of the Holy Spirit is to look deeply into the example given to us by Christ. Learning how Jesus lived the Spirit-filled life, you will discover God's power and presence through your own journey in life. Mark delivers a biblically dependable, expansive work that is sure to spark a fresh movement in your own life and in the church.

—Brandon Thomas
Senior Pastor, Keystone Church
President, Passionate Life Ministries

The Holy Spirit is one of the most neglected conversations in the church, especially the relationship the Spirit had with Jesus. The Bible is not nearly as silent. The Spirit birthed Jesus, baptized Jesus, guided Jesus, empowered Jesus, and raised Jesus from the dead. There's a lot to talk about, and Driscoll takes on the task. We've grown accustomed to Pastor Mark being forthright and biblical. The great delight of this book, however, is that it takes up a neglected conversation with the perspicuity of a pastoral voice. This book is as much about you as it is about Jesus and the Spirit. It gives insight into forgiveness, suffering, and dealing with difficult people. It is as much psychology as theology, as much self-help as Bible study. Our curiosity of the Spirit is rewarded with clarity in our relationships.

—Mark Moore
Teaching Pastor, Christ's Church of the Valley
Author, Professor at Ozark Christian and Hope
International University

Mark Driscoll has done a fantastic job capturing what it means to be deeply Holy Spirit–led. *Spirit-Filled Jesus* is a thorough, masterful, strategic account of Jesus living by the Spirit. It gives us clear, practical guidelines of how we can too, and it comes from an author who practices what he writes. Driscoll's study on the Holy Spirit's leading in relationships, family, suffering, and forgiveness brings surprising clarity to some previously not-so-clear topics. I'm buying this book for my family and friends.

—J. D. Pearring
Director, Excel Leadership Network

Because Jesus lived His life as a perfectly Spirit-filled man, He responded to the challenges of life through the power of the Spirit (Matt. 12:28; Luke 4:18–19; Acts 10:38) rather than by using His divine powers. That means His life is truly exemplary for ours. Like Jesus, we need and have the helper in us. Pastor Mark explores this amazing truth in a most helpful way in this most readable, engaging book. As you read, your understanding of Jesus, who is Emmanuel, will be deepened, and your life as a Jesus follower will be empowered.

—Gerry Breshears, PhD
Professor of Theology
Western Seminary, Portland, Oregon

Mark Driscoll has a unique handle on today's culture. His theological mastery and his keen understanding of current issues facing Christians today come together beautifully in *Spirit-Filled Jesus*. Jesus told His disciples that it was best for Him to go, so He could send His Holy Spirit. Learning to embrace the Holy Spirit in our daily lives is the fundamental aspect of Christianity we must all embrace to be successful. Through this book Mark shows us the way.

—Jimmy Witcher
Senior Pastor, Trinity Fellowship Church
Trinity Fellowship Association of Churches

As a fifth-generation pastor with spiritual roots deeply planted in the soil of classical Pentecostalism, I thought I had a fairly comprehensive view of the person, nature, and work of the Holy Spirit. But *Spirit-Filled Jesus* opened my eyes to a far deeper reality. Using pastoral wisdom and a remarkable ability to bring Scripture to life, Mark Driscoll shares unique insight into Jesus' relationship with the Holy Spirit and teaches us how to have the same. If you let it, this book will better position you to live a Spirit-empowered life.

—TERRY CRIST
LEAD PASTOR, HILLSONG CHURCH, PHOENIX

Spirit Filled Jesus will lead you to understand the role of the Holy Spirit in your life, and lead you to health and wholeness found only in Christ. The depth and understanding of *Spirit-Filled Jesus* will equip you for the battle you are in and help you discover Jesus like never before.

—BIL CORNELIUS
FOUNDING AND LEAD PASTOR, CHURCH UNLIMITED

Jesus Christ is the prototype for living the Spirit-filled life. That may sound radical, but it is a powerful reality that all four of the Gospels lay out for us. In his latest book, *Spirit-Filled Jesus*, Mark Driscoll dives deep into the relationship that Jesus had with the Holy Spirit and gives us practical insight into how we can follow in His footsteps. Read this book, wrestle with its message, and then live the Spirit-filled life like Jesus.

—LEE CUMMINGS
SENIOR PASTOR, RADIANT CHURCH
OVERSEER, RADIANT NETWORK OF CHURCHES

Pastor Mark Driscoll's book *Spirit-Filled Jesus* is a must-read for any Christian wanting to live a Spirit-filled life. Although the Bible says a lot about the Holy Spirit, for many, who the Holy Spirit is and what the Holy Spirit does remain a mystery of faith. Pastor Mark, a learned theologian and one of the most gifted communicators of our generation, drawing from deep scriptural truths and his own life experiences, explains in layman's language who the Holy Spirit is and how believers can experience the nature and power of God's Holy Spirit in their own lives.

—David Middlebrook
Cofounder, The Church Lawyers
Coauthor, Nonprofit Law for Religious Organizations

SPIRIT-FILLED JESUS

SPIRIT-FILLED JESUS

MARK DRISCOLL

CHARISMA
HOUSE

Most CHARISMA HOUSE BOOK GROUP products are available at special quantity discounts for bulk purchase for sales promotions, premiums, fund-raising, and educational needs. For details, write Charisma House Book Group, 600 Rinehart Road, Lake Mary, Florida 32746, or telephone (407) 333-0600.

SPIRIT-FILLED JESUS by Mark Driscoll
Published by Charisma House
Charisma Media/Charisma House Book Group
600 Rinehart Road
Lake Mary, Florida 32746
www.charismahouse.com

This book or parts thereof may not be reproduced in any form, stored in a retrieval system, or transmitted in any form by any means—electronic, mechanical, photocopy, recording, or otherwise—without prior written permission of the publisher, except as provided by United States of America copyright law.

Unless otherwise noted, all Scripture quotations are taken from the Holy Bible, English Standard Version. Copyright © 2001 by Crossway Bibles, a division of Good News Publishers. Used by permission.

Scripture quotations marked HCSB are taken from the Holman Christian Standard Bible®, Copyright © 1999, 2000, 2002, 2003, 2009 by Holman Bible Publishers. Used by permission. Holman Christian Standard Bible®, Holman CSB®, and HCSB® are federally registered trademarks of Holman Bible Publishers.

Scripture quotations marked NASB are from the New American Standard Bible, copyright © 1960, 1962, 1963, 1968, 1971, 1972, 1973, 1975, 1977, 1995 by The Lockman Foundation. Used by permission. (www.Lockman.org)

Scripture quotations marked NIV are taken from the Holy Bible, New International Version®, NIV®. Copyright © 1973, 1978, 1984, 2011 by Biblica, Inc.® Used by permission. All rights reserved worldwide. New International Version® and NIV® are registered trademarks of Biblica, Inc. Use of either trademark for the offering of goods or services requires the prior written consent of Biblica US, Inc.

Scripture quotations marked NKJV are taken from the New King James Version®. Copyright © 1982 by Thomas Nelson. Used by permission. All rights reserved.

Scripture quotations marked NLT are from the Holy Bible, New Living Translation, copyright © 1996, 2004, 2007. Used by permission of Tyndale House Publishers, Inc., Wheaton, IL 60189. All rights reserved.

Copyright © 2018 by Mark Driscoll
All rights reserved

Visit the author's websites at markdriscoll.org and spiritfilledjesus.com.

Library of Congress Cataloging-in-Publication Data:
Names: Driscoll, Mark, 1970- author.
Title: Spirit-filled Jesus : life by his power / Mark Driscoll.
Description: Lake Mary, FL : Charisma House, 2018. | Includes bibliographical
   references.
Identifiers: LCCN 2018029899 (print) | LCCN 2018034467 (ebook) | ISBN
   9781629995236 (ebook) | ISBN 9781629995229 (hardcover)
Subjects: LCSH: Jesus Christ. | Holy Spirit.
Classification: LCC BT205 (ebook) | LCC BT205 .D75 2018 (print) | DDC
   231/.3--dc23
LC record available at https://lccn.loc.gov/2018029899

The names and details of people in some stories have been changed, and any similarity to individuals known to readers is purely coincidental.

While the author has made every effort to provide accurate internet addresses at the time of publication, neither the publisher nor the author assumes any responsibility for errors or for changes that occur after publication. Further, the publisher does not have any control over and does not assume any responsibility for author or third-party websites or their content.

This publication is translated in Spanish under the title *Jesús lleno del Espíritu*, copyright © 2018 by Mark Driscoll, published by Casa Creación, a Charisma Media company. All rights reserved.

18 19 20 21 22 — 987654321
Printed in the United States of America

CONTENTS

FOREWORD

EVERY ONCE IN a while you get the opportunity to meet someone you admire. It's great at first, but then you get to know them and you end up feeling a little disappointed. Perhaps they don't live up to the expectation you had of them, or they aren't the person you had hoped they would be. I can tell you this was definitely *not* the case with Mark Driscoll.

Five years ago I received a phone call from Mark. He called to tell me about some of the pastors from his church who had just attended Gateway Conference, our church's annual conference for pastors and ministry leaders. They came home excited about how God had used the conference in their lives and shared with him about some of the new ideas they learned while here. He was calling to thank me, but he also wanted to connect with me in hopes of learning more.

I had listened to his messages and knew he was an anointed and gifted teacher, but I had never met him or talked to him personally. I was amazed that this man, whom God was using mightily, was still hungry to learn more and was striving to become a better pastor.

Some months later my wife, Debbie, and I had the privilege of meeting Mark and his wife, Grace, and getting to know them. I already thought highly of Mark from our phone conversations, but now that he and Grace were in our home, sitting down and talking with us, I was even more impressed. It was evident that they were the real deal. Now, years later, Debbie and I consider them to be close personal friends, and we love them dearly.

I am honored to walk with Mark as a friend and a co-laborer in the kingdom. I also have the privilege of serving as one of the overseers of The Trinity Church in Scottsdale, Arizona, where he is the founding senior pastor. I've been extremely impressed with his love for the Lord, his love for his family, and his desire to serve the Lord in all he does. He is a great man of God, a man of integrity, and a man of character.

Mark is also uniquely gifted to teach God's Word. He is one of those individuals who can teach on a passage of Scripture and pull out treasures and nuggets I've never seen. Sometimes when he's preaching, I'll think, "I've read that passage a hundred times and never saw that! How did I miss it?"

And that's exactly what you'll find when you read this book. Suddenly the Word of God will come alive in a whole new way as Mark points out something you've never seen before and brings new revelation to what it means to experience a Spirit-filled life.

Most people know the Holy Spirit is *our* helper, but they don't often realize He also helped Jesus. When Jesus was on the earth in human form, He resisted temptation, endured suffering, and over-came Satan all by the power of the Holy Spirit. If Jesus needed the power of the Holy Spirit, then how much more do we? He is our model for walking out a Spirit-filled life and living victoriously.

Perhaps you're like me and you grew up in a church that treated the Holy Spirit like the crazy uncle you have to endure at family gatherings. Maybe you witnessed some abuse of the Holy Spirit and His gifts. Or maybe you're a new Christian and don't know much about Him. No matter what your background is, I want you to know that the Holy Spirit desires to have a relationship with you like the one He has with Jesus. It's my hope that as you read this book, you'll come to know Him in a whole new way and under-stand how victorious the Christian life can be when you have a rela-tionship with Him.

I'm so excited for you to begin this journey. I pray you will open your heart and mind to the Holy Spirit as you begin to see Him for who He really is and gain a deeper understanding of what it means to experience an increase of His presence and power in your life. Once you begin walking in relationship with the Holy Spirit and experiencing the same source of life-giving power that Jesus did, you will never be the same.

—Robert Morris
Founding Senior Pastor, Gateway Church
Best-Selling Author, *The Blessed Life*, *The God I Never Knew*,
and *Frequency*

TWO YEARS LATER...

You will receive power when the
Holy Spirit has come upon you.[1]
—Jesus Christ

VIEW MY BIBLE the same way a person on a capsized ship adrift in the ocean swimming for his life views a life preserver. Without my Bible, I'd be drowned, done, and doomed.

I have numerous Bibles, but one of them in particular is my prized possession. When I was eighteen in 1989, a pastor's daughter I was smitten with gave me my first Bible. She even had my name embossed on the front. (Eventually I bought her a ring, so for any single guys reading this, the moral of the story is: if a nice Christian girl buys you a Bible, you should buy her a ring!) I took that Bible to college with me, started reading it out of curiosity, and became a Christian simply through Bible reading—something I had not done much before. I then found a great church that helped me further learn the Bible.

At a Bible study class I brought my Bible and a big book on systematic theology. I asked my pastor if the theology book was a good one. He pointed at my Bible and asked if I'd read all of it yet. I told him I had not. He took the theology text out of my hand. It was like a stickup without a gun. My wise pastor then told me I needed to read the entire Bible before I read anything else.

I went home and started reading my Bible. I read the whole Bible in a short time—weeks or maybe months. I went back to my pastor to report my finished assignment, fully expecting him to tell me to start reading the theology text. Instead, he told me I needed to read a short book in my Bible, to study it until I had committed much of it to memory and could explain it from my heart, and to continue this process until I died. That's what I've been doing ever since.

I've also been doing four other things I was instructed to do early in my Christian walk. At the time, I had barely started going to church, and I impulsively signed up for a men's retreat, a first for me. On a crisp weekend a group of us drove toward the Washington/Idaho border, stopping at a camp set amidst a rugged landscape of big mountains and rocks.

Being a city kid, this was not the kind of place or crowd where I usually hung out. There was nothing for miles and miles, and the bearded brothers got together to study and sing. They belted out old hymns as if they meant them. Toward the end of a meeting the pastor announced, "I want each of you to schedule some time with God just to talk to Him."

"A meeting with God?" I thought. "OK. I don't know what that means." I just decided to go for a walk.

A big river flowed through the camp, splitting the trees and creating a beautiful sound as the water rushed over rocks raging with whitecaps. I walked upstream alongside the river, enjoying the quiet and sun and raw beauty. I hiked out and back for maybe an hour, talking to God conversationally. "God—it's like—well—I'm supposed to schedule a meeting with You." I talked out loud. I didn't know if that was a good idea. I didn't know how to do this. "So it's me—Mark—and You know—I—um—what do You want me to do now that I'm a Christian?" After a pause I added something like, "I'll do whatever You want."

I waited all by myself.

And God spoke to me audibly.

He said, "Marry Grace, preach the Bible, train men, and plant churches."

God had just told me to do four things, but honestly I had no idea what any of it meant. I had just met Jesus. Grace and I weren't engaged. I didn't really know what pastors did since I grew up Catholic and the only pastor I knew was our priest, a poor virgin who lived at the church and walked around in a bathrobe (or at least that's what I thought as a kid). I hoped maybe there was another kind of pastor.

Imagine where you were at nineteen, just trying to figure out what comes next. I wasn't sure what God had in store, but it sounded like an adventure. I just wanted to obey God—whatever that meant.

> As I worked through each line of Luke's terrific testimony about Jesus, an unexpected theme kept appearing. Page after page talked about the ways the Holy Spirit saturated Jesus Christ's earthly life.

I married Grace in college in 1992, and today we have five kids who all love and serve Jesus. I started preaching out of my Bible and have been preaching ever since.

PREACHING THE WORD

Through the years I've stuck with those early instructions from God and the advice of my first pastor. As a general rule I preach through books of the Bible verse by verse for about an hour each sermon.

In my late thirties I preached the longest sermon series I have ever preached when I taught on the Gospel of Luke.[2] It took me roughly two years to preach that book to an audience comprised largely of college-educated singles who attended late night services because they had a hard time getting up by the crack of dinner. As I worked through each line of Luke's terrific testimony about Jesus, an unexpected theme kept appearing. Page after page talked about the ways the Holy Spirit saturated Jesus Christ's earthly life. By this time, as a bit of a nerd, I had amassed a large library and had completed (or nearly completed) my master's degree in what is basically Bible. But I could find very little written on this theme I found in Luke.

Curious to see what others might think about my discovery, I taught a breakout session on the Spirit-filled life of Jesus Christ at a conference for a group called the Gospel Coalition. It sparked some positive and some negative responses, which were both helpful.

Here's the bottom line of what I discovered: Dr. Luke contributes more content to the New Testament than anyone else.[3] He writes a historical book in two parts with the Book of Luke recording the Spirit-filled life of Jesus and the Book of Acts recording the Spirit-filled life of Jesus' people. His books are written in chronological order as he is "the Indiana Jones of the New Testament" on the hunt to track down the facts about Christ and Christianity.

Sir William Ramsay, former professor of classical art at Oxford University, at one time vehemently opposed the idea of Luke being considered an accurate historian. But after undertaking his archaeological research in Asia Minor, Professor Ramsay changed his position.

> Luke is an historian of the first rank; not merely are his statements of fact trustworthy; he is possessed of the true historical sense; he fixes his mind on the idea and plan that rules in the evolution of history; and proportions the scale of his treatment of the importance of each incident. He seizes the important and critical events and shows their true nature at greater length, while he touches lightly or omits entirely much that was valueless for his purpose. In short, this author should be placed along with the very greatest of historians.[4]

In his first book Luke records how the Holy Spirit descended upon Jesus at His baptism and empowered His entire life and ministry as perfectly Spirit-filled. In his second book Luke records how the Holy Spirit then descended upon the people of Jesus at

Pentecost and empowered them for Spirit-filled life and ministry as Christ lived through them. To rightly understand the Holy Spirit and the Christian life in Acts requires first learning about the Holy Spirit in the life of Christ in Luke. If we only pick up Acts, it is similar to watching the second half of a two-part movie and trying to understand the story line of the sequel without watching the prequel.

The entire point of this book is to help you think deeply about the Spirit-filled life of Jesus so that you can then live by His power. The order is crucial and biblical—first, think about Jesus and then, think about you. This insight from Luke has changed my life, family, and ministry, and I know it will do the same for you if you submit to the Spirit as we walk through the Scriptures.

> To rightly understand the Holy Spirit and the Christian life in Acts requires first learning about the Holy Spirit in the life of Christ in Luke.

A PERSONAL RELATIONSHIP WITH THE HOLY SPIRIT

It is common for Christians to speak about having a personal relationship with Jesus Christ. As a Bible-believing pastor, I absolutely encourage this for people.

Jesus, however, lived His life by a personal relationship with the Holy Spirit. In the rest of this book we will examine together how Jesus was anointed by the Spirit, baptized by the Spirit, filled with the Spirit, led by the Spirit, and more. You'll come to realize that when Jesus needed help, He went to the Helper. The Holy Spirit is our helper and so much more.

- As God's person, the Holy Spirit is fully God and the third member of the Trinity.

- As God's presence, the Holy Spirit is God with us.

- As God's power, the Holy Spirit empowered the life of Jesus Christ and also empowers the life of believers.

If you're a Christian, you already know you have a personal relationship with Jesus. I now invite you to have a personal relationship with the Holy Spirit just as Jesus did.

As I close this introduction, I'd like to share a story from my upbringing. My Catholic union worker dad fed our family of seven by doing hard labor in construction. I started visiting the job site with my dad as a little boy. At an early age, wearing overalls, boots, and a hard hat, I learned that the integrity of anything you build is contingent on first pouring a strong foundation.

As a Bible teacher I noticed the same thing in reading the apostle Paul. In books like Ephesians and Colossians he spends the first part of his book laying a theological foundation. In the ensuing chapters he then builds upon that foundation with very practical applications of the foundational truths in such areas as faith, family, and forgiveness.

In this book I am following that same pattern. Admittedly the next chapter might seem a bit dense, thick, and technical. Hang in there with me as I pour some theological concrete. Once I lay the foundation, you can then begin to build your life as a home in which the Holy Spirit lives with you as He does with Jesus.

Chapter 1

SPIRIT-FILLED JESUS

You think too much about yourself.
You don't think about Jesus enough.
That is the one problem that makes all your problems worse.

SURE, YOU HAVE faults, flaws, and failures. Sure, you have pains, plans, and problems. But thinking more and more about you and then picking up a self-help book isn't going to help. Why? Because self-help is no help. The best thing for you to do is first think more and more about Jesus and pick up a book that helps you learn about Spirit-help. Spirit-help is serious help. The Holy Spirit helped Jesus and wants to help you.

I'm not trying to bum you out, but I need to get honest before I can build you up.

Let's just get to the bottom line of your life—what keeps you awake at night, causes you stress during the day, and floods your mind before your feet hit the floor in the morning? Most of the time you are thinking about you, right? Then you go to church for an hour a few times a month and get frustrated with God because it doesn't seem as if He's doing enough to help you. Meanwhile, the worship leader sings about His goodness, the preacher reminds you of His promises, and you go home wondering what you are missing.

Where are you turning for hope, help, or healing?

Have you ever examined your life in light of these questions: How did Jesus Christ live His life and leave His legacy? If Jesus were living my life, what would He be doing and how would He be doing it? That's the key that unlocks the rest of your life. I don't

1

want you to live your life for Christ. I want Christ to live His life through you! When Jesus needed help, He went to the helper. You need to do the same.

We will think about you in a bit. But first, let's think about Jesus.

The story of Jesus starts rather humbly and quietly with nearly no resources or riches. I've been to His hometown of Nazareth, and it is not impressive. The town reportedly had only one well for its water source, which meant the population it could sustain would have been perhaps somewhere between a few dozen and a few hundred people. His childhood home was likely about the same size as a parking space for an automobile. He was born into a poor, rural, peasant family to parents who were likely teenagers. He never married. He never traveled more than a few hundred miles from home. He never went to college. He never owned a company or made much money. He never wrote a book. He never owned a house. He never held a political office. He never fought in a war. He spent roughly 90 percent of His life in obscurity doing construction with His dad. His three years of public ministry included lots of harassment, constant slander, and vicious attacks trying to wrongly paint Him as a demon-possessed alcoholic whose mother had enjoyed so many men that His paternity remained a mystery.

For someone with no electricity, no media, no social media, no public relations firm, no offspring, no money, no power, no soldiers, no business card, no Twitter account, and no office, Jesus Christ has somehow become the most towering figure in all of human history. He accomplished this feat in three short years of itinerant ministry, walking around and preaching mainly to rural folks, including illiterate peasants, without the benefit of live internet streaming. H. G. Wells, a historian who was not a Christian, said, "No man can write a history of the human race without giving first and foremost place to the penniless teacher of Nazareth."[1]

JESUS' IMPACT ON THE ARTS

The Bible, which records Jesus' teaching and life, is the best-selling book in the history of the world. Furthermore, it is the most translated book in the history of the world because Christianity has always been about educating people and translating documents into languages that people can read for themselves.

A Christian, Johannes Gutenberg, invented the printing press, and the Bible was the first book widely published. More books have been written about Jesus than anyone who has ever lived. In the world of literature undeniable influence of the Christian faith appears in the works of Dante, Chaucer, Donne, Dostoevsky, Bunyan, Milton, Dickens, Hans Christian Andersen, Tolstoy, T. S. Eliot, C. S. Lewis, Tolkien, Sayers, and Solzhenitsyn.

In the world of the arts Michelangelo, Raphael, and Leonardo da Vinci were inspired by Christian faith and depicted Jesus in some of their work. Cathedrals and churches around the world have been beautifully built in His honor.

In the world of music Bach, Handel, and Vivaldi claimed to be worshippers of Jesus. Today an entire genre of worship music devoted to Jesus fills airwaves, stadiums, and churches with people singing about Him and singing to Him.

Pop-culture references to Jesus appear in everything from movies to television shows. His face shows up frequently on everything from T-shirts to stickers. His cross may also be the most popular form of jewelry, worn by everyone from modest holy nuns to immodest Hollywood divas. Historian Philip Schaff said, "He has set more pens in motion and furnished themes for more sermons, orations, discussions, works of art, learned volumes, and sweet songs of praise than the whole army of great men of ancient and modern times."[2]

JESUS' IMPACT ON DIGNITY

No one has inspired more good than Jesus. Since the decree went forth at the First Council of Nicaea in AD 325 that hospitals were to be opened to care for the body wherever churches were opened to care for the soul, Christians have been about caring. For this reason, we have the Red Cross founded by the Christian Henri Dunant and hospitals with Christian affiliations such as Baptist, Presbyterian, and Catholic.

In a day when women were mostly illiterate and considered the property of their husbands, Jesus turned the world upside down by having a friendship with sisters Mary and Martha, forgiving and teaching Mary Magdalene and the Samaritan woman at the well, and including women in His inner circle of disciples. Women were also the first to find His tomb empty.

Since Jesus was technically adopted by Joseph and grew up to care for the widow, orphan, and outcast, Christians have always had a heart for the poor and powerless. Historian and member of the American Antiquarian Society W. E. H. Lecky said, "The character of Jesus has not only been the highest pattern of virtue, but the strongest incentive in its practice, and has exerted so deep an influence, that it may be truly said that the simple record of three years of active life has done more to regenerate and to soften mankind than all the disquisitions of philosophers and all the exhortations of moralists."[3]

Jesus' Impact on History

Jesus looms so largely over history that we measure historical time in the context of His life. BC refers to the time "before Christ," and AD (*anno Domini*) means "in the year of the Lord." Our biggest holidays are dedicated to Him as we celebrate His birth every Christmas and resurrection every Easter.

Nations, causes, and leaders have come and gone. But for more than two thousand years the church of Jesus Christ has spread from one nation to the nations, from the language of Hebrew to thousands of languages, and from one generation to generation after generation. Christianity ranks as the most popular religion and largest and longest-standing movement of any kind in the history of the planet with more than two billion people today claiming to be followers of Jesus Christ.

Napoleon Bonaparte admitted that Jesus greatly surpassed his own conquests saying, "I know men; and I tell you that Jesus Christ is not a man. Superficial minds see a resemblance between Christ and the founders of empires, and the gods of other religions. That resemblance does not exist. There is between Christianity and whatever other religions the distance of infinity....His religion is a revelation from an intelligence which certainly is not that of man....Alexander, Caesar, Charlemagne, and myself founded empires; but upon what foundation did we rest the creations of our genius? Upon force! But Jesus Christ founded His upon love; and at this hour millions of men would die for Him."[4]

Most religions center on a holy place that serves as their headquarters. Christianity centers on a holy Person who serves as our head. Approaching the new millennium, *Newsweek* ran a cover story that said, "By any secular standard, Jesus is also the dominant figure of Western culture. Like the millennium itself, much of what we now think of as Western ideas, inventions and values finds its source or inspiration in the religion that worships God in his name. Art and science, the self and society, politics and economics, marriage and the family, right and wrong, body and soul—all have been touched and often radically transformed by the Christian influence."[5]

Surveying the record of human life on the planet, perhaps historian Kenneth Scott Latourette has said it best, "Jesus is the most influential life ever lived on this planet."[6]

FIVE FALSE CONCEPTS OF CHRIST

When someone does something incredible, we want to learn from them. This explains why we study in detail the lives of great leaders, warriors, athletes, and musicians. It's why we write biographies and record histories. Discovering how someone made a world-changing impact helps us learn their lessons and emulate their example.

Since Jesus is the most important and impactful person in the history of the world, it is not surprising that there is no shortage of speculation about the secret to His success. Needless to say, two thousand years of theorizing has led to many misconceptions about Jesus. For the sake of brevity, we will consider five popular false concepts about Christ.

1. Jesus was an alien.

This view has grown increasingly popular among non-Christians and the theme of a number of documentary-type television shows on networks such as the History Channel. When we think of an alien, we tend to think of the monsters created in science rather than someone like Superman. Consider for a moment the similarities between Jesus Christ and Superman.

- Both are sent to earth by their fathers from other places.

- Both were raised by poor parents in rural areas.

- Neither started to publicize their powers until they were around thirty years of age.

- Both appeared to be ordinary people in every way if you simply saw them going about their business as a carpenter or news reporter respectively.

- Both had exemplary character devoted to truth and justice.

- Both helped people in need by endangering their own lives.

- Neither married.

- Neither fathered children.

- Both brought people back from death.

- Both came back from death themselves.

- Both saved the people of earth.

Of course, Superman is fictitious whereas Jesus actually walked the earth. If they even exist, aliens are not God, and so Jesus was not an alien if the Bible is to be believed. Jesus was opposed and ultimately killed for repeatedly, emphatically, and publicly saying He was God, not an alien.

In John 10:33 the religious leaders sought to kill Jesus "for blasphemy, because you, a mere man, claim to be God" (NIV). Mark 14:61–64 (NIV) says:

> The high priest asked him, "Are you the Messiah, the Son of the Blessed One?"
>
> "I am," said Jesus. "And you will see the Son of Man sitting at the right hand of the Mighty One and coming on the clouds of heaven."
>
> The high priest tore his clothes. "Why do we need any more witnesses?" he asked. "You have heard the blasphemy."

Jesus used the title "Son of Man"—taken from Daniel 7 where God comes to earth as a man—some seventy times. When the religious leaders heard this, they rightly understood Jesus to be saying He was God come from heaven and not an alien visiting from another planet.

Christianity stands alone among the major religions in claiming its founder to be God. Jesus suffered and died for saying He was God, and never intimated that He was an alien or created being from another planet but rather the Creator God who made all the planets and beings.

2. Jesus was an angel.

The group known since 1931 as the Jehovah's Witnesses began with C. T. Russell as the Zion's Watch Tower Tract Society. They teach that Jesus Christ and the archangel Michael are in fact the same being, created billions of years ago by Jehovah God before other beings and then aiding in the rest of creation. Importantly they do not see Jesus as God Almighty.

One theologian says, "Jehovah's Witnesses believe that when Jesus Christ was alive in the flesh He was simply and solely a human being—no more, and no less. From the first Russell [a founder] had dismissed the idea of two natures in the one Christ. Jesus was not 'a combination of two natures, human and spiritual' for such a 'blending' would produce 'neither the one nor the other, but an imperfect hybrid thing, which is obnoxious to the divine arrangement.' That being so, 'when Jesus was in the flesh, he was a perfect human being; previous to that time, he was a perfect spiritual being; and since his resurrection he is a perfect spiritual being.'"[7]

Jesus denied this view. In Luke 24:36–40, following His resurrection, we read that Jesus, "stood among them, and said to them, 'Peace to you!' But they were startled and frightened and thought they saw a spirit [or angel]. And he said to them…'See my hands and my feet, that it is I myself. Touch me, and see. For a spirit does not have flesh and bones as you see that I have.' And when he had said this, he showed them his hands and his feet." Then Jesus had breakfast, hugged His friends, and showed doubters the scars in His hands and side, which are things that an angelic being without a physical body cannot do.

3. Jesus was a good guy but not the God Guy.

This is perhaps the most popular false concept of Christ—not as the God-man but rather just a good man. This view emphasizes the compelling works of Jesus much more than His controversial words about being God. This view recasts Jesus as merely a great humanitarian who loved people, fed the poor, fought for justice, cared for children, empowered women, and exemplified tolerance, inclusiveness, and kindness.

Most if not all major world religions recognize Jesus as a good man and moral example but not God. Some liberal or progressive "Christians" would also hold a similar view of Jesus as the best mere mortal who has ever lived but little more. This would include the presentation of Jesus in *The Da Vinci Code* as a very typical man who marries, lives an ordinary life, and little more.

Jesus denied this false concept. In Luke 18:18 a ruler called Jesus "Good Teacher." To which Jesus replied, "Why do you call me good? No one is good except God alone" (v. 19). Jesus did not allow anyone to call Him good unless they also call Him God.

4. Jesus was a man who became a god.

There are multiple streams of teaching that present Jesus as a mere man who moved up the ladder to the status of deity. This includes an early church heresy called adoptionism. This false teaching said that Jesus was merely a man who was given supernatural powers at the time of His baptism and later raised from death and adopted into the Godhead as the Son of God. Adoptionism sadly continues in a variety of forms.

In New Spirituality (or New Age) teaching Jesus was a man who ascended to a higher level of consciousness and became more integrated with the spiritual life force that runs through all things. As a result, He achieved a higher plane of being and divine status.

Regarding Mormonism, we are told, "Perhaps the most widely divergent teaching from that of orthodox Christianity is the Mormon belief that God and the plurality of gods were men before they were gods. One of the often-quoted statements to this effect...was made by Joseph Smith: "God himself was once as we are now, and is an exalted man, and sits enthroned in yonder heavens!...He was once a man like us...God himself, the Father of us all, dwelt on an earth."[8]

We go on to learn, "For Mormonism, the eternality of God means a prehuman spiritual existence followed by a period of probation in a physical body, and then evolution to a status of godhood once again. The thrust of this idea is that humankind itself is destined to become a god. The widely quoted epigram articulated by Lorenzo Snow, the fifth president of the church, captures this curious and paradoxical equation: 'As man is, God once was; as God is, man may become.' Numerous other statements by Mormon theologians confirm this teaching."[9]

These evolutionary concepts, in effect, see humanity as moving up the spiritual ladder toward godlike status. Satan first used this temptation when he told Adam and Eve, "You will be like God" (Gen. 3:5). The truth is not that we go up a ladder of good works or consciousness to godlike status, but that God in Jesus Christ humbly came down to be with us as prefigured in Jacob's ladder in Genesis. In a world of people fighting to climb the ladder, Jesus, who was at the top, humbly came down.

Jesus Himself says precisely this in John 6:38–42, "'I have come down from heaven, not to do my own will but the will of him who sent me...' [They] grumbled about him, because he said, 'I am the bread that came down from heaven.' They said, 'Is not this Jesus, the son of Joseph, whose father and mother we know? How does he now say, "I have come down from heaven"?'" Jesus clearly said that He was not a man from earth who became a god, but rather God who came down from heaven to earth by becoming a man.

5. Jesus continually lived out of His deity.

Maybe Jesus lived the sinless and perfect life because He was God, and God does things that we cannot? Many people think Jesus avoided sin, defeated the demonic, and walked in spiritual authority this way. But since we are not God, we cannot do those kinds of things. In this line of thinking Jesus is God but not really human.

People holding this view commonly struggle with Jesus' humanity and such things as using the bathroom. For some people, this kind of earthiness seems to border on irreverence.

This thinking stretches all the way back to the ancient Greeks who believed our material body was corrupt, but our immaterial soul was not. The goal was to liberate the soul from the body at death. This led to gnostic thinking, which many believe an entire book of the Bible called 1 John was largely written to combat—repeatedly saying things like, "By this you know the Spirit of God: every spirit that confesses that Jesus Christ has come in the flesh is from God, and every spirit that does not confess Jesus is not from God" (1 John 4:2–3).

The art world commonly overemphasizes Jesus as God and underemphasizes Jesus as human. Who among us has not, after all, seen a painting of Jesus as a baby or grown man with an angelic nuclear glow around Him and halo hovering over His head?

Some of the earliest films made about Jesus also contribute to the overemphasis on Him as God but not man. The History Channel's two-hour documentary titled *The Passion: Religion and the Movies* unfolds the tension between Jesus' humanity and divinity for Christian filmmakers.

Jesus has been portrayed in movies since the silent era, and in 1927 Christian film director Cecil B. DeMille produced the silent Jesus movie *The King of Kings*. That film cautiously portrayed Jesus more as an icon than a man, complete with a glowing aura around Him. This trend continued all the way up until 1965 with George Stevens' Jesus movie *The Greatest Story Ever Told*.

Movies about Jesus are important because they greatly shape the way people view Him. Until the cultural revolution of the 1960s, perhaps every film with a character playing Jesus emphasized His deity over His humanity. This helped to create a strong trend for people to see Jesus as God more easily than to see Jesus as man.

THE HOLY SPIRIT TIES THE JESUS KNOT

Do you remember learning how to tie your shoe as a child? At first, it seemed impossible to pull both laces together so that they were the same length and came together securely, but after a lot of practice, you eventually figured out how to do it.

Learning about Jesus is the same as learning to tie your shoe. The two proverbial laces are the divinity of Jesus as fully God and the humanity of Jesus as fully man. Pulling both of these laces together has eluded many and created a variety of knotty false teachings.

Admittedly there are some scriptures about Jesus that are hard to know how to pull together. Consider these verses in light of the fact that the Bible repeatedly says that Jesus Christ is God:

> James 1:13 says God cannot be tempted with evil.
> Matthew 4:1 says the devil tempted Jesus.
> God cannot be tempted. Jesus is God. Jesus was tempted.

How in the world can this possibly be reconciled? Was Jesus not really tempted since He was God? Or was Jesus tempted but not really God? Countless nights have been spent at every Bible college debating just this one example. Here are a few more examples, starting with God's attribute of being unchanging (immutable):

> In Malachi 3:6 God says, "I the LORD do not change."
> Luke 2:52 says Jesus grew in wisdom, stature, and in
>   favor with God and man.
> God does not change. Jesus is God. Jesus changed.

Or how about this one regarding God's attribute of being all-knowing (omniscient)?

> First John 3:20 says God knows everything.
> Mark 13:32 says "Concerning that day or that hour [of
>   Jesus' second coming], no one knows, not even the
>   angels in heaven, nor the Son, but only the Father."
> God knows everything. Jesus is God. But Jesus says there
>   is something He does not know—namely when His
>   second coming will occur in history.

Lastly, how about this one regarding God's infinite energy?

> Isaiah 40:28 says the Lord does not grow faint or grow
> weary.
> John 4:6 says Jesus, weary from a journey, sat beside a well.
> God does not grow tired. Jesus is God. Jesus grew tired.

To deal with these types of questions, over five hundred Christian scholars gathered for the Council of Chalcedon. As a result of their time in prayer, Bible study, and focused debate, they released the Chalcedonian Creed in AD 451. It included the "hypostatic union," which means that Jesus Christ is one person with two natures—fully God and fully man. The Bible conveys this exactly when it says that Jesus is Emmanuel, which means God with us.

In the Old Testament things such as a divine ladder, a cloud by day and a pillar of fire by night, a tabernacle, and then a temple that housed God's presence closed the distance between the holy God and the unholy people. All of this prefigured the coming of Jesus Christ as the connecting point between God in heaven and people on earth. First Timothy 2:5 describes the fulfillment this way, "There is one God, and there is one mediator between God and men, the man Christ Jesus." In Jesus Christ, God humbled Himself for the special task of reconciling people to Himself. Regarding the "why," legendary preaching evangelist George Whitefield said, "Jesus was God and man in one person, that God and man might be happy together again."[10]

Jesus lived forever in glory as the second member of the Trinity, but for the mission of bringing salvation to the earth He humbled Himself. The holiest person is also the humblest person. The Creator entered the creation, the eternal God stepped into human history, the omnipresent God walked from place to place—all to reveal God and redeem people, as it says in Philippians 2:5–8.

> Have this mind among yourselves, which is yours in Christ
> Jesus, who, though he was in the form of God, did not

count equality with God a thing to be grasped, but emptied himself, by taking the form of a servant, being born
in the likeness of men. And being found in human form,
he humbled himself by becoming obedient to the point of
death, even death on a cross.

Jesus did not lose His divine attributes; He simply chose not to use them at certain times.

In becoming a human being, Jesus did not lose anything but rather added humanity to His divinity.[11] Therefore, Jesus Christ retained all of His divine attributes. He did not, however, avail Himself of the continual use of His divine attributes. Perhaps this was for two primary reasons.

One, on occasion Jesus would reveal His divinity as God. Matthew 9:35 says, "Jesus went throughout all the cities and villages, teaching in their synagogues and proclaiming the gospel of the kingdom and healing every disease and every affliction." In Mark 4 some sailors on a boat with Jesus were exhausted from rowing all night until Jesus awoke and commanded the storm to stop, which it did. Those present "were filled with great fear and said to one another, 'Who then is this, that even the wind and the sea obey him?'" (v. 41). In John 2:11 Jesus turned water into wine, and we read, "This, the first of his signs, Jesus did at Cana in Galilee, and manifested his glory. And his disciples believed in him." In sum-mary, sometimes Jesus performed miracles to reveal the kingdom of God and Himself as King.

Two, Jesus would use His divine characteristics to benefit others but not Himself. For example, we read in Mark 2:5–7, "Jesus...said to the paralytic, 'Son, your sins are forgiven.' Now some of the scribes were sitting there, questioning in their hearts, 'Why does this man speak like that? He is blaspheming! Who can forgive sins but God alone?'" Ultimately we sin against God; therefore, only God has the authority to truly, completely, and eternally forgive our sin. When Jesus forgave sin, the religious critics who heard Him were correct; He was doing divine work reserved for God alone to benefit a needy sinner.

In summary, while on the earth Jesus did retain His divine attributes, but He did not continually avail Himself to the use of His divine attributes. Furthermore, Jesus did not use His divine characteristics (e.g., all knowing, all powerful, all present) in a way to benefit Himself. When suffering, Jesus suffered as we do; when learning, Jesus learned as we do; and when tempted, Jesus faced temptation as we do. In no way did Jesus cheat to make His life easier by using divine attributes that we do not possess.

In this regard Jesus was not the same as Clark Kent. Superman had special powers that other people did not have, but he lived in disguise as Clark Kent, pretending to be like the rest of us when in fact he was not. Jesus is not like that. Jesus was not pretending to be a humble, homeless, hated peasant who was faking His suffering, learning, and tempting. When the Bible said Jesus was hungry, tired, wept, bled, and died, it was in His full humanity without an ounce of fakery. Hebrews 2:17–18 talks about this.

> He had to be made like his brothers in every respect, so that he might become a merciful and faithful high priest in the service of God, to make propitiation for the sins of the people. For because he himself has suffered when tempted, he is able to help those who are being tempted.

If Jesus did not use His divine attributes to live His life and leave His legacy, how did He do it? He received help from the Helper. Can you access the same life-giving, destiny-altering, God-revealing power and help for your life?

If we look to the ancient church creeds (doctrines) that are very helpful for many things, there is one thing missing—how Jesus lived His life. Notice how each creed moves from the birth of Jesus to the death of Jesus and omits the entirety of His life. The Apostles' Creed (fourth century AD) says Jesus was "born of the Virgin Mary; suffered under Pontius Pilate, was crucified…."[12] The Nicene Creed (fourth century AD) says Jesus "was incarnate by the Holy Ghost of the Virgin Mary, and was made man, and was crucified also for us under Pontius Pilate..."[13]

What is missing? Jesus' earthly life.

Are You Living Your Eternal Life Today?

This omission may have contributed to the focus in Christianity that if you accept Jesus, you will go to heaven when you die. That is indeed true, but when does eternal life begin? Is eternal life a duration of life that only begins once you die? If so, then Christianity is about dying and not much about living. Christianity is, therefore, something for old people to think about at the finish line and nothing for young people to fret about at the starting line. This may explain why churches are filled with grandparents but not their grandchildren.

On the other hand, is eternal life a quality of life that starts at the moment of your salvation, infects and affects all of your life, and culminates at your death? If so, then Christianity is about living a new life from the moment you meet Jesus and receive His Spirit that continues forever and ever. If eternal life is the Spirit-filled life of Jesus empowering your entire life, then any day lived any other way is a wasted day.

I believe in heaven. I look forward to heaven. I hope that in my resurrection body my hair will not be as thin as it is right now, venturing home to be with the Lord before the rest of me. I hope that my current two-inch vertical leap will be replaced by the ability to dunk a basketball and that when I sing it will not sound as if I was captured by al Qaeda as is currently the case. In heaven, I also look forward to skateboarding on the streets of gold and discovering what a perfect cheeseburger actually tastes like.

Even if there were no heaven, I would want to be a Christian solely for the benefits in this life. If I died and became nothing more than mulch, or if everyone went to hell including me, I would still want to know Jesus and be filled with the Spirit in this life because it is the only way to truly live. The Spirit-filled life with Jesus is so wonderful that even one day of it makes life

> If eternal life is the Spirit-filled life of Jesus empowering your entire life, then any day lived any other way is a wasted day.

worth living. In the next chapter we will learn what this looks like for you and your family.

Chapter 2

HOW A SPIRIT-FILLED FAMILY FULFILLS THEIR DESTINY

Without the Holy Spirit, I might have been a pirate instead of a pastor.

My family name is O'Driscoll. We come from County Cork in southern Ireland. Although a fire in Dublin destroyed many records pertaining to our family history, my dad and I reconstructed some of our family heritage by visiting Ireland together. *O'Driscoll* means "the messenger of God," and it can refer to a preacher. For hundreds of years, we were a land-owning warrior clan with fortified castles and a small empire.

Things changed when new political leadership arose. In the country where our ancestors battled with Vikings, Norsemen, Spaniards, and assorted smaller European tribes, the English government upended everything when they passed laws banning all who didn't belong to the Anglican Episcopal Church from owning land or homes. Apparently dispossessed, we lost our land, houses, and fortified castles, presumably along with our dignity.

Our clan chose a new family business and became pirates. I'm not sure what the family meeting looked like—"All in favor of looting and pillaging, say aye!" We gained fame for robbing ships that passed through Baltimore Harbour in southern Ireland. On at least one occasion, we boarded and overtook a ship from Algeria carrying a cargo of wine. That seizure touched off an international incident, with Irishmen taken as slaves in retribution. When the only skills listed on your LinkedIn page are fighting and stealing alcohol, it's a sure bet that the story will not end happily ever after. When the Great Famine hit Ireland, a number of relatives died, and a few men from our family boarded coffin ships—which were not built to transport human beings—and risked their lives to land in America.

We then became potato farmers on a family homestead. That's where I was born.

In recent years at least one of my cousins has been on the television show *Cops*—and he was not one of the cops. I've been told that my uncle died of gangrene because he would not stop drinking and an infection overtook his healthy organs until it killed him.

I grew up in a community with two serial killers—Ted Bundy and the Green River Killer. Drug and alcohol abuse, along with prostitution and gang violence, ran my neighborhood growing up. The first funeral I remember attending for someone my age was that of a young teenage girl from my school who died of a drug overdose.

My parents started a new legacy that I intended to continue. They did not do drugs or abuse alcohol and worked hard to keep my four siblings and me out of trouble. I'm deeply grateful to my parents for keeping me out of harm's way growing up. My mom got saved in the Catholic Charismatic Renewal of the 1970s, was healed at a women's prayer meeting, and the Spirit began His work of transforming our lives and legacies through the faith of my mom. By God's grace and my mom's prayers, today I am a pastor instead of a pirate.

Which kind of family do you descend from in past generations? What kind of legacy do you want to leave for your family in future generations?

JESUS' FAMILY WAS SPIRIT-FILLED

Jesus' family had a godly legacy. Luke 1:5–7 says, "There was a priest named Zechariah....And he had a wife from the daughters of Aaron, and her name was Elizabeth. And they were both righteous before God, walking blamelessly in all the commandments and statutes of the Lord. But they had no child, because Elizabeth was barren, and both were advanced in years."

Luke tells us Elizabeth comes from generations of ministers and Zechariah is a priest—the equivalent in those days of a rural pastor in a small town—also born into a ministry family. Zechariah and Elizabeth love the Lord, serve faithfully in ministry, and wait until old age for God to bless them with a child without getting bitter or committing adultery as Abraham and Sarah had done previously. They are simple and sad but still steadfast.

For years—even decades—Zechariah travels all the way to Jerusalem, but the dice never fall in his favor for the once-in-a-lifetime opportunity to enter the temple, throw some incense on the coals, and say a prayer.

Then one day Zechariah's big moment finally arrives—it's the day he's waited for most of his adult life! The angel Gabriel informs Zechariah and Elizabeth they are going to have a baby boy. Gabriel's credentials are unparalleled: "I stand in the presence of God," he says (v. 19).

Gabriel tells them the baby will be named John (God is gracious); "And he will turn many of the children of Israel to the Lord their God, and he will go before him in the spirit and the power of Elijah...to make ready for the Lord a people prepared" (vv. 16–17).

Jesus' cousins do not have fame, money, or power, but they both have the Holy Spirit. In Luke 1:41 we read that "Elizabeth was filled with the Holy Spirit" and then prophesied over Mary. In Luke 1:67, "Zechariah was filled with the Holy Spirit and prophesied" over his son at birth. Not only are Jesus' cousins Spirit-filled, but so is Jesus' mother.

Jesus' Mother Was Spirit-Filled

Mary is a relative of Elizabeth, but when Luke picks up the narrative, Mary does not yet know her elderly cousin is pregnant. Mary is merely a young woman living a quiet life in Nazareth.

Neither the Old Testament nor other significant historical texts mention Nazareth. Have you ever been on a long road trip and stopped in the middle of nowhere to get gas, grab a beef jerky, use the bathroom, clean the bugs off your windshield, and drive away as fast as you can, praising God you don't have to live there? That's Nazareth.

After Gabriel's visit with Zechariah within the sacred walls of the temple in Jerusalem, where does God send the angel next? Nazareth, to meet with Mary.

> Mary's response to God's plan is…"let it be to me according to your word."…Her son will one day emulate this simple, courageous resolve. In the Garden…He says, "Your will be done."…There are moments in His life when Jesus echoes His godly mother.

Mary is betrothed to Joseph, meaning they have pledged to marry each other in an arrangement far more serious and binding than what we understand as engagement today. In a small rural town like Nazareth where most everyone would operate as one big extended family, to publicly declare engagement would only be done if the bride- and groom-to-be are fully committed to walking down the aisle.

Most theologians believe Mary is somewhere between twelve and fourteen years old when Gabriel pays her a visit. Let that sink in. Everything is riding on a teenage girl. Now that's faith.

Gabriel tells Mary the amazing news: your son will be named Jesus, which means God saves from sins. Her son will be God's Son and her Savior.

Mary's response to God's plan is legendary: "Behold, I am the servant of the Lord; let it be to me according to your word" (v. 38). She is a humble young woman with simple but sincere faith. Mary believes God. Her son will one day emulate this simple, courageous resolve. In the Garden of Gethsemane, as Jesus atones for the sins of the world through the shedding of His blood, He says, "Your will be done" (Matt. 26:42). There are moments in His life when Jesus echoes His godly mother.

Unmarried. Poor. Young. Pregnant with God.

Mary has a lot to worry about.

Rather than worrying, Mary starts worshipping. Her beautiful, spontaneous, anointed, song begins with the words, "My soul magnifies the Lord (Luke 1:46)." Her spirit and the Holy Spirit intersect to worship.

Culturally we may not completely appreciate what Mary and Joseph are willing to sacrifice at this juncture. Mary risks losing her fiancé and her reputation. (Small town religious gossip can be brutal.) Joseph probably realizes his boy Jesus will be called illegitimate, his wife will be called unfaithful, and he will be called a fool for the rest of his life. He doesn't have to accept this fate and can cancel the wedding. He is seemingly a strong and steady kind of guy who does a lot more than he says. We know he has numerous angelic visits, and every time he is told to do something, he obeys the Lord no matter the cost.

Since Jesus will not be his biological son, Joseph stands as a hero for foster parents, adoption, and blended families. He appears to be a quiet, humble, godly man whose most significant ministry will turn out to be working an honest job, loving his wife, obeying God, and raising godly kids who change the world. Thanks to Joseph's humble obedience, Jesus will have a devoted dad.

The Spirit is so active in the life of this family that even their pastor prophesies at Jesus' baby dedication at the temple. Mary and Joseph travel from Bethlehem to Jerusalem to dedicate Jesus in the temple, so we know that this very devout family does "according to what is said in the Law of the Lord" (Luke 2:24).

Once in Jerusalem, Joseph and Mary meet an old covenant pastor named Simeon who loves God. Luke 2:26–27 says, "It had been revealed to him by the Holy Spirit that he would not see death before he had seen the Lord's Christ. And he came in the Spirit into the temple." Simeon then praises God for Jesus and prophesies salvation and suffering for the Savior.

Joseph and Mary encounter another Holy Spirit–inspired

prophecy during their trip. Anna, a prophetess, praises God for the opportunity to witness "the redemption of Jerusalem" (v. 38). After these powerful encounters with the Spirit of God, Joseph, Mary, and Jesus complete their ceremonies and start home again for Nazareth.

> Mary and Joseph travel from Bethlehem to Jerusalem to dedicate Jesus in the temple.

Not only were Jesus' mom, dad, baby-dedicating pastor, and prophetess Spirit-filled, so was Jesus' cousin.

JESUS' COUSIN WAS SPIRIT-FILLED

Excited to see her relative Elizabeth and celebrate their pregnancies, Mary walks about a hundred miles, likely in the hot sun, alone.

As we pick up the story, we see Mary's immediate obedience to God's word in Luke 1:39–40: "In those days Mary arose and went with haste into the hill country, to a town in Judah, and she entered the house of Zechariah and greeted Elizabeth."

In the culture of the New Testament, society would often marginalize women, particularly the young, poor, and single, and the elderly, poor, and childless—especially those living away from major urban centers and lacking connections to influential families. Mary and Elizabeth fit all these criteria. They are among the least likely to be chosen for something significant.

About 25 percent of our Bible was prophetic (predicting future events) when written. Sometimes prophecy is a personal message; God wants someone to know something, so He sends a messenger to deliver a word to that individual. This is the kind of prophecy we see from Elizabeth. Luke 1:41–42 tells us, "Elizabeth was filled with the Holy Spirit, and she exclaimed with a loud cry, 'Blessed are you among women, and blessed is the fruit of your womb!'"

Elizabeth continues to honor Mary, which is unusual since it would be customary for the younger to honor the older. Not only does Elizabeth honor Mary, but she also honors Mary's baby.

"And why is this granted to me that the mother of my Lord should come to me?" asks Elizabeth (v. 43). She hasn't seen Jesus walk on water, raise the dead, heal people, die on a cross, or resurrect from death—she hasn't even seen Him be born—but Elizabeth is astounded to come near Jesus, and she worships Him and claims Him as her Lord. Being in the presence of the pre-born Lord is all she needs to be inspired to worship Him. In fact, Elizabeth is the first person in the New Testament to worship Jesus Christ!

In the next moment the two women draw near one another, and with them the two sons who represent the old covenant and the new covenant; the promises and the fulfillment; the prophet and the Lord. Their bellies come together—and Elizabeth's unborn son John worships along with his mother! Luke 1:41 reports that "the baby leaped in her womb. And Elizabeth was filled with the Holy Spirit."

This is incredible.

John is known by God, filled with the Spirit, and named with a calling of destiny on his life—all before he's ever seen the sunshine, felt the wind, or sipped fresh air into his lungs. He is filled with the Holy Spirit, and we get our first glimpse of John as an in-utero worship leader, dancing and celebrating in the womb. I can't think of a stronger portrait of personhood in the womb than that.

Luke, a medical doctor, writes under the inspiration of God the Holy Spirit. What does it mean when he says of Elizabeth that "the baby leaped in her womb"? What does the Bible mean by the word *baby*?

An examination of every time Luke uses the Greek word *brephos* shows a consistency. (I've added the italics for emphasis.)

- "When Elizabeth heard the greeting of Mary, the *baby* leaped in her womb" (Luke 1:41).

- "The *baby* [John the Baptizer] in my womb leaped for joy" (Luke 1:44).

- "You will find a *baby* [Jesus] wrapped in swaddling cloths and lying in a manger" (Luke 2:12).

- "They...found Mary and Joseph, and the *baby* lying in a manger" (Luke 2:16).

- "They were bringing even *infants* to [Jesus] that he might touch them.... Jesus called them to him, saying, 'Let the *children* come to me'" (Luke 18:15–16).

- "[The godless Pharaoh] dealt shrewdly with our race and forced our fathers to expose their *infants*, so that they would not be kept alive" (Acts 7:19).

The same word, *brephos*, is used for an unborn baby, a newborn baby, and young children because God sees them all the same—as people bearing His image and likeness, worthy of all rights and dignity. A baby in a womb is known by God as John was, named by God as John was, and can be filled with God the Holy Spirit as John was (Luke 1:15). How wonderful is it that God cares about unborn children? How encouraging is it that even when children are miscarried or aborted, we see the possibility that God can know them, love them, name them, and fill them with the Spirit even from the womb as He did John?

If we took a poll to name the most significant person history has ever known, it's highly unlikely that John the Baptizer would even crack the top ten or top thousand. Jesus is in a category of His own: God incarnate. Regarding John's greatness, we read in Luke 1:15, that John "will be great before the Lord." Jesus makes it even clearer saying, "I tell you, among those born of women none is greater than John" (Luke 7:28).

What's so great about this bug-eating, honey-chugging, gospel-preaching, sinner-baptizing, Jedi robe–wearing eccentric? John lives his entire life by the Spirit's power. Before John's birth, the angel Gabriel says, "He will be filled with the Holy Spirit, even from his mother's womb" (Luke 1:15). The Bible also says, "The hand of the Lord was with him" (v. 66). That's another way of saying that the Holy Spirit would be present *with* him, *in* him, and *through* him for his entire life. John would become the greatest man who ever lived by the power of the Holy Spirit.

John is a bit of a wild man who grows up in the wilderness and is not owned by the religious establishment. He is young, charismatic, strong, eccentric, and fearless. Crowds flock to him like a breakout rock star or revolutionary young politician.

John is not all about John; John is all about Jesus. "After me comes he who is mightier than I," John says, "the strap of whose sandals I am not worthy to stoop down and untie" (Mark 1:7). In that day a student would do anything and everything for their teacher with one exception—remove their sandals, a job reserved for the lowest ranking slave. Even with his stock at an all-time high, his first tour just starting, and the T-shirts rolling off the press, John says he is unworthy to do the work of a slave for Jesus Christ. When his fame is hotter than ever and he can cash it all in for a huge ministry, he sets it all aside, sends all his disciples to follow Jesus, and says, "He must increase, but I must decrease" (John 3:30).

John's public ministry lasts roughly six months—shorter than an academic freshman year at a Bible college. He preaches a lot of sermons, baptizes perhaps thousands of people, hands his ministry to Jesus, and gets martyred—all by the age of about thirty.

Many, if not most, of Jesus' early followers are originally part of John's ministry. Yet John accepts his role as the opening band and exits the stage once the crowd is warmed up and Jesus is ready to take the stage. The Holy Spirit helps John to have a humble spirit. The same is true of Jesus' brothers.

JESUS' BROTHERS WERE SPIRIT-FILLED

Beyond a few of their names, we know very little about Jesus' brothers and sisters except for His half-brothers James and Jude.

Although he is Jesus' brother (Matt. 13:55), James is not a believer until Jesus appears to him following the resurrection (Mark 3:21; 1 Cor. 15:7). He is with the apostles at Pentecost (Acts 1:14) and becomes a leader of the Jerusalem church (Gal. 1:19, 2:9; Acts 12:17, 15:12–21). His two nicknames are "James the Just" for his character and "Camel Knees" from praying so much.[1]

In Jude 1 the author introduces himself as, "Jude, a servant of Jesus Christ and brother of James." In Galatians 2:9 Paul calls James a pillar holding up the church along with Cephas (Peter) and John. Both James and Jude go on to be devoted Christian pastors, worshipping their big brother Jesus and writing books of the Bible bearing their names. James also presides over the conference held in Jerusalem to welcome Gentile converts in the church (Acts 15). His work opens up the gospel beyond the Jewish people and can be credited in large part for the existence of Christianity as a global movement of the Spirit to this day.

We know that both James and Jude live by the power of the Spirit because they write Scripture. To write Scripture, you must have the Spirit (2 Pet. 1:21; 2 Tim. 3:16).

In his brief letter Jude mentions the Spirit in verses 19–20, "It is these who cause divisions, worldly people, devoid of the Spirit. But you, beloved, building yourselves up in your most holy faith and praying in the Holy Spirit..." Not only is Jude empowered by the Spirit, as a pastor he teaches his people to pray in the Spirit as well.

The Book of James is all about wisdom. When James frequently speaks of wisdom he is saying the same thing as when other New Testament writers mention the Holy Spirit.[2] The Bible makes this connection between the presence of the Spirit and possessing of wisdom in both the Old and New Testaments.[3]

Jesus' brother James is filled with the Holy Spirit, writes the Scriptures by the power of the Spirit, and instructs Christians that it requires wisdom from the Holy Spirit to know and follow the will of God. Additionally James dies a martyr's death in service to his half-brother. We read that "James the half-brother of Jesus was executed…he was thrown off the temple and, still alive, was stoned to death."[4] Dying, James echoes his big brother Jesus from Luke 23:34 saying, "Forgive them, for they know not what they do."

One archaeological expert says, "When James is murdered…it is Simon…who takes over leadership of the movement."[5] History seems to indicate that to replace James, another one of Jesus' brothers named Simon (sometimes called Simeon) is chosen to assume leadership. If accurate, Mary and Joseph have at least three children in significant ministry roles in addition to their son Jesus Christ. Most of us are familiar with Jesus' ministry and its impact on history, but we often overlook the enormous role Jesus' family played in His ministry. Jesus had no ministry without His family!

Is Your Family Spirit-Filled?

I've talked about my family. We've studied Jesus' family. What about your family? If your family is godly, how can you continue that legacy? Even if your family is ungodly, how can you chart a new course for future generations? If you want your family to be godly, you need to learn three lessons from Jesus' family and start applying them today.

1. God was the gravitational center of the universe for Jesus' family.

Your life and family are like the earth. Just as our planet continually orbits the sun, our souls were created to revolve around God. Apart from God we do not know who we are, where we belong, why we are here, or what our purpose is.

Tragically, because we are sinners, we forget, ignore, or leave the God around whom we were created to orbit. When this happens, we pick someone or something other than God to function as the center of our lives. This explains why the Bible denounces idolatry, which is replacing God's position as the center of our lives.

Whatever we choose to revolve around—ourselves, our children, our jobs, our spouses, our ministries, our hobbies, our friends, or

God—has massive and potentially miserable implications. Like a solar system, every family needs a gravitational center. Everyone gathers around the center as the highest priority, serving it as the place that pulls everyone and everything together.

Jesus' family had the Lord as their gravitational center. Mom and dad, brothers and sisters, and cousins all remained steadfastly devoted to the Lord. This held their family together and kept it healthy.

2. Each family member was filled with the Holy Spirit.

The presence of God directed them, and the power of God sustained them. The power of the Spirit enabled Jesus' cousins to serve God faithfully for decades even though they endured poverty and infertility. The power of the Spirit enabled Jesus' mother and father to accept the complicated calling of raising the Lord, knowing from the Scriptures that they would shed tears watching Him suffer for sinners. The power of the Spirit enabled Jesus' cousin John to set the world on fire for a few months, hand his ministry to Jesus, and get his head chopped off to God's glory. The power of the Spirit enabled Jesus' siblings to serve in ministry, write books of the Bible, and carry forth the message and mission of their brother and Savior until they died as martyrs for their brother. It just goes to show, more than money, fame, or power, the key to a good family is each member continually being filled with the Holy Spirit.

3. Each member of Jesus' family was a servant.

Jesus told us that He came not to be served but to serve, and He learned this from His family. (See Matthew 20:28.) The opposite of a servant is a consumer. A servant gives; a consumer takes. A servant does what is best for others; a consumer or customer takes what they want for themselves.

One of the most egregious flaws in modern Christianity occurs when the church appears as a business providing religious goods and services to families who act like customers. Worshippers worship God; customers expect to be worshipped as gods. When this happens, the customer determines the message and mission. Instead of serving in ministry themselves, people shop for a church that tells them what they want to hear and provides the services they want to receive. This is the spiritual equivalent of trying to get physically healthy by paying an athlete to work out while you sit down and watch them exercise.

WHAT MINISTRY DOES GOD HAVE FOR YOUR FAMILY?

Jesus lived a Spirit-filled life, and Jesus' Spirit-filled family served. Period. This was a ministry family. There is no way to mature spiritually without serving. Otherwise we often seek to make ourselves the gravitational center of our universe, wanting everyone to orbit around us and serve us and call it ministry when it's really idolatry. The kingdom of God works in the exact opposite way. A great family with a great legacy only happens when the Lord is the center and each family member surrenders to the Spirit and serves.

In closing, this has become most apparent to me with my own family in recent years. My wife, Grace, and I have five kids—three boys and two girls. We moved to Arizona for a hard reset of life and ministry after years of feeling like crash test dummies in a car with no airbags. After about two decades in ministry

> There is no way to mature spiritually without serving.

we took some time off to heal up before entering the next season of God's will for our lives.

For several months we had church in our home as a family on Sunday mornings before we relocated. Our kids got it organized with one leading singing, one reading Scripture, one leading prayer, one collecting the offering (our youngest wanted to gather money for a single mom), one organizing communion, and me being the Bible teacher. Before long some family and friends were joining us. Our kids added a children's nursery in our playroom and started cooking breakfast for those who came to visit. Soon our kids were running a fun little house church that grew to be a full house before we moved out of state. This joyful season allowed our kids and other people to heal up from a rough season.

Our kids enjoyed that experience so much they started brainstorming about planting a church together as a family project some months after we landed in Arizona. The first church Grace and I planted, we were just twenty-five years of age with no children. Over the years when the kids came along, complex and challenging situations made it increasingly difficult for my wife and our kids to be much involved. This time, however, could be different, and we could plant a church as a family ministry.

So we started meeting over dinner to brainstorm the new church. The kids picked the name The Trinity Church to honor their grandparents on Grace's side who planted and pastored a church by that name for more than forty years until Grandpa passed away. Amazingly the domain thetrinitychurch.com was available for cheap, so we bought it. We prayed about how to start a church as a family that welcomed other families. It was a lot of fun, and the kids helped architect the entire church. I will never forget the dinnertime conversation where one of the youngest children asked me, "Dad, am I on the church board?"

And I chuckled, smiled, and said something like, "Yeah, I guess you are, but since you are a minor, it has to be unofficial."

Each night at dinner we prayed for specific things. We didn't really have anything or know anyone beyond a few people, so we needed God to figure out everything.

Our big prayer was for a building. God did a miracle. The first time I saw our church plant home was with our youngest son. He'd just finished baseball practice one night, and we drove by to see it. He said he felt that it was God's will for us to have that building, so he took off his ball cap, raised his hand, and standing out front in the dark, he asked the Lord to give it to us.

God answered my little buddy's prayer, and in a crazy God story we got a church building. It was a fifty-year-old church that needed a lot of work, so my kids put on work gloves and spent the hot Arizona summer doing demolition to renovate the old building. I came downstairs early one Saturday, and sitting on the couch were our sons wearing gloves and prepared to go to work. I asked them what they were doing up so early, and they said they were my associate pastors ready to go to work for the day. I smiled and choked back tears. There is nothing more encouraging than seeing the Spirit at work in your family. There is nothing better than serving the Lord with your family.

Before long other families joined us at our work projects. We are not a perfect family, and like all kids and parents, we work through our stuff. But it has been one of the great joys of my life to see the Spirit at work in our kids and to be able to serve the Lord together in ministry.

God may not call your family to plant a church, but part of your destiny does include ministry. We don't know much about Jesus' father, Joseph, or His other siblings because they served more quietly, but we have no reason to believe they did not serve God faithfully. The family of God is the same as any family—everyone has an important part to play, with some people serving in ways that are seen by people and others helping in ways that are only seen by God.

How has God used your family to minister to others in the past? Have you taken time as a family to invite the Holy Spirit to reveal to you and your family what your ministry call might be? How and where would God have you to serve? Which gifts has the Spirit given your family members for the ministry He has for you? God loves you and your family, and He invites you to do Spirit-filled ministry as Jesus and His family did!

Chapter 3

MATURE LIKE YOUR MESSIAH

ADULTS CAN LEARN a whole lot about God through the questions children ask. One night I was reading a children's Bible story to the three young children we had at the time (the other two were taxiing up to the runway).

I don't remember what Bible story I read from the children's Bible with all the pictures, but I do remember the conversation that ensued. The children started asking what Jesus was like at their age and got pretty excited about the subject. It suddenly felt like a Jesus-themed episode of a *Jeopardy!* kids' tournament.

"Did Jesus have chores when He was a kid?"

"Did Jesus have to go to school when He was little?"

"Did Jesus wrestle with His brothers?"

"Could Jesus throw a perfect curveball when He was a kid?"

"When Jesus got the flu as a kid, did He heal Himself or just skip school and wait it out?"

I'd not given much thought to this issue previously, but the kids were onto something. I explained to our children that, yes, our God Jesus knew what it was like to be their age. Jesus had to learn to take His first step, drink from a cup, say words, read words, obey His parents, get along with His siblings, and figure out how to both climb up and down a tree. Jesus experienced all of the life stages that we do, including the prenatal in Mary's tummy, the first year as a baby, the toddler years (ages one to three), the preschool years (ages three to five), the grade school years (ages five to twelve), the teen years (ages thirteen to eighteen), and the ensuing young adult and adult years. Jesus knew what it was like to trip and fall, start to grow facial hair, have your voice crack awkwardly in puberty, and eventually become an adult.

As I sat on the bed with the kids getting ready to lay hands and pray over each of them, it dawned on me how wonderfully helpful it is that Jesus Christ is a God everyone can relate to at whatever life stage they find themselves. Furthermore, Jesus can relate to and understand what we are going through at every life stage, making Him the perfect person to lead and guide us forward.

THREE LESSONS FROM
THE WAY JESUS MATURED

Regarding maturity and reflecting on the life of Jesus, it is important to note three things:

1. We should determine maturity by such characteristics as age and life stage.

There is nothing wrong with acting childish if you are a child. For example, if both a parent and a toddler failed to get a good night's sleep, both would be tired. But if both threw themselves on the floor thrashing about and screaming at the grocery store, we would be more troubled by the behavior of the parent because we would expect him to be more mature. This was the gist of Paul's writing in 1 Corinthians 13:11, saying, "When I was a child, I spoke like a child, I thought like a child, I reasoned like a child. When I became a man, I gave up childish ways."

2. Physical and spiritual maturity do not happen in the same way.

As a general rule for most people, physical maturity occurs a lot more naturally and easily than spiritual maturity. To mature spiritually takes a great deal of work to cultivate character whereas physical growth happens more naturally and with far less conscious intentional effort.

3. At every age and life stage, Jesus was perfectly mature for that season.

At two years old Jesus was perfectly mature for that age. At ages twelve, twenty-two, and thirty-two He was more mature than He had been at previous life stages. One Bible commentator says it this way, "The intellectual, moral, and spiritual growth of the Child, like the physical, was real. His was a perfect humanity developing perfectly, unimpeded by hereditary or acquired defects. It was the first instance of such a growth in history. For the first time a human infant was realizing the ideal of humanity."[1] An expert in the original language of the New Testament says, "His physical, intellectual, moral, spiritual development was perfect. 'At each stage he was perfect for that stage.'"[2]

JESUS MATURED
THROUGH TRIAL AND ERROR

A sermon I once preached about the sinlessness of Jesus got me in more trouble than usual. His perfection, I argued, doesn't mean He never learned by figuring out how to do something via trial and error.

This idea struck home when Grace and I were sitting at a burger joint surrounded by our young kids, basking in a night out just a notch above fast food. The next table was jammed with little kids too, and a drink showed up for the two-year-old. Anyone who's ever been in charge of a toddler in a restaurant should know to serve all beverages in a sippy cup or at least a cup with a lid and a straw. But that little man was handed a big glass, all icy and sweaty.

The glass should have had a warning label, "SLIPPERY WHEN WET," but the little guy was too young to read it anyway. He reached for it, picked it up, and it slipped out of his hand. He spilled the whole glass all over the table. What did his dad do? Barked at the kid and disciplined him.

I looked at our kids' huge eyes around the table, watching this dad make a scene. I was caught somewhere between stunned and trying to figure out how to frame the situation into a teachable moment. One of our kids said, "Everybody makes mistakes. That kid didn't do anything wrong. He's just got little hands, and that was a big glass."

As we discussed the scene with our kids, it dawned on me. I asked, "What's the difference between a sin and learning through trial and error?"

"Um," they said. "A sin is when you do something wrong, and it's a bad thing. But you learn to do things right sometimes by doing it wrong."

I agreed. "If anything," I said, "that father should've disciplined himself because he didn't ask for a cup with a lid and a straw. He was the one who failed, not the boy."

That scene inaugurated a saying at our house. We always want our kids to know, "There's a big difference between committing a sin and making a mistake."

When as Christians we declare that Jesus is perfect, it seems to me that we acknowledge His sinlessness while giving lip service to His humanity. I want to be clear—Jesus never sinned, perfectly obeyed all of Scripture, and was morally perfect without any sin of any kind. But I don't think that means it was impossible for Jesus in His full humanity while on the earth to learn from trial and error. For example, when Jesus was a little kid, did He ever spill a drop from a cup? Did He ever put a cookie in His mouth as part of it crumbled on the floor?

We say, "Don't cry over spilled milk." "That's the way the cookie crumbles." It's all part of being human. But people get theologically anxious when we apply this common sense to Jesus. What do you say? Jesus was and is fully God. Was Jesus really human or not?

Jesus wasn't sinful, yet He was entirely human, enjoying and coping with the fullness of human experience like the rest of us. As followers of Jesus, we all know that we should seek to be perfect as our heavenly Father is perfect, be holy as He is holy, be good as He is good, without change or shifting shadows. Yet there's a gaping difference between a moral perfection and an absolute life perfection. Jesus never sinned, but I don't think the Bible requires us to say He never learned through trial and error. When Luke 2:52 says "Jesus grew in wisdom and stature, and in favor with God and man" (NIV), it means He grew, learned, changed, progressed, hit His thumb with a hammer a few times on the job with His dad, and learned to write by messing up, messing up, and messing up until His motor skills caught up with His brain. God does not need to learn or grow, but the God-man Jesus Christ temporarily set aside the continual use of His divine attributes to experience full humanity and identify with us mere mortals.

God deals with our sins, but God doesn't discipline us for learning through our trial and error efforts. He is a Father who makes the most of our mistakes to teach us. I'm confident He actually expects us to fumble and fail, just as you don't expect your kid to get the notes right the first time you hand them a trombone. It might be years before you feel like all those lessons you paid for were worth the money.

We figure out how to do something well by trial and error. My son recently swung at a curveball but missed it because he opened his front side too early. I'm not sure Jesus went to the cross to atone for his missed swing. Next time up, my son made the adjustment and hit the same pitch.

To learn means you have to fail. To fail, you have to risk. If you do not risk, you will not fail, but you also cannot learn.

Critics like to point out how you fail so they can laugh and sneer. Coaches point out how you fail so you can learn and succeed.

Grace and I—and our growing kids—frequently see parents disciplining their children for mistakes rather than coming alongside them to teach. It's easy to see how people perceive God by the way they parent. Our parenting reflects our understanding of God, and so does our treatment of ourselves and anyone who makes mistakes.

Ditto for the church family where mistakes should be opportunities to learn and grow but instead are often scarlet letters to wear.

You and everyone under your care are forever God's children. He's not demanding perfection today in this life, but rather progress toward the perfection that never comes until the first day of the next life. He merely aims for teachable hearts, kids who learn and grow. I believe that God invites you to stretch, grow, try, and even fail as you experiment with doing difficult things for His glory. Spend your energy avoiding sins and learning through trial and error.

How Jesus Matured

The Bible tells us very little about how Jesus matured in the earliest seasons of His life. We find most of the details in the second half of chapter 2 of Luke's Gospel, which is also the only one of the four Gospels written in chronological order. Four things in this chapter that largely contribute to Jesus' maturity also contribute to our maturity:

1. Jesus matured because He knew the Scriptures.

Luke 2:46–47 says that at the age of twelve in the temple in Jerusalem, Jesus was "sitting among the teachers, listening to them and asking them questions." Jesus' knowledge of the Scriptures was so insightful that "all who heard him were amazed at his understanding and his answers." To mature in the ways of God, you have to know the Word of God.

2. Jesus lived in relationship with God the Father.

When Jesus' parents asked why He had been in the temple discussing theology for days, Jesus said in Luke 2:49, "I must be in my Father's house." In the Old Testament there are roughly only fifteen references to God as Father. Most, if not all, of those occurrences are not in reference to individuals but instead to the nation of Israel.

However, everything changed regarding our understanding of God as Father with the coming of Jesus Christ. Jesus' favorite name for God was *Father*, a term of endearment often referred to in the original language Jesus spoke as *Abba*. It appears roughly 165 times in the four Gospels.

One reason Jesus matured was His constant, warm, loving, and intimate relationship with God the Father as the beloved Son. Jesus encouraged us to have this same kind of relationship with the Father, teaching us to pray in Matthew 6:9, "Our Father...."

Building on the theme of maturing through a personal relationship with God the Father, Paul says this in Romans 8:14–16: "For all who are led by the Spirit of God are sons of God. For you did not receive the spirit of slavery to fall back into fear, but you have received the Spirit of adoption as sons, by whom we cry, 'Abba! Father!' The Spirit himself bears witness with our spirit that we are children of God." By being Spirit-empowered like Jesus, you can know God as Father and mature as Jesus did.

3. Jesus matured because He had respect for authority.

Luke 2:51–52 summarizes Jesus' years from age twelve onward saying, "He went down to Nazareth with them [His parents, Joseph and Mary] and was obedient to them.... And Jesus grew in wisdom and stature, and in favor with God and man" (NIV).

Though perfect, Jesus submitted to imperfect parents and honored His mother and father as the Ten Commandments required. If there was ever anyone who had the right to refuse to submit to any human authority, it was Jesus Christ. If there was ever anyone who did not need to be under human authority, it was Jesus Christ. If there was ever anyone who could have said that they were under God's authority alone and none other, it was Jesus Christ. But Jesus Christ matured, in part, because He honored and submitted to the parental authority that God placed over Him. The same is true of our maturing. Those who do not submit to authority (e.g., parent, teacher, boss, government, pastor, Scripture, Holy Spirit, etc.) do not mature. God works through authority and blesses those who honor authority. In our age of rebellion and independence, which is the essence of sin, it is no surprise that so many are so immature.

4. Jesus matured by the power of the Holy Spirit.

For starters His name *Christ* literally means the one anointed with the person, presence, and power of the Holy Spirit. One Bible dictionary explains it this way:

> Israel anticipated the arrival of the Anointed One, who would not be anointed by men and with oil prepared by human hands, but by God, with the Holy Spirit (Matt. 3:16–17 par. Mark 1:10–11; Luke 3:21–22). For that reason Jesus could testify of himself: "The Spirit of the Lord God is upon me, because the Lord has anointed me…" (Luke 4:18 quoting Isa. 61:1; cf. Acts 10:38). Thus, the name "Christ" connotes not only his sacred commission as Mediator and Redeemer of his people, but also the authority and power through which he was able to complete this mission.[3]

In the Old Testament we read about the boy Samuel maturing through the power of the Holy Spirit by growing up in the presence of God. In 1 Samuel 2:21 it says, "Indeed the LORD visited Hannah, and she conceived and bore three sons and two daughters. And the boy Samuel grew in the presence of the LORD." The Bible uses the same kind of language here as it does to explain Moses dwelling in the Spirit to such a degree that he has an intimate and personal transforming connection with God (Exod. 34:29–35 cf.; Num. 11:25). In 1 Samuel 2:26 it says, "Now the boy Samuel continued to grow both in stature and in favor with the Lord and also with man."

Similar to Samuel, Luke 2:40 says of Jesus, "And the child grew and became strong, filled with wisdom. And the favor of God was upon him." Regarding His age, most Bible commentators agree that this refers to Jesus as a younger child under the age of twelve. In the following section of verses Luke 2:52 says, "Jesus increased in wisdom and in stature and in favor with God and man."

THE HOLY SPIRIT
DESCENDED UPON JESUS

We've now set the stage for the next major event in history, the public unveiling of Jesus Christ as the Son of God living by the power of the Holy Spirit. Until this event Jesus lives in relative obscurity. We know very little about His life during His teens and twenties, but all that changes at His baptism.

The baptism of Jesus Christ is so significant that it appears in all four of the New Testament Gospels. Luke 3:21–22 reports, "Now when all the people were baptized, and when Jesus also had been baptized and was praying, the heavens were opened, and the Holy Spirit descended on him in bodily form, like a dove; and a voice came from heaven, 'You are my beloved Son; with you I am well pleased.'"

This event was not Jesus receiving the Holy Spirit for the first time. In the previous chapters Luke clearly tells us that the Holy Spirit was intimately involved in the life and ministry of Jesus Christ from the womb. Mary, His mother, conceived Jesus by the power of the Holy Spirit. Therefore, at every moment of His journey into human history through the womb of Mary, the Spirit was present in power with Jesus. Jesus' baptism was not where He received the Spirit, but rather it was a public event where the Father "revealed" to the crowd what Jesus already knew—that He lived in loving and constant relationship with God the Father and God the Spirit (John 1:31). This was crucially important because God's people had long awaited the fulfillment of Isaiah's promises that their Savior would come in the power of the Spirit.

> The Spirit of the LORD shall rest upon him, the Spirit of wisdom and understanding, the Spirit of counsel and might, the Spirit of knowledge and the fear of the LORD.
>
> —ISAIAH 11:2

My servant, whom I uphold, my chosen, in whom my soul delights; I have put my Spirit upon him.

—Isaiah 42:1

The Lord God has sent me, and his Spirit.

—Isaiah 48:16

The Spirit of the Lord God is upon me, because the Lord has anointed me.

—Isaiah 61:1

Since there is no authority higher than God the Father, His public validation was the highest validation possible to launch Jesus' public ministry following His baptism. The presence of the Spirit like a dove reminds us of the days of Noah. In that day salvation from God's wrath came through deliverance via a wooden boat carrying God's people, and in Jesus' day salvation from God's wrath would come via a wooden cross carried by God Himself.

Looking back at Jesus' baptism, Peter preaches in Acts 10:36–38:

Preaching good news of peace through Jesus Christ (he is Lord of all), you yourselves know what happened throughout all Judea, beginning from Galilee after the baptism that John proclaimed: how God anointed Jesus of Nazareth with the Holy Spirit and with power. He went about doing good and healing all who were oppressed by the devil, for God was with him.

Peter clearly states that one of the primary purposes of Jesus' baptism was to publicly announce that Jesus' entire ministry—including preaching, healing, and delivering—would be accomplished by the power of the Holy Spirit. Matthew 3:16 reveals a curious detail that those present "saw the Spirit of God descending like a dove and coming to rest on him." In John 1:32–33 John the Baptizer says, "I saw the Spirit descend from heaven like a dove, and it remained on him....he who sent me to baptize with water said to me, 'He on whom you see the Spirit descend and remain, this is he who baptizes with the Holy Spirit.'" The language of the Spirit "coming to rest" and "remain" on Jesus reveals an ongoing, abiding, and relational presence where everything in Jesus' life will be under the control and by the power of the Spirit.

How Can Maturity Happen in Your Life?

Since the Spirit rested and remained upon Jesus, as we study His life we need not demand that every biblical scene include the mention of the Spirit. It has already been stated that Jesus lived every moment with the Spirit. In the same way, when I tell people about meeting Grace on March 12, 1988, and that we have done life together every day since, it would be odd for me to mention her every single time I say or do anything for the rest of my life. By knowing of our relationship, you should rightly assume she is involved in all my life whether I directly state that fact or not. The Son and the Spirit have a similar relationship—they do all of life together, and the Spirit empowers everything Jesus does. For example, we read that Jesus was "full of the Holy Spirit," "led by the Spirit," and came "in the power of the Spirit."

In the synagogue after Jesus reads Isaiah 61:1–2, "The Spirit of the Lord God is upon me," He says, "Today this Scripture has been fulfilled in your hearing" (Luke 4:18–21). Luke continues by revealing that Jesus also "rejoiced in the Holy Spirit" (Luke 10:21). Jesus and Holy Spirit continually do life and ministry together, and occasionally the Bible reminds us of this fact by stating it plainly.

Some scholars have noted that the power of the Spirit in the life of Jesus does not receive the attention it deserves. Theologian and former prime minister of the Netherlands Abraham Kuyper has written about the relationship between Jesus and the Holy Spirit.

The Church has never sufficiently confessed the influence of the Holy Spirit exerted upon the work of Christ. The general impression is that the work of the Holy Spirit begins when the work of the Mediator on earth is finished, as tho [sic] until that time the Holy Spirit celebrated His divine day of rest. Yet the Scripture teaches us again and again that Christ performed His mediatorial work controlled and impelled by the Holy Spirit.[4]

Former Wheaton College professor Gerald Hawthorne has also written on the subject of Jesus' relationship with the Holy Spirit.

Not only is Jesus their Savior because of who he was and because of his own complete obedience to the Father's will (cf. Heb. 10:5–7), but he is the supreme example for them of what is possible in a human life because of his total dependence upon the Spirit of God.[5]

Since Christ matured by the power of the Holy Spirit, it follows that Christians who take His name also mature by the same power. To put it simply: the only way for a Christian to become *like* Christ is by the power of the same Holy Spirit who empowered the life *of* Christ.

Where do you need to mature? What do you need to learn? What temptation do you need to overcome? Where are you weak and falling short? Where are you proud and needing to grow humble? Where are you foolish and needing to grow wise? Where are you lazy and needing to find discipline? You need the Helper, the Holy Spirit, in every area, every day, for every need. You cannot and will not mature as Jesus did without the help of the Spirit.

> The only way for a Christian to become *like* Christ is by the power of the same Holy Spirit who empowered the life *of* Christ.

We will further examine this subject later in the book, but now we've set the stage for the people of Jesus to live by the power of Jesus. It all starts by living in the love of the Spirit.

Chapter 4

LEARN TO LOVE

L OVE.

It's a little word with big implications.

When we were kids in school, teachers taught us that we need food, water, air, and shelter to live. But we also need love. Without love, we literally die.

Some years ago beautiful medical facilities were built to house newborn orphans. They provided the infants with a clean environment, sunlight, healthy food, fresh water, a comfortable bed, and fun toys, but the children grew sick and died in staggering numbers. The doctors did research but could not figure out why the healthy children were dying. An outside group was brought in to investigate the crisis.

Can you guess what they concluded?

The children needed to be loved. They required human contact—to be held, coddled, and spoken to multiple times every day. Without love, newborns fail to thrive and can actually die.

God made us for loving relationship and human connection. Knowing this, God who created us and knows what we need says over and over in the Bible, in places like 1 John 4:21, "Whoever loves God must also love...."

When you tell someone that you love them and mean it from the heart, something profound and priceless has happened in your relationship. Once Grace and I decided that we not only loved each other but that we would also *say*, "I love you," our relationship was never the same.

The Old Testament in a Tweet

In the midst of Jesus' ministry a group of religious folks who were having a bit of a debate asked Him what the most significant section of the Bible is. They wanted Him to give them the boiled-down bottom-line summary of the entire Old Testament. Since Jesus is the most significant person who has ever lived, and the Bible is the most significant book ever written, Jesus' answer would be most significant. Mark 12:28–31 records what I like to refer to as Jesus' "tweet" of the Old Testament.

> And one of the scribes came up and heard them disputing with one another, and seeing that he answered them well, asked him, "Which commandment is the most important of all?"
>
> Jesus answered, "The most important is, 'Hear, O Israel: The Lord our God, the Lord is one. And you shall love the Lord your God with all your heart and with all your soul and with all your mind and with all your strength.' The second is this: 'You shall love your neighbor as yourself.' There is no other commandment greater than these."

According to Jesus, to mature we need to focus on five things:

1. Love God emotionally with all your heart.

2. Love God spiritually with all your soul.

3. Love God mentally with all your mind.

4. Love God physically with all your strength.

5. Love your neighbor as much as you love yourself.

Living a Spirit-filled life begins with love. That love changes your heart, saves your soul, renews your mind, and refreshes your strength. It then spreads to those around you. When the Bible talks about love, it is talking about the very essence of God. The Holy

Spirit for all eternity lives in perfect love with the Father and Son. While on the earth, this loving relationship continued as the Holy Spirit journeyed with Jesus like a friend through every moment of every day. Despite being hated by mobs, used by crowds, denied and betrayed by friends, Jesus still had one loving relationship that He could always count on—His friend circle with the Father and Spirit. This loving friendship helped Jesus to live in love and have the grace to be loving toward others.

The church father Augustine says something that applies to Christ and the Christian, "Whoever loves already has the Holy Spirit, and by having him he becomes worthy of having even more of him. And the more he has the Spirit the more he loves."[1] Augustine rightly says that no one can love like God without the Spirit of Love.

> Apples come from apple trees, grapes come from grape vines, and Christian love comes from the Holy Spirit.

When we see God's love, we know God's Spirit is the source of that love. For this reason, when the Bible speaks of love, it points to the Holy Spirit as the source of love in Jesus' life and our lives. Romans 15:30 speaks of "the love of the Spirit." Colossians 1:8 speaks of "love in the Spirit." First Thessalonians 4:7–9 speaks of the "Holy Spirit" who causes "brotherly love" so that we can "love one another." Apples come from apple trees, grapes come from grape vines, and Christian love comes from the Holy Spirit.

Have you ever seen a successful person explain their success? A world-class athlete, musician, or leader often explains their success by talking at length and with great affection for the people who loved them, supported them, and sacrificed for them. They talk about their moms, dads, grandparents, best friends, spouses, or other people who loved them the best and remained with them as supporters in the toughest of times. While Jesus was on the earth, this role was filled by the Holy Spirit who loved Him and empowered Him to love others.

LOVE

If someone told you to name the most important thing someone could do, what would your answer be? Jesus' answer in Mark chapter 12 is to first love God and then love your neighbor.

His emphasis on love tells us three things. First, we need to know who God is. Second, we need to know that God loves us. Third, we need to know that God's love for us is a gift to both be enjoyed and shared with God and others.

When Jesus tells us that God is one, He quotes from the ancient book of Deuteronomy 6:4. God's people would have memorized this section of the Bible and spoke it each day as a prayerful reminder of who God is. The Hebrew word for one God, *echad*, is a curious one; it often means multiple people who are so unified they are one. Genesis 2:24 uses the same word as God's intention for married couples, beginning with Adam and Eve—to be one even though they are two. In this we see the Trinity. The Trinity is the Christian teaching from the Bible that there is one God who is three persons— Father, Son, and Holy Spirit.

Because the three persons of the Trinity are one, the Bible can say in 1 John 4:8, "God is love." God is not lonely. Throughout all eternity the Father, Son, and Spirit live in loving relationship. They communicate with one another, care for one another, and continue with one another. In some regards, the One God resembles a loving family, which may explain why the language of Father and Son is used to describe their loving relationship.

Not only is God loving, but God loves you! Apart from your performance God loves you and accepts you as you are. God loves you so much that through His Son Jesus Christ, He gladly for- gives all your past, resides within you for hope, help, and healing in your present, and will walk with you hand in hand like a loving parent for the rest of your life and into eternity. God's love is mind bending, heart changing, and destiny altering. God loves you! God cannot love you more! God will not love you less!

God and His love for you are gifts for you to enjoy and share with others. Jesus talks about this, and His best friend John (nicknamed "the one Jesus loved") echoes it in 1 John 4:11, "Beloved, if God so loved us, we also ought to love one another."

Love—undoubtedly one of the most significant words in the Bible—appears roughly eight hundred times. In our culture, though, it can be one of the most misunderstood and misused words. For example, people "love" their mamas, the New York Yankees, and pizza, and they *really, really* love it when their mamas make them pizza while they are watching the Yankees.

Simply put, when the Bible says that God is love, it means that He is relational. God wants a relationship with each one of us. This is why He speaks to us through Scripture and listens to us through prayer. Furthermore, God made us like Him, in a limited sense, to be in loving relationship with Him and others, starting with what Jesus calls our "neighbor." Therefore, our loving relationships are supposed to start at home with our family members sleeping in the rooms next to ours.

> Our God is *all about* loving relationships. This is not merely what God does; this is how God is!

Here's how God explains it in Genesis 1:26: "Let us make man in our image, after our likeness." Did you catch the "our" language? Again, this is the Bible's way of letting us know about the Trinity, that there is one God made up of the three persons—Father, Son, and Spirit. It's important to remember that our God is *all about* loving relationships. This is not merely what God does; this is how God is!

Our God is a loving and relational God, and He made us to be loving and relational people. We are handmade and hardwired for loving relationships. We are not supposed to live life alone. In fact, while the world was still perfect and before sin occurred, God said it was not good for us to be alone in Genesis 2:18. Today, in our sin-infected and corrupted world, we have an even greater need for loving relationships.

GETTING GOD'S LOVE

If you have ever flown on an airplane, you have likely heard the safety speech given at the beginning of the flight. The crew always tells you that in case of an emergency, oxygen masks will drop. The attendant tells you to put your own mask on first before you assist anyone else.

Life is like a flight. Jesus is our captain. Our relationship with Him is our proverbial oxygen mask. On Jesus Airlines, when the storms hit and lightning strikes, there will be times of turbulence until we land in His kingdom. When these times occur, we need to get

> Love is sometimes what you feel, sometimes what you say, but always what you do.

our proverbial oxygen mask on first. We need to live in the healthy, life-giving power of God's love before we can be helpful to those around us. Jesus talks about this in Mark 12:28–31, saying that we need to love God first and love our neighbor second.

Christianity is about many things, but one of the most important things is love. In 1 Corinthians 13:13 Paul says that the greatest thing in all the world is love. Love is sometimes what you feel, sometimes what you say, but always what you do. Ultimately love shows forth in action. True love unselfishly acts in the best interest of the beloved. This results in acts of service and sacrifice, much like Jesus Christ who served by sacrificing His own life as the greatest act of love the world will ever know.

How do we access the love of God? We obtain the love of God by the Spirit of God. The Bible teaches this in Galatians 5:22, "The fruit of the Spirit is love." The Spirit of God has experienced eternal love in relationship with the Father and Son. The person, presence, and power of the Holy Spirit brings us this love and makes it available to believers.

Today my family lives and ministers in Scottsdale, Arizona. For most of the year it's a beautiful, dry, barren desert with red clay dirt and green cactus as far as the eye can see. But everything changes during monsoon season. When the monsoons hit, the sky opens up and rain comes down in a flood that feels like the days of Noah. Very quickly the rain from above transforms the landscape below. Seemingly out of nowhere, desert wildflowers explode from beneath the dry clay, and the desert bursts forth in life and vibrant color. The results are stunningly beautiful.

Just as monsoon rain pours down from above, love floods down upon us from God. Romans 5:5 says, "God's love has been poured into our hearts through the Holy Spirit who has been given to us." The Holy Spirit is God's version of monsoon rain. When God the Holy Spirit rains His love down on you, it cools and refreshes, washes away filth, and brings beautiful life. You need God's love because without it, you wither and die in a desert.

Furthermore, the people in your family and life need God's love to flow through you to them. When you are filled with the Spirit, God's love begins to transform you into a loving person. In this way, God's love flows down on you, wells up in you, and then flows through you to others. Let's take a closer look at the ways Jesus told us to love.

LOVE GOD EMOTIONALLY WITH ALL YOUR HEART

When people want to get to the bottom of something, they speak of getting to the *heart* of a matter. When someone suffers, we say that our *hearts* go out to them. When someone acts generously or kindly, we describe them as big*hearted* and say that their actions are *heart*warming. When someone feels devastated, we call it being broken*hearted*. When someone regrets a decision they made, they say they had a change of *heart*. And when we see someone who is loving and kind, we say that they are good*heart*ed and they warm our *hearts*.

The heart is the essence of who you are. Proverbs 27:19 says, "As a face is reflected in water, so the heart reflects the real person" (NLT). In a very real sense, the life you live is just a reflection of the heart you have.

When Jesus said to love God and others with "all your heart," it shows that we need to pay attention to and work on our hearts continually. This is especially true when it comes to our relationships. We need to examine our heart toward God and others regularly.

In life the "want to" precedes the "how to." Good advice on *how* to do something serves no purpose unless we *want* to do it. This is the heart of Christian living. Only after we want to do what is right are we then ready to learn how to do that very thing.

> In a very real sense, the life you live is just a reflection of the heart you have.

Be honest, how is your heart toward God? If you could pick one word (e.g., tender or hard, loving or angry, obedient or defiant, etc.) to describe your heart toward God what would it be?

Too often, especially when it comes to parenting or counseling, it's easy to move too quickly to behavior without considering the deeper matter of the underlying heart condition. When it comes to your internal heart and external behavior, there are four options.

1. Bad heart, bad behavior

Bad people do bad things. Sometimes the bad behavior merely reveals a bad heart. Jeremiah 17:9 is referring to this when it says, "The heart is deceitful above all things, and desperately wicked" (NKJV). This one is straightforward. Water is wet, politicians lie, and bad people do bad things.

2. Bad heart, good behavior

Bad people do good things. Jesus speaks of people like this, saying in Matthew 15:8, "This people honors me with their lips, but their heart is far from me." This one is a bit trickier as the sneaky person hides who they are by playing a role, pretending to be someone they are not—like the religious person who is an arrogant son of the devil and thinks hypocrisy is a spiritual gift but still says "bless you" when you sneeze.

3. Good heart, bad behavior

Good people do bad things. We can really discourage someone if we wrongly assume that a bad motive inspired the bad outcome. In 1 Samuel 16:7 God says, "For the LORD sees not as man sees: man looks on the outward appearance, but the LORD looks on the heart." Sometimes a person genuinely wants to do the right thing, but somehow does the wrong thing. One single mom I know was making dinner when she got interrupted by a business call. Wanting to help, her little girl tried her best to finish cooking dinner, but she just made a mess and burned the food. When her mom finished the call and returned to the kitchen, her little girl, covered in flour, said with a proud smile, "I'm sorry you have to work so hard, Mommy. I love you, and I am helping you by making dinner!" Sometimes God's kids are like that kid.

4. Good heart, good behavior

Good people do good things. The Bible refers to this when God says in Ezekiel 11:19–20, "I will give them one heart, and a new spirit I will put within them. I will remove the heart of stone from their flesh and give them a heart of flesh, that they may walk in my statutes and keep my rules and obey them." If you know more of these kinds of people than you can fit in your car at one time, you are blessed. They are like unicorns—we hear about them, but it's hard to find one.

Which of these four categories would most accurately describe your internal heart condition and external actions?

LOVE GOD SPIRITUALLY
WITH ALL YOUR SOUL

We tend to spend a lot of time, effort, money, and energy on our outer life. We fret about our physical appearance—our weight, our flaws, and the best angle for a selfie we plan to post online. We spend our whole lives worrying about the car we drive, clothes we wear, house we live in, and possessions we own. This external stuff does not satisfy us, save us, or soothe us.

Tragically it is not uncommon for the news to erupt with a tale about someone who has everything great in their outer life—good looks, nice car, huge home, beautiful spouse, healthy kids, lavish vacations, adoring fans—only to take their own life. Your inner life affects your outer life much more than your outer life affects your inner life. A peaceful soul, forgiven and loved by God, does more good than anything you could ever own, any achievement you could ever have, or any award you could ever earn.

Jesus says that loving God is the most important of all human activities. This is what your soul was made to do. As you love God from your soul, you are then able to love your neighbors and help them to love God from their souls.

Tending to your own soul means maintaining a healthy diet of Bible reading, prayer, worship, giving, serving, and building healthy relationships with God's people to remain in God's presence. As your soul becomes healthy through a loving relationship with God, you are best able to lovingly help others do the same.

In addition to your outer world you also have a mysterious inner world to explore. The Bible speaks of your inner life in terms of your soul. Unlike your visible body, you cannot see your invisible soul through a microscope or a telescope. It is only seen by the God who made it so that you can have a relationship with Him at the deepest level for your being for all eternity.

In Genesis 2:7 we read that we too were made by God with a soul: "The LORD God formed the man of dust from the ground and breathed into his nostrils the breath of life, and the man became a living creature." Admittedly human life is multifaceted and complex; for the sake of simplicity, the Bible here says that we—at the most basic level—have a visible physical outer life and an invisible spiritual inner life.

You do not just have a soul; you *are* a soul. This explains why even when your body dies, your soul does not. Your soul goes into the presence of the Lord until it rejoins the body and rises from the dead as Jesus did.

Our cultural problem is that we have replaced the soul with the self. The soul that was made by God and for God is now disconnected from God and replaced with the self. When it comes to helping people, including raising children, our culture tragically has no concept of the soul. In his book *Soul Keeping* John Ortberg even noted that the *Diagnostic and Statistical Manual of Mental Disorders* never once mentions the soul. To effectively help people, we need to help the whole person, including the soul, which integrates all aspects of a person together.

There are two main takeaways here:

1. **You have a soul.** Your soul was made by God and for God's Spirit. You are the steward of your soul. Nothing in your outer life matters as much as your soul, and nothing in your outer life will be healthy unless your soul is healthy. How healthy is your soul?

2. **Just as the body needs air, so the soul needs the Spirit.** You cannot live spiritually without God's powerful presence. Your soul needs to receive the life and love of God's Spirit, so you can teach your

neighbors—starting with your family and friends—
to love God from their souls in response to His love
for them from His soul. This explains why worship
remains so vital. Yes, it's fine to listen to a podcast,
but to be healthy, your soul needs to get into a room
with the souls of other people to sing from the
depths of your collective souls and connect with the
Holy Spirit.

Our world talks a lot about the soul. We can eat soul food while listening to soul music and looking into the eyes of someone we love because, as the old saying goes, the eyes are the windows to the soul. We even call Christian evangelists soul winners.

But what does the Bible have to say about the soul? Jesus provides perhaps the most famous statement about the soul in Matthew 16:26: "For what will it profit a man if he gains the whole world and forfeits his soul? Or what shall a man give in return for his soul?" Jesus wants you to understand that investing all your energy into your outer life is a complete waste of time if you have neglected your inner life. When this happens, people can sense it. Maybe you've heard someone say that a person seemed soulless and empty, or they might ask that person, "Have you lost your soul?"

Jesus' point is very simple—life is not mainly about what you have, where you go, what you achieve, who you know, or what awards you receive. Life is first and foremost about what you and your soul become as home to the Spirit.

How is your soul?

LOVE GOD MENTALLY
WITH ALL YOUR MIND

The Bible repeatedly says that everyone plays a part in a very real spiritual battle. That war often wages in the battlefield of the mind.

In our minds we struggle with lies, temptation, and condemnation. In our minds we wrestle to determine truth and lies, right and wrong, and God and Satan. Romans 12:2 makes this point when it says, "Do not be conformed to this world, but be transformed by the renewal of your mind." Not only is it sinful to *act* in ways that are contrary to God, it is also sinful to *think* in ways that are contrary to God. Furthermore, sinful thoughts often precede sinful actions, which means that if our minds are renewed our behavior will be as well.

Our mind was made to love God. Jesus says that we should love God with all our mind. God wants mindful Christians, not mindless Christians.

The key to a renewed mind is spiritual. Romans 8:5–6 says, "Those who live according to the Spirit set their minds on the things of the Spirit. For to set the mind on the flesh is death, but to set the mind on the Spirit is life and peace." God the Holy Spirit alone can renew your mind to love God's truth, learn God's ways, and live for God's glory. Without the Spirit, your mind becomes proud and "puffs up" with mere knowledge that does not love God or others (1 Cor. 8:1). In a world where the smartest person is the most respected, it is humbling and helpful to remember that it is not the smart mind, but rather the Spirit-surrendered mind that is pleasing in God's sight.

Is your mind surrendered to Scripture?

LOVE GOD PHYSICALLY
WITH ALL YOUR STRENGTH

Jesus is God in a body as John 1:14 says, "The Word became flesh and dwelt among us." Furthermore, as we have studied, Jesus matured physically—He was physically healthy.

Sometimes Christians can over-spiritualize things. Some things are very practical and not that spiritual.

Grace and I have five healthy children who all love the Lord. We travel a lot with the children, having started when they were little. Most of the time they do really well on airplanes, but I will never forget the worst flight of our lives. Our oldest daughter was just a few years old, and her brother was a newborn. We were traveling from Seattle to Orlando and had to run to catch a connecting flight. The first leg of the flight started early in the morning, so the kids did not get much sleep. Once we landed, our daughter assumed the trip was over, and she was very sad to hear that we had one more flight to board.

The flight was full, so my wife sat near the front with a newborn on her lap, and I sat near the back in a middle seat with a toddler on my lap. Dehydrated from a cold, exhausted, and with air pressure hurting her ears and giving her a headache, my daughter was just plain physically done traveling and needed a nap. During the second flight, she started crying, and our usually well-behaved child became "that kid." Eventually it seemed as if everyone around us was giving me the cold, hard stare, and I could tell that they were thinking, "Put the child in the overhead bin." Trying to prevent a nuclear meltdown, I looked at my crying little girl and asked what I could do.

She said, "Get me a pumpkin."

It was officially over. Why she wanted a pumpkin, I will never know. But I had not packed an emergency pumpkin.

The truth is, we all have pumpkin days. On pumpkin days the solution is often far more practical than it is spiritual.

Many things—hunger, tiredness, dehydration, only eating foods that end in "itos" (e.g., Doritos, burritos, taquitos), suffering with a cold or illness, or not having a day off since Gettysburg—can affect the rest of your being (heart, soul, mind). You exist in two parts. One is visible, external, and material; and the other is invisible, internal, and spiritual. The two parts of you affect each other positively and negatively.

You will find that you are likely more tempted to sin when you are exhausted or more tempted to despair when you are sick. There are some very practical reasons at the level of your physical well-being for this reality. As a result, you need to take a Sabbath day off as Jesus did. You also need to take a nap now and then as Jesus did.

Loving God means that you love God with your body. You should feed it healthy food, hydrate it with water, tuck it in at night, get it some exercise, and not get naked with people you are not married to.

One day your body will rise from the grave and be completely and eternally healthy. Until that day, loving God with the strength of your body will require having a body ruled by the Spirit. If your body governs itself, you will feed your physical desires until you self-destruct by eating, drinking, and indulging until you suffer and die. Paul talked about this in Romans 8:11–13 when he said, "If the Spirit of him who raised Jesus from the dead dwells in you, he who raised Christ Jesus from the dead will also give life to your mortal bodies through his Spirit who dwells in you....For if you live according to the flesh you will die, but if by the Spirit you put to death the deeds of the body, you will live."

In the old covenant the holiest place on earth was the temple. People would journey to that place to be near the presence of God, the Holy Spirit. In the new covenant your body becomes the holiest place on earth, the temple of the Holy Spirit. Therefore, you must love God with all the strength of your body by tending to your temple. In 1 Corinthians 6:19–20 Paul says, "Do you not know that your body is a temple of the Holy Spirit within you, whom you have from God? You are not your own, for you were bought with a price. So glorify God in your body." How are you doing at tending to the bodily temple that God has given you? Does your eating, drinking, and exercising glorify God? What changes do you need to make?

How Is Loving God Going?

Grace and I have been together since March 12, 1988. For years of our marriage I wrongly assumed that just because she had not said anything, we had no problems and all was well. Then one day I threw out what I thought were simple questions, "How are we doing in our relationship? How can I be a better friend to you?" I was expecting her to tell me that she felt like she was married to Jesus and she was blessed. Much to my surprise, she took that opportunity to gently let me know that I had a lot of room for improvement.

In all honesty I got a bit defensive. I asked why she had not told me these things before. She kindly reminded me that she had on various occasions and that I was not really listening or acting upon what she was saying. She was right. I needed to be more loving.

I took the words of my wife to heart and scheduled a day alone with the Lord. My goals were to (1) pray to the Lord, asking Him how I could love better in my relationship with my wife, (2) listen, (3) journal out my thoughts with the Lord, and 4) study scriptures that pertained to what He would say to me.

God was faithful to meet with me that day, but before He talked to me about my relationship with Grace, He spoke with me about my relationship with Him. The Lord kindly but firmly convicted me that if I loved Him better first, then I would love Grace better, so I needed to start working on my relationship with Him first.

I believe that much of the time, God feels like my wife did. God loves you, and He wants a loving relationship with you. He has spoken to you through Scripture, your conscience, and the wise counsel of godly people about some areas you need to improve in order to nurture a loving relationship with Him and others. Have you been listening?

If you need help with loving God or loving others, I would encourage you to spend some time with the Lord and invite the Holy Spirit to reveal to you the truth in these areas.

How are you doing at loving God with all your heart?

How are you doing at loving God with all your soul?

How are you doing at loving God with all your mind?

How are you doing at loving God with all your strength?

How are you doing at loving your neighbors, starting with the family and friends who are closest to you?

God invites you to love with all your heart, soul, mind, and strength by His Spirit. But there is a very real enemy who is all about hate and not love, who wages war against your heart, soul, mind, and strength. You will learn more about him and how to defeat him the same way Jesus did in the next chapter.

FIVE WEAPONS TO DEFEAT THE DEMONIC

I N AN INTERESTING moment, a kind, easygoing, and heartfelt pastor revealed to me that his previous job had been in the United States military as a SERE (Survival, Evasion, Resistance, and Escape) specialist. As I understand it, he prepared troops to survive if they were stranded in a harsh environment or captured by the enemy. I asked him if he ever had to waterboard people at work, and his answer was a stoic, "I can neither confirm, nor deny." Then he smirked, which was the poker tell.

I asked him what a typical day looked like. If I remember the conversation correctly, he said that they would pick up an unsuspecting trainee from say, their home, remove all their personal belongings (e.g., cell phone, wallet, watch, keys). Then they would rough them up a bit, throw them in the back of a dark, windowless box truck, and drive them around for a few days until they were good and disoriented. The goal was to combine isolation, disorientation, and exhaustion so that the trainee felt weak and weary.

Then they would try to psychologically press the trainee to the limits of their humanity to find their breaking point. He went on to explain that every human being has a limit to how much stress and duress they can physically and mentally endure, and once you push a person over that line they break. His job was to find that line and help military personnel push beyond their limits and move that line.

The Bible is, in many regards, a battlefield report of a war that has been raging for all human history. According to the Bible, angels are spirit beings created by God to serve His purposes. However, one angel became proud, which is the root of many sins, and preferred to be his own god rather than worship and obey the real God (Isa. 14:11–23; Ezek. 28:12). We now know him by various biblical names such as Satan, the dragon, the serpent, the enemy, the devil, the tempter, the murderer, the father of lies, the adversary, the accuser, the destroyer, and the evil one.

Tragically one-third of the angels sided with Satan to declare war on God and become the army devoted to destroying God's kingdom (Isa. 14:12; Luke 10:18; Heb. 12:22; Rev. 9:1, 12:3–9). Their rebellion culminated in a great battle against God and His holy angels. Satan and his demons lost and were kicked out of heaven without the possibility of ever being forgiven or reconciled into a right relationship with God (2 Pet. 2:4).

After the great war in heaven, continuing with the story of Scripture, the scene shifts to a new battlefield—earth. The Bible opens with a wedding between Adam and Eve, and by the time you turn the page, Satan the serpent shows up to declare war on their marriage and family. From this we learn that Satan always shows up to ruin what God made wonderful and turn people away from loving relationships with God and one another. The next thing you know, the family is at war against itself as Adam and Eve hide from God, attack each other verbally, and one of their sons murders the other.

Tragically our first parents surrendered to Satan and sinned, and ever since everyone has suffered. Every one of us born since the fatal, foolish fall has entered into a spiritual war between the kingdom of God and spiritual terrorists seeking only to kill, steal, and destroy.

After our first parents, Adam and Eve, surrendered through sinning, a promise was made. God Himself foretold the coming of Jesus to crush Satan saying in Genesis 3:15, "I will put enmity between you and the woman, and between your offspring and her offspring; he shall bruise your head, and you shall bruise his heel." The battle was brewing.

Many years later Jesus was born. Like Adam, He was not openly attacked by the evil one until there was a public ministry calling on His life. The temptation of Jesus is so important that all three Synoptic Gospels (Matthew, Mark, and Luke) include it.

Jesus (also called "the last Adam" in 1 Corinthians 15:45) picks up the war where the first Adam fell in battle. Adam began with no sin nature, lived in a paradise, enjoyed a close friendship with God, endured temptation, failed, and was cast into the lonely wilderness. Jesus came with no sin nature, left a paradise, enjoyed a close friendship with God, endured temptation, succeeded, and defeated the dragon in the lonely wilderness.

> Every one of us born since the fatal, foolish fall has entered into a spiritual war between the kingdom of God and spiritual terrorists seeking only to kill, steal, and destroy.

Just prior to facing the toughest temptation in history, Jesus experienced the most remarkable revelation in history. Shortly after the incredible high of having the Spirit descend upon Him at His baptism and the Father speaking from heaven for all to hear that He is the beloved Son of God, Jesus faced the incredible low of forty days without food or companionship. It just goes to show that sometimes our greatest temptations come after our greatest success. Sometimes success is harder to manage than failure, and wins are harder to navigate than losses. Why? Because the serpent slithers in to strike at success.

Before graduating to His public ministry, Jesus had to take one final test. That test was His temptation. We learn from the account in Luke 4:1–15 that to walk with God is to walk into a war. Thankfully God gives us five weapons for spiritual war.

Your First Weapon: The Holy Spirit

The story of Jesus' temptation begins in Luke 4:1–2, "And Jesus, full of the Holy Spirit, returned from the Jordan and was led by the Spirit in the wilderness for forty days, being tempted by the devil. And he ate nothing during those days. And when they were ended, he was hungry."

Unlike God, Satan is not omnipresent. He cannot be in more than one place at a time. Satan himself went to war with Jesus, but for the rest of us, he sends someone else on his behalf. As is often the case with the demonic, no one invites it, but instead, it rudely shows up in a pushy and bossy way, demanding to be dealt with immediately.

Like Moses (Exod. 34:28) and Elijah (1 Kings 19:8) Jesus spent forty days alone in the wilderness. By the time the dragon showed up for war, Jesus had reached the limits of His humanity. In this we learn when our enemy is likely to HIT—when we are *hungry, isolated*, and *tired*.

- When we are physically unwell and in need of food or some other provision, we are more open to temptation since we lack the energy we need to fight.

- When we are isolated because we live alone, have no close friends or family living nearby, and can live a life filled with secrecy because of privacy, we are also more vulnerable to sinful temptation.

- When we are tired, our energy levels are low because we are burned out, not sleeping well, sick, injured, overconsuming alcohol, using illegal drugs, or experiencing poor health for any reason, the enemy sees us as wounded prey that he can more easily devour.

Living out of His full humanity, the Lord Jesus was vulnerable. We are as well, anytime we find ourselves hungry, isolated, or tired.

To make matters worse, Satan and demons do not share the limitations of our humanity. They do not get the flu, need a day off, or age. The demons are fallen angels. We read of the angels in Revelation 4:8, "Day and night they never cease to say, 'Holy, holy, holy, is the Lord God Almighty, who was and is and is to come!'" No human being could sing in worship day and night without ceasing forever. Our humanity has limits that spirit beings do not share.

We read the same thing in Revelation 7:15, which says of the angels, "They are before the throne of God, and serve him day and night." Satan also works twenty-four-hour shifts as we read in Revelation 12:10, he "accuses them day and night."

> It is better to have the Spirit and nothing else than to have everything but the Spirit.

How can you as a human being with finite energy possibly win a battle against spirit beings who have the benefit of being able to war against you day and night without needing a meal, nap, glass of water, or day off? Your power is finite, but the Spirit's power is *infinite*!

Where did Jesus' temptation occur? In a barren, lonely, desolate wilderness. Sometimes following the leading of the Holy Spirit means we, like Jesus, will find ourselves in poverty rather than prosperity, trouble instead of tranquillity, and hardship instead of happiness. It just goes to show that the surest place to be is in God's will, even if it's in a wilderness. It is better to have the Spirit and nothing else than to have everything but the Spirit.

Your Second Weapon: Identity

The way you see yourself is your identity or what is commonly referred to as self-image or self-esteem. You form your identity in one of two ways: you achieve it by yourself or you receive it from God.

When you achieve your identity by yourself, there are numerous problems. For starters, if you wrap up your identity in your role (mother, wife, husband, father, winner, beauty queen, etc.), when your role changes, you fall into an identity crisis. When the kids move out, the marriage crumbles, you lose your job, or age comes to diminish your beauty, you become devastated. You no longer know who you are, and your life begins to spin into chaos.

When you receive your identity from God, you are able to remain healthy no matter what happens in your life. When you know that you are a loved child of God and your identity in relationship to your heavenly Father cannot be changed, you are free to stop living *for* your identity—something that is never secure—and start living *from* your identity, which is eternally secure.

Who you think you are determines what you do. Because of this, when Satan attacks, he starts by undermining your sense of identity. In the first attack on humans Adam and Eve were told that if they did something (partake of the forbidden fruit), they would then achieve their identity by becoming "like God." That, however, was a lie. God had already made them in His "likeness." They had already received an identity of being like God, but somehow got spiritual amnesia and forgot who they were. They wrongly believed the satanic lie that they could achieve an identity by their own efforts.

Satan used this same tactic when he attacked Jesus. We read of the assault on Jesus' identity in Luke 4:3, "The devil said to him, 'If you are the Son of God, command this stone to become bread.'" Satan questioned Jesus' identity as the Son of God. God the Father spoke this very thing from heaven over Jesus at His baptism forty days prior saying, "this is My Son." Jesus did not need to do anything to achieve His identity as the Son of God. Unlike Adam, thankfully and perfectly, Jesus did not forget who He was.

The role of Satan is to be our accuser (Rev. 12:10). As the accuser, Satan said to Jesus, "If you are the Son of God..." Notice the word *you*. Just in case you missed English class the day they covered this, *you* is a pronoun referred to as "second person" in grammar and writing. When you hear the second person *you* as Jesus did, it means someone else is speaking to you—either another person, God, or the demonic. This can be an audible conversation or a thought. If it is a negative thought you have not related to anyone, you might be experiencing a demonic attack on your identity. Common examples are: "God does not forgive you, and what you have done is beyond forgiveness." "You are a failure." "You are a loser." "You are worthless." "You are hopeless." "You should kill yourself."

God never speaks to one of His children this way, but the demonic realm does, and they hope you believe who they say you are and forget who God says you are. Sometimes negative self-talk and negative self-image are a demonic attack on you and your identity, as was the case with Jesus. Knowing who God says you are as a loved, forgiven saint with a Father who never fails is the key to your victory, just as it was to Jesus.

Jesus was likely beyond hunger and feeling the early effects of starvation after forty days of fasting. When Satan asked Jesus to turn stones into bread, the act itself was not sinful. God had provided manna bread for His people after their Exodus from Egypt into the wilderness. Jesus was born in Bethlehem, which means house of bread. Later He said He was the "bread of life" (John 6:33, 48) and frequently broke bread over meals with friends all the way up to the Last Supper. If Jesus could turn water into wine, then He could also turn stones into bread.

The temptation was not to commit a sinful act, but rather to enter into a sinful relationship. Satan was inviting Jesus to enter a relationship where they would do evil together. We often think of all the relationships that Jesus had while walking on the earth, but we need to also consider all the relationships He *refused* to have because those alliances would have been ungodly. For example, the religious leaders constantly harassed Jesus, demanding that He agree with them, join them, and advance their cause. Jesus repeatedly refused their demands until they murdered Him for refusing to join them. For Jesus to have joined such a group in a supportive relationship would have been sinful. Jesus entered into relationships where He could make sinful people godly but did not enter into relationships where sinful people could make Him ungodly.

Too often we see sin solely in terms of actions, and we overlook sinful relationships. There are people you should not be romantically or intimately involved with. There are people you should not be in business with, allow into your home, or provide access to your children, spouse, or private details of life. There are people you should not do ministry with. The enemy sends such people and trains them according to his battle plan. They are pushy, bossy, ask questions that make you feel uncomfortable and insecure, and press for an unholy, unhelpful, unhealthy relationship just like the devil did in the desert.

Do not be discouraged or feel defeated when this happens. The same thing happened to Jesus. There is a difference between temptation and sin. When you are tempted, especially by a sinful relationship, remember Jesus and Hebrews 4:15–16, which says, "We do not have a high priest who is unable to sympathize with our weaknesses, but one who in every respect has been tempted as we are, yet without sin. Let us then with confidence draw near to the throne of grace, that we may receive mercy and find grace to help in time of need." When the enemy comes to HIT you with sinful temptation, often starting through an ungodly relationship with someone, you can invite Jesus to be with you, bring empowering grace through the Holy Spirit to you, and help you. Jesus has experienced the same things you experience, and He won His war and will help you win your fight as well.

I find it curious to ponder why Satan continues his war against God even though the Scriptures are abundantly clear that he will be forever defeated. Perhaps not only is the devil a deceiver, but he is also self-deceived. In the past he refused to accept his God-given identity as a created being made to honor, glorify, and obey God. Unhappy with the identity God gave him, he instead wanted to achieve his own identity, be a god himself and be honored, glorified, and obeyed by the real God, Jesus Christ.

Satan may have proudly deceived himself into thinking that he can defeat God, rewrite the Bible, and make his chosen identity an eternal reality. This explains why he tempts us with pride to live a life in which we reject the identity we have received from God and instead achieve our preferred identity for ourselves apart from God, thinking that God is wrong and we are right. It's all demonic deception from the deceiver who has deceived himself.

Your Third Weapon: Godly Perspective

Fishing is pretty easy because fish are not very smart. The key to catching fish is knowing what kind of bait they like. Once you get the right bait on the hook, the rest is pretty easy. You drop it in front of the fish, and they get so excited that they swim up, bite the bait, and overlook the hook.

You would think that at some point the fish would catch on to this ploy. Since fish have a school, you think that by now they would have classes on how to avoid hooks. Nope. The fish never learn, and the same old bait-and-hook method works every time.

People are a lot like fish. The devil and his demons figure out what bait we like and dangle it in front of us. Like a fisherman, the devil couldn't care less what bait we prefer. He will gladly give us sex, money, power, success, comfort, drugs, alcohol—pick a preference. Like dumb fish, we continually swim right on up and take the bait, forget about the hook.

The Bible calls Satan "the prince of the power of the air" (Eph. 2:2). One Bible commentator explains this phrase saying, "Basically his thought was of an evil power with control in the world…but whose existence was not material but spiritual."[1] Cultures and nations are not morally or spiritually neutral. At work in and through various physical peoples and places are powerful spiritual beings who are encouraging and promoting sin and suffering.

In tempting Jesus, Satan loaded every cultural bait on the hook at the same time. We read in Luke 4:5–7, "And the devil took him up and showed him all the kingdoms of the world in a moment of time, and said to him, 'To you I will give all this authority and their glory, for it has been delivered to me, and I give it to whom I will. If you, then, will worship me, it will all be yours.'" I believe that when Satan showed Jesus every temptation in every nation and culture, in an instant, He felt the combined level of temptation that everyone on the earth was facing at that moment. Can you imagine how you would fare under the same circumstances?

If we are honest, each of us must confess to the existence of some bait the enemy could put on a hook and dangle in front of us, and we would likely bite. Yet Jesus Christ didn't even nibble. He was offered every human desire for no price and no pain so long as He was willing to allow Satan instead of the Father to be His highest authority. Whether His loyalty was to the Father or Satan, Jesus' sitting on a throne ruling over a kingdom would be the same. He would remain the second in charge at the right hand. Satan and the Father offered Him rulership over the kingdoms of the earth from the second chair. Satan's offer did not require any suffering or crucifixion as the Father's plan did. Jesus, however, chose the Father's painful plan over the enemy's pleasurable plan.

Why? Because He had perspective. Jesus was offered two options in that instant:

- Option 1 was the temptation to have no pain and all pleasure in exchange for losing His relationship with God the Father and God the Spirit.

- Option 2 was the invitation to have all pain and no pleasure in exchange for keeping His relationship with God the Father and God the Spirit.

Simply stated, Jesus valued His relationship with God the Father and God the Spirit more than literally anything else. When tempted, you need to keep the perspective of Jesus and remember that your most valuable treasure is your relationship with God. Trading it for anything resembles the foolish and impetuous Esau who sold his birthright for a bowl of soup.

Your Fourth Weapon: Scripture

In college Grace and I had an eccentric and entertaining professor. Disheveled with long hair, a wild-eyed look, unkempt beard, cowboy boots, and a large knife always in his belt holster, he was quite a character. His lectures were electric. He had a razor-sharp mind, quick wit, and larger-than-life personality. He was nuttier than a PayDay bar.

He also liked to quote Bible verses—a lot. He would sprinkle in random scriptures from memory, including entire

> Just because you know the Bible that does not mean you know the Lord.

chapters of the Bible. One time after class we asked him if he was a Christian. He laughed loudly, threw his head back, and said something like, "Of course not. I don't believe any of that foolishness about Jesus!" Shocked, we asked why he knew so much Bible if he hated Christ and Christianity. He went on to explain to us that his brother was a pastor, and he memorized the Bible so he could mock his brother and win Bible arguments with him even though he was an atheist.

As a brand-new Christian, I learned an important lesson that day: just because you know the Bible that does not mean you know the Lord. In fact, Satan and demons know the Bible very well. We read about a Bible debate between Jesus and Satan in Luke 4:8–11, where Jesus said, "It is written, 'You shall worship the Lord your God, and him only shall you serve.'"

Satan then said, "If you are the Son of God, throw yourself down from here, for it is written, 'He will command his angels concerning you, to guard you,' and 'On their hands they will bear you up, lest you strike your foot against a stone.'"

The Bible is a spiritual sword. Like any weapon, you'd better know how to use it so that when you are attacked, you can defend yourself. When Satan attacks Jesus, he tries to use the Word of God against even God. But as he often does through false teachers and false prophets, he quotes it falsely.

One Bible scholar says, "The tempter cleverly misquoted Psalm 91:11–12 by leaving out the phrase 'to guard you in all your ways.' This passage teaches that God provides his angels to watch over his people when they live in accordance with His will (see Exod. 19:4–5; Deut. 32:10–11). Satan claimed that the Father would protect the Son as He plummeted to the ground. But since such a stunt would not be within the will of God, the promise of divine protection would not apply."[2]

In this battle with the devil Jesus repeatedly quotes from memory the Book of Deuteronomy. Jesus models a very vital principle: we must combat sinful temptation with biblical meditation. Paul warns us, saying in Colossians 2:8, "See to it that no one takes you captive by philosophy and empty deceit, according to human tradition, according to the elemental spirits of the world, and not according to Christ."

In every age there are people who want to say yes to sin and temptation, so they search for what sounds like a biblical justification for inexcusable behavior. Many times this is in relation to sexual sin with demonically empowered arguments supporting such behavior, often with a philosophically compelling and popular case.

Why? Because when new cultural norms disagree with the Bible, they tell us it's OK to change the Bible rather than change our behavior. That's demonic. As a general rule, when anyone's interpretation of the Bible concludes with them getting naked with someone other than their spouse of the opposite gender, you know that they studied at Satan's seminary. Most theological debates are just fancy ways for people not to exercise dominion over their drawers.

Your mind is the battlefield in your war with the devil and his demons. The enemy wants a mental stronghold or a fortified head-quarters for war. He most often finds a place in your life where you have suffered significant emotional and spiritual pain and seeks to convince you to believe a lie in that painful place. Once you believe any lie or embrace any wrong interpretation of Scripture, you have opened a stronghold for the devil and his minions in your mind. From there he can expand the war against you until you are increasingly thinking thoughts that are against the Word of God. Second Corinthians 10:3–5 explains it this way, "Though we walk in the flesh, we are not waging war according to the flesh. For the weapons of our warfare are not of the flesh but have divine power to destroy strongholds. We destroy arguments and every lofty opinion raised against the knowledge of God, and take every thought captive to obey Christ."

Any tempting thought that we do not take captive to Christ will take us captive. In ancient battle when a suspected enemy was captured, they would be taken into custody, brought to the highest-ranking officer, and interrogated at spearpoint to see if they were friend or foe. Part of our spiritual warfare is doing the same to our thoughts—especially thoughts about God. We are to take those thoughts captive, march them to Jesus, hold the sword of the Scriptures to their throat, and see if they tell the truth or lies. Paul refers to this in 1 Thessalonians 5:21–22 when he says, "Test everything; hold fast what is good. Abstain from every form of evil."

Jesus modeled for us how to combat sinful temptation with bib-lical meditation. He so filled His mind with the Scriptures that when tempted He could quote the exact Scripture correctly. This allowed Him, and allows us, to defeat the enemy.

YOUR FIFTH WEAPON: FAITH TO TRUST

Jesus not only defeated the devil but also got the last word. Luke 4:12–13 says, "And Jesus answered him, 'It is said, "You shall not put the Lord your God to the test.'" And when the devil had ended every temptation, he departed from him until an opportune time."

It is demonic to demand that God must be tested by us, prove Himself to us, or perform a miracle for us. God is in control, and we are not. We are not to test God, but rather trust God unless He tells us otherwise. Throughout the entire battle with the devil, Jesus refused to test God and instead chose only to trust God.

The essence of faith is trusting God. Trusting God is always important, but never more important than when we find ourselves tempted. In those moments the Holy Spirit wants to help us as He helped Jesus continue to trust in God and not succumb to the temptation to test God. This kind of faith surrenders the outcome of events to God and accepts whatever future God determines is best.

For Jesus, this kind of trust meant that He would face a very difficult future. He would have to trust the Father and the Spirit for His life of poverty, ongoing vocal public opposition, betrayal by Judas, shameful arrest, and brutal execution.

When the enemy comes to tempt us, he seeks to get us to surrender to him. Jesus surrendered to God, and eventually the enemy surrendered and departed. James 4:7 promises this to all of God's people saying, "Submit yourselves therefore to God. Resist the devil, and he will flee from you."

The devil fled from Jesus but not forever. Satan would return, and like a sniper lying in wait, he kept his site scoped on Jesus, hoping for another opportunity to take a kill shot. The same goes for the Christian. This war with the devil and his demons has many battles, so we must remain vigilant and on guard for an enemy attack.

You must understand that being tempted does not mean you are ungodly, unspiritual, or unloved by God. Jesus experienced temptation, and you will too. When this happens, do not believe the lie that it is sinful or shameful to be tempted. Jesus was perfect, and while on the earth He was persistently tempted.

Jesus overcame demonic temptation by living in the continual presence of God, the Holy Spirit. Jesus' temptation account begins in Luke 4:1, "Jesus, full of the Holy Spirit...." The temptation account ends in verses 14–15, "Jesus returned in the power of the Spirit." Jesus' spiritual victory begins and ends with being Spirit-filled. This is the key to spiritual warfare and defeating demonic temptation. Jesus said the same thing in Matthew 12:28, "If it is by the Spirit of God that I cast out demons, then the kingdom of God has come upon you." Jesus clearly stated that He defeated demons by the power of the Holy Spirit—the same power we have access to as Christians.

To defeat a spiritual enemy, you need the energy of the Spirit of God. In 1 John 4:4 it says precisely this: "He who is in you is greater than he who is in the world." In context John means that the same Holy Spirit who dwells in the believer and dwelt in Jesus is more powerful than any and every demon, including Satan himself. For this reason, if you

> Jesus' spiritual victory begins and ends with being Spirit-filled. This is the key to spiritual warfare and defeating demonic temptation.

maintain a humble spirit, then you allow an opportunity for the Holy Spirit to give you a power you do not have to defeat an enemy that you cannot otherwise defeat—by saying no to temptation and yes to triumph.

In many circles today talk of the devil and his demons is not popular. In *The Screwtape Letters* C. S. Lewis wrote, "There are two equal and opposite errors into which our race can fall about the devils. One is to disbelieve in their existence. The other is to believe, and to feel an excessive and unhealthy interest in them."[3] In the world of general spirituality there is a reticence to even think in terms of holy and unholy angels in favor of seeing all spirits and spirituality as equally positive. Others reject talk of the demonic because they have seen irresponsible and hyper-spiritual people blame shift their poor life decisions onto the devil and his demons.

Some Christian theologians feel such academic pressure to surrender the supernatural they actually teach that biblical miracles are mere myths. For example, one noted theologian has said, "It is impossible to use electric light and the wireless and to avail ourselves of modern medical and surgical discoveries, and at the same time to believe in the New Testament world of demons and spirits."[4]

In short, he means that in the world of the telescope and microscope, belief in "primitive" notions of the spirit world that cannot be examined by science are outdated since we've become too smart to believe in the devil. Meanwhile, the devil laughs at how proud and foolish we are to ignore him. Some years ago there was an insightful line from an intriguing movie called *The Usual Suspects* that said, "The greatest trick the devil ever pulled was convincing the world he didn't exist."[5]

Christians should not act surprised when trouble comes into their lives. Perhaps the trouble begins with how we're invited to become Christians. In varying ways we're told, "Confess your sins to Jesus, and He will take you to heaven." While true, we often leave out the time between our commitment to Christ and the day we see Him face to face—also called life. In reality, in this life there's a war between two kings, Jesus and Satan; two kingdoms, light and darkness; and two armies, those of Jesus and Satan. While the Bible promises us that King Jesus is victorious, we're on a pilgrimage to get to Jesus' eternal kingdom. Along the way, we are preaching the gospel by the power of the Holy Spirit in hopes of setting some war captives free from their bondage to Satan, sin, and death. Christians seeking to serve their King Jesus and His kingdom need to know that an eternal vacation is coming, but only after the long war.

> Our goal cannot be to become spiritual. Our goal must be to become Spirit-filled.

Our goal cannot be to become spiritual. Our goal must be to become Spirit-filled.

TAKING YOUR TEST

As I've mentioned, I am the father of five children. Each year, to graduate to the next grade, our three boys and two girls undergo an intense season of testing. Those tests are intended to reveal the maturing in their learning and qualify them to move to the next level. During those testing seasons, the kids are understandably tired, a bit stressed, and exerting a lot of energy to pass their tests.

Once you graduate from school in the natural, you quickly forget that your spiritual testing continues. There will be seasons in life when you face many tests, trials, and temptations. In those trying times you need to remember something you learn from the example of Jesus: Satan's temptation to get you is God's test to *graduate* you. In reality a temptation and a test are two sides of the same coin. Satan wants you to fail the test by surrendering to temptation and thereby not graduate to the next level of spiritual maturity and ministry opportunity. Conversely God wants that temptation to be a test that you pass, certifying that you are ready to graduate spiritually to another level of maturity.

We read that Jesus graduated by surrendering to God rather than surrendering to temptation. Not only did the devil leave Him, but the Spirit filled Him and brought Him from the wilderness into town to begin His public ministry. Luke 4:14–15 says, "And Jesus returned in the power of the Spirit to Galilee, and a report about him went out through all the surrounding country. And he taught in their synagogues, being glorified by all."

Between the glorious baptism of Jesus and the beginning of Jesus' public ministry, we find the scene of temptation. This order is incredibly important. In Luke's chronological account we see that Jesus needed to pass the temptation test to graduate to His next level of public ministry.

I want this to be an encouragement to you. Satan may come to tempt you, but the Spirit will empower you to pass that test and graduate to a higher level of maturity and ministry. Jesus' brother

James connects this concept of a temptation or trial being a test, saying, "Count it all joy, my brothers, when you meet trials of various kinds, for you know that the testing of your faith produces steadfastness. And let steadfastness have its full effect, that you may be perfect and complete, lacking in nothing" (James 1:2–4). In 1 Peter 1:6–7 it says, "In this you rejoice, though now for a little while, if necessary, you have been grieved by various trials, so that the tested genuineness of your faith—more precious than gold that perishes though it is tested by fire—may be found to result in praise and glory and honor at the revelation of Jesus Christ."

> Satan's temptation to get you is God's test to *graduate* you. In reality a temptation and a test are two sides of the same coin.

When you see temptations and trials sent by your enemy as tests that God uses to graduate you, you can "count it all joy" and rejoice.

Why?

Jesus took your test and passed by the Spriit's power, and sends the same Spirit to empower you to pass your test.

If you have failed your temptation test in the past, God is gracious. He will forgive you, teach you, and help you get ready to retake the test. God is so gracious that you can keep retaking a test until you pass it and graduate to the next level of life and ministry. You *can* pass the temptation test, and by the Spirit's power, you *will*.

After you have passed your temptation test, you can look at the demonic realm and say the same thing Joseph said to his brothers in his epic final scene, "As for you, you meant evil against me, but God meant it for good" (Gen. 50:20). Once you have passed your temptation test, you can then become emotionally healthy, as we will study next.

Chapter 6

JESUS' SECRET TO EMOTIONAL HEALTH

W<small>E WERE BORED</small> little boys—until we discovered the blue tarp in the garage at our buddy's house. Unsure what lay beneath, one of the boys yanked the tarp and revealed, in all its glory, a blue minibike with white pinstripes.

We stood breathless, motionless, and speechless as we looked in disbelief at this uncovered treasure. We had no idea where it came from or why it was there. Perhaps it was a gift from God like the chariot that took Elijah into heaven?

In the life of every boy there are magical moments where the glory of God descends as it did on the temple in the days of Solomon. For a boy, when a motor and wheels come together, something supernatural and sacred happens.

One boy who got good grades, ate his vegetables, and got beat up a lot at recess, shared his safety concerns and suggested we get parental permission before riding. We immediately declined his proposal since we knew that no sane parent would let little boys who had barely figured out how to ride bicycles without training wheels graduate to a motorized mode of transportation.

With the quiet precision of ninjas, we slyly rolled our little hog out of the garage and tried to figure out how to start it. The old compression motor required a kickstart, and we took turns sitting on the seat and kicking the starter down without any luck. The old bike was like my buddy's dad who usually watched television half asleep in his chair—it rumbled and sputtered but didn't quite have enough energy to fire and get going.

Finally one of the boys jumped as high as he could and came down full force on the kick starter. Like Lazarus getting out of his grave in full glory, the old bike roared to life. Unfortunately the throttle was stuck open, and our buddy lasted mere seconds on the seat. Like an old bronco rider, he was quickly bucked off. The minibike, however, was stuck on full speed as it took off down the street with no one steering it.

Chasing after it down the road, we were screaming at the other kids in the neighborhood to get out of the way of the runaway minibike. Eventually the street beast tilted to the right and veered into a fence where it fell over as a tire kept spinning. We pulled enough wires until we slew the beast and it puffed its final breath. We had to murder our minibike. It felt like a funeral. If only we could have stayed in the saddle, we could have ridden our trusty steel steed into the sunset.

There's a parallel we can learn from this story. People are like that minibike. Experiences in life are like fuel. Emotions are like the motor. The will is like the handlebars. Without a driver, things get crazy fast.

Experiences in our lives spark our emotions, and very quickly our lives start operating out of anger, depression, joy, or whatever emotion we are feeling. The problem is, without a driver staying in the seat and holding the handlebars, things quickly escalate, and we are a lot like that minibike—out of control and barreling forward. If our feelings drive everything we say and do, it's only a matter of time before the bad crash happens.

You know what this feels like, right? When was the last time you got emotional and the story of what followed sounds a lot like my minibike memory? Who do you know that lives a lot like that story—their emotions get fired up and off they go, out of control and rolling fast with no one steering or driving?

JESUS' EMOTIONAL LIFE

How did Jesus maintain emotional health? If anyone had reason to be like our out-of-control minibike, Jesus did.

Jesus had some very real enemies. They had a constant public plan to ruin His reputation. They said He was a drunk, a glutton with no self-control, and a demon-possessed party animal who spent a lot of time with the kind of folks who like to wear underwear as outerwear while breaking the commandments with full zeal. That's a rough public relations nightmare for a single, homeless guy trying to launch a brand-new ministry from scratch. Jesus, who never sinned, did call them hypocrites, white-washed tombs, serpents, and blind guides, and said that their daddy was the devil—all of which probably got pretty emotional. How have you responded to enemies who continually harangue and harass you publicly?

Religious neat nicks, who were more conservative than God, regularly attacked Jesus in public. They would wait for a crowd to surround Jesus, and then pick a fight, start an argument, or try to incite a riot. Quite frequently Jesus had to make a run for it because things got so dire that He was in real danger. This harassment included threats of legal action and culminated with Jesus being falsely arrested, tried, and convicted of a crime so heinous that He got the death penalty. How would you respond if you were beaten beyond recognition, stripped nearly naked, and hung up to bleed before a cheering crowd while your mom stood there crying?

Jesus had a constant parade of people who drained His life energy. Crowds followed Him wherever He went, wanting Him to answer their questions, cast out their demons, heal their infirmities, fix all their problems, pay their bills, and be their friend. Jesus had no assistant to schedule any of this nor any office for them to come to, so they just followed Him around like a swarm of mosquitos continually buzzing day and night wherever He went.

How do you respond when people get on your last nerve and refuse to give you your space? How is your relationship with the most annoying, frustrating, and exhausting family members? How have you responded when people started talking trash about your mama?

Jesus' disciples were not a big help either. Peter liked to boss Him around and deny Him. Thomas doubted Him. James and John kept asking if they could sit with Him in heaven and rule over the cosmos for all eternity as His wingmen. Judas stole money from the ministry account the entire time he was the bookkeeper.

How have you responded to friends, coworkers, and ministry partners who made your life miserable?

People wore Jesus out. On one occasion He took a nap on a boat during a massive storm. That's a yawning Yahweh.

What is your emotional response to people when you are flat out weary, sick, tired, and burned out? How would you respond to all of this constant public pressure for three years? Would you default to rage, depression, or some other emotion?

How did Jesus maintain emotional health? There is surprisingly very little written about the emotional life of Jesus in comparison to such things as His teachings, miracles, and parables. Theologians have struggled with the emotions of God in general, and Jesus in particular. One theologian reports, "The Thirty-Nine Articles of the Church of England and the Westminster Confession of Faith described God as 'without body, parts, or passions.'"[1]

Perhaps this misconception explains the prevalence of passion-less Christianity. If God is "without...passions," then our relationship with Him should also be one "without...passions."

How in the world could anyone who reads the Bible end up at that conclusion? In the first book of the Bible alone God floods the earth and drowns everyone but one family of hillbilly moonshiners led by naked Noah; sends an unlimited supply of free, flaming road tar upon Sodom and Gomorrah; turns Lot's wife into a pillar of salt big enough to salt the rim of every margarita poured on the earth today; and sends a parade of plagues on the entire nation of Egypt. I'm guessing that the folks who got the flood, road tar, salty spouse, or plague would tell us that to them, it seemed like God was a wee bit passionate.

God is a passionate Person who wrote the Bible through passionate people to be read and obeyed by us passionately! Our emotional God made us in His image with emotions to have a loving relationship.

FOUR REASONS FOR
PASSIONLESS CHRISTIANITY

Sadly, many have arrived at a passionless Christianity, and I believe there are four reasons why.

People are emotionally unhealthy.

Some people are so emotionally unhealthy and untethered that their spirituality becomes little more than chasing experiences devoid of any real study or knowledge of God. It's as if the Holy Spirit were a bartender and the church an open bar. Overreacting, others want to downplay the emotions because of unhealthy emotionalism, and if the dead in Christ shall rise first, as Paul says, these folks are at the front of the line. An old preacher says that this kind of error is like a drunk peasant who climbs on one side of a horse only to fall off the other side of the horse.

People place mind over emotions.

The modern era of rationalism, which roughly corresponds with the time since the Protestant Reformation, so shaped some people that they read the Bible through the lens that the mind is more trustworthy than the emotions. This tendency started with Rene Descartes making the mind the center of our being with his *cogito ergo sum*, which is Latin for "I think, therefore I am."[2]

Therefore, *Star Trek*'s Spock is the ideal being we should aspire to become. Theologians of this ilk like to say that we should think God's thoughts after Him—which is perfectly fine if we also aspire to feel God's feelings after Him.

This passionless problem was present in the early church as well. Bible commentator William Barclay says of the New Testament:

> We must remember that it was written for Greeks.... To the Greek the primary characteristic of God was what he called apatheia [apathy], which means total inability to feel any emotion whatsoever. How did the Greeks come to attribute such a characteristic to God? They argued like this. If we can feel sorrow or joy, gladness or grief, it means that someone can have an effect upon us. Now, if a person has an effect upon us, it means that for the moment that person has power over us. No one can have any power over God; and this must mean that God is essentially incapable of feeling any emotion whatsoever. The Greeks believed in an isolated, passionless and compassionless God. What a different picture Jesus gave. He showed us a God whose heart is wrung with anguish for the anguish of his people. The greatest thing Jesus did was to bring us the news of a God who cares.[3]

People make God non-relational.

In an effort to preserve God's unchanging nature (which is true and called immutability by theologians), they made God non-relational. In a relationship there are emotions between persons in response to one another, and so it is in our relationship with God. Nonemotional Christianity is also non-relational and nonbiblical.

People don't connect the Holy Spirit with emotional health.

There has not been sufficient emphasis on the biblical connection between the ministry of the Holy Spirit and emotional health. For starters, God the Father, Son, and Spirit have emotions. The Bible clearly teaches that the Holy Spirit is a person with emotions—contrary to much false teaching in other religions that follow a *Star Wars* story line with an impersonal force or an unemotional divine being.

EMOTIONS AND THE HOLY SPIRIT

We can "grieve the Holy Spirit of God" (Eph. 4:30) as others before us have "rebelled and grieved his Holy Spirit" (Isa. 63:10). When people have no regard for Jesus, the Bible says they have "outraged the Spirit of grace" (Heb. 10:29). When we have "loved righteousness and hated wickedness," God anoints us with the Holy Spirit as the "oil of gladness" (Heb. 1:9). For those who want to end the turmoil in their emotional life, God tells us that "righteousness and peace and joy" are found "in the Holy Spirit" (Rom. 14:17). The Bible tells those who are struggling with hopelessness, cheerlessness, and restlessness, "May the God of hope fill you with all joy and peace in believing, so that by the power of the Holy Spirit you may abound in hope" (Rom. 15:13). When our souls become dehydrated and need God's love to fill them, we can drink deeply of "the love of the Spirit" (v. 30).

As a case study of a Spirit-filled emotional life, in 2 Corinthians 6:4–10 the apostle Paul tells us that his external physical life was marked by "afflictions, hardships, calamities, beatings, imprisonments, riots, labors, sleepless nights, hunger…dishonor…slander… treated as impostors…unknown…dying…punished…poor… having nothing." With this kind of constant battering and suffering, we would expect Paul to be incredibly emotionally unhealthy. But in that same passage, he describes his internal emotional life with words such as "purity, knowledge, patience, kindness…genuine love…truthful speech" and goes on to worship, saying, "Behold, we live…always rejoicing."

Paul endured the same kinds of trauma that Jesus experienced and that often destroy other people. Yet, like Jesus, Paul responded with great emotional health and peace. How did Jesus and Paul do it? What was the secret to their internal emotional health despite their external death? In this same section of Scripture the Holy Spirit through Paul pointing back to Jesus reminds us of the emotional "power of God," which is made possible only by "the Holy Spirit."

I know this is a strong statement, but it's true: there is no possibility of being emotionally healthy without a deep, intimate, personal relationship with the Holy Spirit. Did you get that? There is no emotional health apart from the Holy Spirit.

How do I know that's true? Because what is true of Jesus is true of you. Let's consider Jesus' emotional life. For the first time as a man, Jesus dealt with physical exhaustion, the adrenaline rush that can compel us to a fight or flight response, and the kind of dishonor, disrespect, and disregard from people that can quickly push a person toward being emotionally unwell. Add to that the fact that Jesus did not have a loving wife and fun kids to come home to, and the pressures He faced would crush anyone else. Nonetheless, Jesus maintained a perfect emotional life in a world filled with circumstances that were far from perfect.

> I know this is a strong statement, but it's true: there is no possibility of being emotionally healthy without a deep, intimate, personal relationship with the Holy Spirit.

Part of the Holy Spirit's ministry in the life of Jesus was directing His emotions. As one example, Jesus' joy came from the Holy Spirit according to Luke 10:21, which reveals, "Jesus, full of joy through the Holy Spirit..." (NIV). Later on we read the same thing of the emotional life of Jesus' disciples in Acts 13:52, "the disciples were filled with joy and with the Holy Spirit."

One Bible commentator discussing the Holy Spirit as the source of Jesus' emotional joy says, "By mentioning the fact that Jesus rejoiced greatly 'in the Holy Spirit' Luke means that this Spirit, by which the Savior had been anointed (4:18), was the cause and originator of his joy and thanksgiving."[4] Another widely respected Bible commentator says of Jesus' emotional life, "The Holy Spirit caused this exultation and jubilant outburst on the part of Jesus."[5] Admittedly the subject of this chapter deserves an entire book. For the sake of brevity, we will examine as much of Jesus' emotional life as I can pack into one chapter, and I want you to remember that the Holy Spirit's anointing remained on Jesus through all of His life experiences and emotional responses.

Jesus' Emotions in the Gospels

One theologian summarizes the place where Christian study has fallen short, saying, "Unfortunately, contemporary evangelicals have paid little attention to the development of a theology or biblical anthropology of the emotions, affections, and feelings."[6] To help correct this error, we need to examine the emotional life of Jesus Christ.

For starters, Jesus' very emotional teaching appeals to our emotions. The parables are incredibly emotionally compelling. Seeing the father running to embrace the prodigal son who has returned home and calling for a feast of celebration is intended to capture our hearts and turn them toward our heavenly Father. Over and over—from the heartwarming story of the good Samaritan to the terrifying tale of the rich man who is tormented in eternity while Lazarus is blessed—all are emotionally appealing, compelling, and transforming. Why? Because loving God with all our hearts is emotional.

Regarding the emotional life of Jesus Christ, a *Christianity Today* article said, "The Gospel writers paint their portraits of Jesus using a kaleidoscope of brilliant emotional colors....In our quest to be like Jesus we often overlook his emotions. Jesus reveals what it means to be fully human and made in the image of God. His emotions reflect the image of God without deficiency or distortion. When we compare our emotional lives to his, we become aware of our need for a transformation of our emotions so we can be fully human, as he is."[7]

Renowned Princeton theologian B. B. Warfield is one of the few people to teach in any detail about Jesus' emotional life in the entire twentieth century. He says, "It belongs to the truth of our Lord's humanity, that he was subject to all sinless human emotions. In the accounts which the Evangelists give us of the crowded activities which filled the few years of his ministry, the play of a great variety of emotions is depicted."[8]

More recently theologian Wayne Grudem has said, "Jesus had a full range of human emotions. He 'marveled' at the faith of the centurion (Matt. 8:10). He wept with sorrow at the death of Lazarus (John 11:35). And he prayed with a heart full of emotion, for 'in the days of his flesh, Jesus offered up prayers and supplications, *with loud cries and tears*, to him who was able to save him from death, and he was heard for his godly fear' (Heb. 5:7)."[9]

Jesus' emotions hit their climax in all four Gospels at the cross. This odyssey begins in the Garden of Gethsemane, which Luke, the medical doctor, reports in Luke 22:44, "Being in agony he prayed more earnestly; and his sweat became like great drops of blood falling down to the ground." A study Bible explains Jesus' emotional state saying, "Probably perspiration in large drops like blood, or possibly hematidrosis, the actual mingling of blood and sweat as in cases of extreme anguish, strain or sensitivity."[10]

Other scriptures emphasize the point of heightened emotional distress and agony for Jesus as He headed to the cross. In the Old Testament, Isaiah 53:3–11 refers to Jesus with these words: despised, rejected, a man of sorrows, acquainted with grief, stricken, smitten, afflicted, crushed, oppressed, and anguish in His soul.

In Hebrews we learn more about Jesus as the Suffering Servant. In Hebrews 5:7 we learn, "Jesus offered up prayers and supplications, with loud cries and tears." Nonetheless, on the other side of the cross was also great emotional joy. In Hebrews 12:2 we read that Jesus "who for the joy that was set before him endured the cross."

Perhaps the most overlooked aspect of Jesus' personality is His perfect sense of humor. Writing in *The Humor of Christ*, theologian Elton Trueblood says:

There are numerous passages...which are practically incomprehensible when regarded as sober prose, but which are luminous once we become liberated from the gratuitous assumption that Christ never joked....Once we realize that Christ was not always engaged in pious talk, we have made an enormous step on the road to understanding."[11]

Trueblood goes on to say:

Christ laughed, and...He expected others to laugh....A misguided piety has made us fear that acceptance of His obvious wit and humor would somehow be mildly blasphemous or sacrilegious. Religion, we think, is serious business, and serious business is incompatible with banter.[12]

Other scholars say, "If there is a single person within the pages of the Bible that we can consider to be a humorist, it is without a doubt Jesus....Jesus was a master of wordplay, irony, and satire, often with an element of humor intermixed."[13] In the appendix of *The Humor of Christ*, Trueblood lists thirty humorous passages of Jesus in the Synoptic Gospels alone (Matthew, Mark, and Luke).[14]

Scholars in the area of humor say, "The most characteristic form of Jesus' humor was the preposterous exaggeration."[15] Examples include (1) pointing out the speck of sawdust in someone else's eye while overlooking the huge wooden beam in your own, which was funny for the guys on the job site, and (2) the fact that you simply cannot shove a camel through the eye of a sewing needle no matter how hard you pull from the front and push from the rear.

Jesus used humor to show how silly religious people can be. In poking fun at solemn religious types and their traditions, Jesus invites us to resist the thinking that the most pious people are also the most saintly.

After all, it was the religious types who took themselves too seriously and did not take Jesus seriously enough, which explains why they kept criticizing Jesus for breaking the rules of their traditions.

How ironic that religious people killed God for not being godly enough for them. As a general rule, if you are more conservative than God, you should scoot to the left. And if you are more liberal than God, you should scoot to the right.

One significant book related to the full breadth of Jesus' emotions is *Jesus' Emotions in the Gospels* by Stephen Voorwinde. He notes that "Jesus is seldom thought of in emotional terms."[16] He continues by saying that there are only sixty references to Jesus' emotions in all four Gospels, and His emotional intensity increases as He approaches the cross.[17]

We will now examine each mention of Jesus' emotions in the four Gospels of the New Testament where, interestingly enough, we find compassion is the most commonly mentioned.

Jesus' emotions in Matthew

Theologian Stephen Voorwinde says, "With his ten references to the emotions of Jesus, Matthew captures a wide range of feelings."[18] Here are the mentions of Jesus' emotions in Matthew's Gospel in the English Standard Version (ESV) translation of the Bible, with some other translations included to help provide a richer and fuller understanding.

- 8:10—"marveled" (ESV, NASB, NKJV), "amazed" (NIV, HCSB, NLT)

- 9:30—"sternly warned"

- 9:36, 14:14, 15:32—"compassion"

- 20:34—"pity" (ESV), "compassion" (HCSB, NASB, NKJV, NIV), "felt sorry for them" (NLT)

- 26:37–38—"sorrowful and troubled"; "My soul is very sorrowful, even to death."

- 27:46—"Jesus cried out with a loud voice, saying…
  'My God, my God, why have you forsaken me?'"

Jesus' emotions in Mark

Regarding Jesus' emotions in Mark, Voorwinde says, "No Gospel writer allows us to gaze more deeply into Jesus' soul than Mark. If a psychological analysis of Jesus' personality were possible, this would be the place to begin. Mark captures a wider range of Jesus' emotions than any other Gospel. To describe the variety of Jesus' emotional reactions he uses fourteen different expressions, compared with seven in Matthew and five in Luke.…Although there are twenty-eight references to Jesus' emotions in John (compared with sixteen in Mark), only nine different words are used."[19] I've provided the following list of Jesus' emotions in Mark, with various translations included that help to provide hue and color to His emotional life.

- 1:41—"pity" (ESV), "compassion" (HCSB, NASB, NKJV, NLT), "indignant" (NIV)

- 3:5—"anger, grieved" (ESV, NASB, NKJV), "anger and sorrow" (HCSB), "anger and, deeply distressed" (NIV) or "angrily…deeply saddened" (NLT)

- 6:6—"marveled" (ESV, NKJV), "amazed" (HCSB, NIV, NLT), "wondered" (NASB)

- 6:34, 8:2, 9:22—"compassion"

- 7:34—"He sighed" (ESV, NLT, NKJV); "He sighed deeply" (HCSB); "deep sigh" (NASB, NIV).

- 8:12—"sighed deeply in his spirit"

- 10:21—"loved" (ESV), "felt a love" (NASB), "with love" (NIV), "genuine love" (NLT)

- 14:33–34—"greatly distressed and troubled… 'My soul is very sorrowful, even to death.'"

- 15:34—"Jesus cried with a loud voice… 'My God, my God, why have you forsaken me?'"

Jesus' emotions in Luke

Regarding the emotional life of Jesus in Luke, Voorwinde says, "Although Luke is the longest Gospel,[20] it has the fewest references to Jesus' emotions. This is somewhat surprising because Luke mentions the emotions of others more often than each of the other Gospels."[21] Take a look at the list of Jesus' emotions in Luke's Gospel.

- 7:9—"marveled" (ESV, NASB, NKJV), "amazed" (HCSB, NIV, NLT)

- 7:13—"compassion" (ESV, NKJV, HCSB, NASB), "his heart went out to her" (NIV), "his heart overflowed with compassion" (NLT)

- 10:21—"rejoiced in the Holy Spirit" (ESV), "full of joy through the Holy Spirit" (NIV), "filled with the joy of the Holy Spirit," (NLT)

- 12:50—"Great is my distress" (ESV); "what constraint I am under" (NIV); "how distressed I am" (NKJV); "I am under a heavy burden" (NLT).

- 19:41—"He wept."

- 22:44—"in agony" (ESV, NASB, NKJV), "in anguish" (HCSB, NIV), "in such agony of spirit" (NLT)

Jesus' emotions in John

Regarding Jesus in John, Voorwinde says, "Of the sixty specific references to the emotions of Jesus in the Gospels, twenty-eight are found in John…although the Fourth Gospel refers to the emotions of Jesus more often than each of the others, the range of emotions it records is comparatively modest. The most frequent references are to Jesus' love (18*x*).[22] Three times it says that he is troubled, twice that he is deeply moved, and once that he rejoices and sheds tears. There are also two references to his joy and one to his zeal. This represents a total of only six different emotions."[23] Among the disciples, John likely had the closest relationship with Jesus as "the one whom Jesus loved." His reporting of Jesus' emotional life is listed below.

- 2:17—"zeal" (ESV, HCSB, NASB, NIV, NKJV), "passion" (NLT)

- 11:3, 5—"love…loved"

- 11:15—"I am glad."

- 11:33—"deeply moved in his spirit and greatly troubled" (ESV), "angry in His spirit and deeply moved" (HCSB), "groaned in the spirit and was troubled" (NKJV), "a deep anger welled up within him, and he was deeply troubled" (NLT)

- 11:38—"deeply moved again" (ESV), "angry in Himself again" (HCSB), "deeply moved within" (NASB), "again groaning in Himself" (NKJV)

- 12:27—"Now is my soul troubled."

- 13:1—"He loved."

- 13:21—"troubled in his spirit" (ESV), "deeply troubled" (NLT)

- 13:34—"I have loved you."

- 14:21—"I will love him."

- 15:9–12—"I loved you…my joy…I have loved you."

Christians have always confessed that Jesus is the only perfect person who has or will walk the earth. His life is the portrait of what healthy humanity is supposed to be. His emotional life while among us was perfect.

BECOMING EMOTIONALLY HEALTHY

Tom and Nancy had been married many years. They had a few kids, a dog, and brought more baggage and carry-ons into their marriage than most commercial airline flights. They did not get any counseling before or during their marriage, and by the time we sat down they were considering divorce.

I prayed a quick prayer, then asked Nancy what she thought their biggest problem was. She said, "Tom is our biggest problem." She answered without taking a breath, much like a highly skilled auctioneer who can rattle off words at a superhuman speed. The phrases I caught from the hurricane included, *arrogant, domineering, overbearing, proud, rude, selfish, cold, distant*, and a few naughty words that the publisher will edit, so I won't bother typing them.

I did not dare ask Tom what he thought the biggest problem was. He did not need the prompting. He said, "Nancy is our biggest problem." Like watching a punch get thrown in slow motion, he then carefully and slowly called her such things as *insecure, weak, emotional, broken, depressed, hopeless*, and then made fun of the fact that she was always crying and way too emotional. She started crying. Then he bellowed, "See what I'm talking about!"

A very long and awkward silence followed as they had what seemed to be a staring contest and glared at each other. It seemed to me that perhaps a good old-fashioned pistol duel would have been more appropriate than meeting in my office.

I was a young pastor, and I was in way over my head. I just sat there dumbfounded.

So I got honest. I said, "Um, you guys are a mess. I'm in over my head. Since I'm being honest, can you do me a favor and be honest? I'm going to ask you both to each answer my question on the count of three at the same time. Tom, are you emotionally cold, distant, aloof, and uncaring? Nancy, are you emotionally broken, hurt, sad, and depressed?" Then I counted to three, and they both said, "Yes."

These people loved God and loved each other. They were just emotionally unhealthy—and in opposite ways. As we talked some more, they were initially drawn to each other because they were so different. She was drawn to his lack of emotion as a stoic man with the emotional spectrum of an oak coffee table, but eventually it made her feel lonely. He was drawn to her deep and complex emotional life, but after a while it made him feel overwhelmed and worn out as if he were an extra in the cast of a weepy daytime soap opera minus the melodramatic sound track.

As we discussed their very different emotional lives, they finally agreed that they were both unhealthy. This admission started their healing.

We began discussing what it would be like for them not to push each other to become like themselves, but rather pull each other in love to both become emotionally like Jesus. They agreed that Jesus had the perfect emotional life, and that if they could both become like Him, they would be healthy and happy together. So we opened the Bible and started examining the emotional life of Jesus.

One scripture that we stumbled upon, thanks to the Spirit, that I had never much considered before was Luke 10:21, which says, "He rejoiced in the Holy Spirit." This is an amazing insight. Since the Holy Spirit inspired the Bible to be written, He chose this instance to reveal that Jesus' emotional life was grounded and guided "in the Holy Spirit."

In God's providence, as I write this sentence I am sitting on a plane flying to New York with Grace on the thirtieth anniversary of our first date. We are spending a few days to celebrate together. Since the day we met, we have lived life together.

The Bible says that though we are two, we are in fact "one." Practically this means that all of life is lived together and all emotions are experienced together. Grace has literally been a means of God's grace in my life. She helps me process what we experience in life, and without her devotion to me, my emotional life would be darker and far more despairing.

Jesus and the Holy Spirit did life together a bit like Grace and I, although they did it perfectly. They did everything together, experienced everything together, and responded to everything together. The Holy Spirit kept Jesus emotionally healthy, and now He comes to bring the emotional health of Jesus to you. Some people struggle to think of how the Trinity operates, but once we understand that the three members of the Trinity live together relationally and emotionally, it makes a lot more sense.

One commentator says of Luke 10:21: "*Rejoiced* is far too colourless a translation for...a positive exultation ('thrilled with joy'...). Next time you see a fan jump up and start shouting when the game turns in their direction and see chips and Coke flying off their lap, remember that Jesus was pretty much that excited."[24] The source of Jesus' strong emotion is the Holy Spirit. One New Testament scholar says, "This holy joy of Jesus was directly due to the Holy Spirit."[25]

That simple conversation with Tom and Nancy when I was a young pastor opened up a whole new understanding of Jesus' emotional life. It's what got me started on over two decades of study that has led to writing this book.

Rather than ignoring our lack of love and emotional health or excusing it by blaming circumstances and other people for our condition, we should first look to Jesus and then examine ourselves in light of His emotional profile. One of the most influential Christian devotional writers of the entire twentieth century, Oswald Chambers, says, "The reason some of us are so amazingly dull and get sleeping-sickness is that we have never once thought of paying attention to the stirring up the Spirit of God gives the mind and our emotional nature. How many of us are terrified out of our wits lest we should be emotional! Jesus Christ demands the whole nature, and He demands that part of our nature the devil uses most, viz., the emotional part. We have to get the right bedrock for our nature, the life of Jesus Christ, and then glean the things which awaken our emotions, and see that those emotions are expressed in ways like the character of our Lord."[26] Sadly, most of us do not do that very thing.

THE HOLY SPIRIT IN YOUR EMOTIONAL LIFE

Are you emotionally healthy? Would you like to become more emotionally healthy? The good news is that every believer has the potential for improved emotional health that increasingly manifests the character of Jesus Christ. How? Not by the latest self-help book. We need to follow Jesus' example and seek the help of the Holy Spirit.

Near the end of his powerful letter to the Galatians, Paul, under the inspiration of the Holy Spirit, reminds us that our emotional life and character flow from only one of two streams—the flesh or the Spirit. Because Jesus lived by the Spirit and sent the Spirit to empower our lives, we can live by the same power, growing in the same character and emotional health of Jesus Christ. Paul teaches this in Galatians 5:25 when he says, "If we live by the Spirit, let us also keep in step with the Spirit." Paul takes his language here from the military. When a platoon goes out for a hike, everyone follows the highest commanding officer, keeping in step and staying in line. Otherwise, a soldier can wander off and get shot by the enemy. So it is for each Christian, the Holy Spirit is our commanding officer, and we must follow His leadership over our entire lives—including our emotional lives—or risk becoming taken captive by our enemy (the devil).

It is common to think that God is not sovereign, but rather our emotions are. Whatever we feel, it is as if those feelings have a life unto themselves and we cannot be held responsible for them but only for our thoughts and actions. People who are feeling or acting ungodly will say something like, "That's how I feel." That kind of statement is often a conversation stopper because it wrongly assumes that our feelings are like the laws of gravity—beyond our control, overwhelming, and unchangeable.

But God expects His Spirit to rule over all of our lives, including our emotions. Oswald Chambers rightly says, "God holds the saints responsible for emotions they have not got and ought to have as well as for the emotions they have allowed which they ought not to have allowed. If we indulge in inordinate affection, anger, anxiety, God holds us responsible; but He also insists that we have to be passionately filled with the right emotions. The emotional life of a Christian is to be measured by the exalted energy exhibited in the life of our Lord. The language applied to the presence of the Holy Spirit in the saint is descriptive of the energy of emotion that keeps the inner and outer life like our Lord's own life."[27]

God Commands Your Emotions

The God of the Bible is not afraid to command the behaviors we choose, thoughts we believe, and feelings we have. Consider these commands in the Bible for our emotions:

- "Put on...compassionate hearts, kindness, humility, meekness, and patience, bearing with one another... forgiving each other...put on love...let the peace of Christ rule in your hearts....And be thankful" (Col. 3:12–15).

- "Love one another earnestly from a pure heart" (1 Pet. 1:22).

- "Love your enemies" (Matt. 5:44).

- "You shall love the Lord your God with all your heart and with all your soul and with all your mind.... You shall love your neighbor as yourself" (Matt. 22:37–39).

- "Love one another with brotherly affection. Outdo one another in showing honor...be fervent in spirit.... Rejoice in hope, be patient in tribulation.... Bless those who persecute you; bless and do not curse them. Rejoice with those who rejoice, weep with those who weep. Live in harmony.... Do not be haughty, but associate with the lowly.... Repay no one evil for evil" (Rom. 12:10–17).

The Bible often tells us to do something because we are not doing that thing and do not want to start doing it. How can we possibly feel something we don't feel like feeling? We must bring our feelings and emotions to the Holy Spirit and invite Him to change them as He would our thoughts or desires. Theologian and pastor John Piper says it this way, "Jesus does command the feelings. He demands that our emotions be one way and not another."[20]

LION AND LAMB

Let's get very practical. When you are emotional and feeling things at a deeper level than usual, it is vital to submit those emotional feelings to the Holy Spirit. Just as you would bring your thoughts or desires before the Lord, you must do the same with your emotions and feelings to see if they align with God's Word or need to be changed by the Spirit.

It will be vital for you to compare your emotions to the emotional life of Jesus Christ to determine if your feelings are right or wrong. This can be challenging because almost everyone has an imbalanced view of Jesus' emotional life. Practically we tend to see

Him as either Lion or Lamb and not both. Those of us with more Lamb personalities will focus on the parts of the Bible where Jesus was meek, kind, patient, loving, and appears more passive if not even timid. Those of us with more Lion personalities will focus on the parts of the Bible where Jesus was strong, firm, urgent, controversial, and appears more active if not aggressive.

Are you more of a lion or a lamb? Do you see Jesus more as a Lion or a Lamb?

The Bible presents Jesus as *both* a Lion and a Lamb.

In Revelation 5:5 John calls Jesus "the Lion of the tribe of Judah." A lion is the king of the jungle. A lion eats whatever it wants—buffalo, hogs, and even elephants or alligators. A male lion lives in a pride or pack with mainly females and children, and if another male comes around, the lion who is head of the pride will go to war and slaughter anything that threatens his pack. Sometimes Jesus is a Lion.

In John 1:29 John calls Jesus "the Lamb of God." Lambs are meek creatures who run from danger and stick together with their flock because they are very social animals. Lambs are vulnerable and so comforting and safe that we invite our kids to count them at night until they fall asleep. Lambs eat grass and are not a threat to other animals because they are vegetarians and do not feast on other animals. As pacifist homeless wandering vegetarians, lambs are basically the first hippies.

The key to your emotional life is twofold: (1) you need the Holy Spirit to help you discern when to be a lion and when to be a lamb, and (2) you need the Holy Spirit to empower you to be a lion when the time is right and a lamb when the time is right. People who are always lions not only protect others from harm, but they also harm those who are for them and with them. People who are always lambs are loving, kind, and safe people who avoid conflict—even while the lions rush in and devour the other lambs.

Going back to our couple in counseling, Tom was invariably a lion. Nancy was always a lamb. Thankfully, through time and tears, the Holy Spirit has healed their past hurts and taught them how and when to be a lion or lamb.

How about you?

Where do you need to invite the Holy Spirit to empower your emotional life so that you feel the fullness of Jesus in your feelings? As you become more emotionally healthy, you will be ready for healthy relationships, as we discuss in the next chapter.

Chapter 7

REDEEM YOUR RELATIONSHIPS

LOOKING BACK ON my teen years, if I'm honest, I think my odds of becoming a mother were higher than my odds of becoming a pastor. As a fifteen-year-old non-Christian, I lied about my age, falsified my birth certificate, and started making minimum wage as a clerk at a 7-Eleven down the street from a strip club. Yes, as a minor I would dutifully check adults' identification to see if they were old enough to buy items such as cigarettes, lottery tickets, and beer.

My first car was a 1956 Chevy that I bought from the owner of the convenience store after saving up my paychecks. I then started driving myself to work before I was old enough to have a driver's license.

If this all sounds bad, I feel inclined to explain to you why this all sounds bad. It sounds bad because it *is* bad.

Anyway, my first car had four tires that were balder than most grandfathers. When it rained, driving the car felt eerily similar to sledding down a hill in the snow spinning round and round on a garbage can lid as a kid. On the freeway the car would drift, and it was hard to keep in one lane. Driving it in the rain felt like trying to ride an ice-skating elephant.

I thought driving couldn't get any worse until many years later as a pastor on a mission trip when I traveled internationally for the first time. I will never forget the drive from the airport.

There were no lanes. Traffic sped in every direction, and people

107

just seemed to go wherever they wanted. Vehicles would suddenly stop for no reason, quickly change directions, and veer in front of one another without any warning. It was chaos, and how anyone survived remains a mystery to me. It felt like the entire nation had too much to drink and decided to go for a drive.

TWELVE RELATIONSHIP LANES

In life, relationships are like drivers on a highway. Unless everyone understands what lane they're in, there are bound to be collisions that lead to disappointment when unspoken expectations go unmet. I'm not even talking about emotional codependence. Just plain old confusion and interpersonal hurt.

Jesus was constantly overwhelmed with people who wanted to get and stay close to Him. Mark 1:21–37 records the relational chaos Jesus had to deal with on what was supposed to be a day off. It was the Sabbath, and He taught in the synagogue, cast a demon out of a dude, "And at once his fame spread everywhere throughout all the surrounding region of Galilee." Not even taking a siesta break for chips and salsa, "immediately he left" to Simon's house to heal his dying mother-in-law. Then "that evening at sundown they brought to him all who were sick or oppressed by demons. And the whole city was gathered together at the door." Imagine it's Halloween and rather than pretend zombies, demons, and witches, they are the real deal knocking on the door. He had to be exhausted and worn out. Nonetheless, "he healed many who were sick with various diseases, and cast out many demons."

I think it's fair to assume that Jesus slept soundly that night, but also woke early to try to avoid the rush of people. "Rising very early in the morning, while it was still dark, he departed and went out to a desolate place, and there he prayed." Makes you wonder if He prayed for the rapture so He could leave earth and get some peace. But "they found him and said to him, 'Everyone is looking for you.'"

How did Jesus possibly manage these kinds of complex, needy, urgent relational demands?

Building on the concept of relational lanes, here's how I see a dozen distinctions between various personal, professional, and spiritual connections after surveying the relationships of Jesus.

1. Enemies

People who want to be in your life to cause pain, harm, and chaos—and who might once have been close friends or family but are now unsafe. In the life of Jesus this group would include Satan and various religious and political leaders who hounded and harassed Him, seeking to harm Him.

2. Former acquaintances

People you no longer have meaningful contact with, such as former coworkers, former classmates, or former neighbors. Jesus lived in Egypt for a while as a child as well as in the small town of Nazareth before moving His ministry to the big city of Jerusalem. As a result, some people knew Him from the past but did not retain a close relationship with Him into the future.

3. Distant relatives

People you rarely see except for major events such as weddings, funerals, or reunions. For Jesus, this group likely included relatives who lived some ways away, such as Zechariah and Elizabeth.

4. Professionals

People you have a relationship with that doesn't involve socializing, such as a doctor, attorney, accountant, or counselor. For Jesus, this group would have included people who employed Him and His dad for carpentry jobs.

5. Neighbors

People you engage in surface conversation, but you don't spend time in one another's homes or lives. These were some of the people who struggled to see Jesus as anything more than the kid who grew up playing ball with their kids.

6. Acquaintances

People you meet in loose circles such as school, kids' sports, or people you bump into at church or simply know because your lives casually intersect. Jesus had a lot of these relationships as crowds numbering perhaps as many as ten thousand or more came to hear Him preach, with some getting to meet Him.

7. Coworkers

People you spend time with on the job without a deep relationship apart from work. The Bible mentions several people who were part of Jesus' ministry and with Him for various projects and seasons.

8. Friends

People you do things with as a group, such as sports, Bible studies, or hobbies. For Jesus, this would have been His twelve disciples and others such as the siblings Mary, Martha, and Lazarus, in whose home He spent time.

9. Mentors

People moving ahead of you who create safe places to open up part or all of your personal, professional, and spiritual life—and who also share at least part of their lives with you. For Jesus, this would have been primarily His parents who helped Him mature from childhood to manhood.

10. Close friends

People you choose to spend one-on-one time with as peers, revealing parts of your life you don't share with others. Jesus' closest three friends were Peter, James, and John who were with Him at the most intimate moments of life. John is also likely Jesus' closest friend since he's called, "the one Jesus loved."

11. Close family

People you feel most connected and committed to and devote significant parts of your life to, such as spouse, kids, or parents. Jesus' family struggled to believe His claims of deity until after His resurrection from death. Then, His brothers James and Jude became pastors, and we find His mom as part of the early church in the opening chapters of the Book of Acts.

12. The Lord

The Person you share the most important relationship with, and unless this relationship is nurtured all other relationships suffer. The Bible says in Luke 5:15–16 that "great crowds gathered to hear him and to be healed of their infirmities. But he would withdraw to desolate places and pray." The more people wanted access to Jesus the more Jesus had to spend time with His eternal community of the Father and Spirit.

Jesus' life was like your life—filled with people who drive in whatever lane they choose and seek to merge into the next lane of importance and closeness in your life. This happened to Jesus, and it happens to you and me.

You can see there's a vast range between your enemies and your ultimate friend. No doubt you can immediately identify people you relate to in most of those categories. Now flip it around and examine it from another vantage point. How do people see you? What expectations do they have of your relationship? How are you clarifying or messing with their perceptions?

Wisdom teaches us to treat different people differently. Our problem comes from our tendency to develop a relationship pattern that works for us and then apply it to everyone only to find it working some of the time and failing some of the time.

EIGHT LAWS OF RELATIONSHIPS

How did Jesus determine what kinds of people He would and would not have relationships with? How did Jesus pick the twelve disciples to be in close relationship with Him for three years? Luke 6:12–13 says of Jesus, "He went out to the mountain to pray, and all night he continued in prayer to God. And when day came, he called his disciples."

Have you ever pulled an all-nighter? Perhaps for school or work? You know that something is incredibly important when you stay up all night to work on it. For Jesus, picking who would be in relationship with Him as disciples required that He spend the whole night in prayer. You might ask why it took so long. Could they not have simply made a list and let Jesus go to bed? No, the Father, Son, and Spirit are relational and take relationships very seriously. It would not be surprising that they had some long conversations about Peter the denier, Thomas the doubter, and Judas the betrayer. Jesus spent all night talking to the Father and the Spirit about the list. You and I need to do the same. Do you invite the Lord to help you pick your closest relationships?

When looking at the disciples, we can rush to the assumption that Judas was a mistake and should not have been chosen, but he was part of God's plan. In John 17:12 Jesus again prays to the Father saying, "While I was with them, I kept them in your name, which you have given me. I have guarded them, and not one of them has been lost except the son of destruction, that the Scripture might be fulfilled." Jesus was a perfect friend to Judas, and Judas betrayed Him. It just goes to show that relationships can be painful even if we did not do anything sinful.

Surveying the life of Jesus, it is insightful to see how He managed so many diverse, complex, and shifting relationships with the help of prayerful time with the Father and Spirit. The following are eight laws of relationships observed in the life of Jesus.

1. The law of hospitality

Consider for a moment how many people you've had something to eat or drink with in the past twelve months. Don't overlook school parties, sporting events, music concerts or recitals, church events, relationships at work, neighborhood events, holidays, birthday parties, anniversaries, wedding and baby showers, meals and coffee with friends, etc. How long is your list? Dozens of people, hundreds of people, or thousands of people? Many people experience hospitality with you, but not all are your friends.

Jesus was friendly to all people, but He was friends with only a few people. People often approached Him, and He was kind, emotionally present, and welcoming. Crowds large and small often surrounded Him. People also invited Him to a lot of parties, which irked fundamental religious folks who did not believe in fun. However, Jesus did not have close friendships with everyone.

2. The law of capacity

Relationships are costly. A close relationship costs time, money, and energy. In the Bible we read of all the people Jesus met with, prayed for, taught, and healed. But there is an even longer list of all the people that Jesus did *not* meet with, pray over, teach, or heal. At times Jesus was so tired that He snuck away and took a nap. Jesus had capacity limits due to His humanity. You too are finite and cannot give to everyone who would like to receive something from you. In the age of technology and social media where accessibility replaces privacy, people feel the law of capacity at levels higher than any other time in human history.

3. The law of priority

Some researchers say that many people interact with five hundred to twenty-five hundred different people in a typical year.[1] If you are a high extrovert or have a job that requires a lot of interaction with the public (e.g., ministry leader, health care, sales, or customer service) that number might even be higher. Some researchers also report that we spend roughly 40 percent of our time with the same five people—the five people to whom we are closest.[2]

If you have a spouse and a few children, you've already filled the quota of five people. For Jesus, His inner circle of three disciples plus a few friends and perhaps His family got the majority of His personal time and energy. He would lovingly help and serve people but then move on, not unlike a doctor or counselor who attends to patients all day but does not invite them all over for dinner at his house.

4. The law of seasonality

Most relationships are seasonal. Few are for life. Jesus grew up with people in a small town, but we don't hear much of anything about those people. Perhaps Jesus had classmates in school, teammates in sports, or workmates on the job, but we don't find anything about them. Many, if not most relationships, are for a season of life. Very few relationships, if any, endure through every season of life. Rather than mourning this fact, we should accept it and thank God for the deposits people make at any point along life's journey. We can cause a lot of mutual grief when we try to drag every past relationship into every future season of life.

5. The law of safety

When it comes to people, we should love all but trust few. Love is free. Trust is earned. Jesus loved everyone but did not trust everyone. People trusted Jesus, but Jesus did not trust all people. He knew that not everyone is safe. Some people are dangerous and others just selfish. In a relationship trust is like a bank account that requires deposits over time to prove valuable.

6. The law of clarity

You know that someone is driving in the wrong relationship lane when things start becoming awkward, causing you to avoid or dread him. You know that pit in your stomach when the phone rings or text dings and his name comes up. You might even avoid certain places out of fear of running into him. At times like these, you need to have what counselors sometimes refer to as transition talks and closure conversations.

Transition talks

A transition talk is an opportunity to lovingly but clearly define (or redefine) the lane the relationship will be. Jesus had this kind of transition talk with Peter. As Jesus neared crucifixion, Peter cowardly denied Jesus. After His resurrection, Jesus met face to face with Peter to have a transition talk in which Jesus was clear that Peter's unloving behavior was unacceptable and would need to change in order for their relationship to continue.

In John 21:15-19, in response to Peter's three denials Jesus asks three times, "Do you love me?" This intense and probably awkward—emotional scene ends with Jesus telling him, "Follow me." Jesus was clear that for their relationship to continue, Peter needed to worry less about himself and try caring more for God's people and following Jesus.

This transition talk worked. Peter went on to be a bold servant of Jesus and author of Scripture. History outside the Bible records that, at the end of his life, when Peter was given the option to (1) deny Jesus and live or (2) confess Jesus and die, he chose to confess Jesus. He asked to be crucified upside down because he saw himself as unworthy to die like Jesus.

Sometimes God uses a transition talk to change someone's destiny. Other times we need to follow up with a closure conversation.

Closure conversations

A closure conversation is the talk we have to be clear that we are not talking anymore. In old movies you know the film has concluded when "The End" come up on the screen. A closure conversation is like that. It is a kind and clear way to end a relationship. Jesus had precisely this kind of discussion with Judas. Like the other disciples, Judas was with Jesus for a few years. Jesus loved him, served him, taught him, cared for him, befriended him, and never sinned against him. Jesus was (and is) the perfect friend. As the bookkeeper for Jesus' ministry, Judas stole money the entire time, and in the end he agreed to betray Jesus for thirty pieces of silver.

Judas was a user and abuser. Judas was a pretend friend. Judas opened himself to Satan to fulfill his plot, which is when (over dinner in front of the other men) Jesus said, "What you are going to do, do quickly" (John 13:27). Jesus said, in effect, there's nothing more to talk about. We are done. You go and do what you want, and we part ways now.

The final scene between Jesus and Judas is literally the kiss of death. It just goes to show that sometimes the worst people hide in ministry because the devil knows it's the last place most believers look for them.

7. The law of idolize-demonize

Arguably the greatest theologian America has ever produced is Jonathan Edwards. He said, and I'm paraphrasing, that those who idolize you will then demonize you. Sometimes when people think they have found the person who can take their pain away, make their dreams come true, and usher them into whatever their false concept of heaven right now looks like, they idolize that person. They lift that person up, shout their praises, and await their blessing, but as soon as they do not get what they want, they stop idolizing and start demonizing. These are the people who love you one minute and hate you the next. They defend you one day and destroy you the next.

This very thing happened to Jesus. In a short amount of time the enthusiastic crowd shouting, "Hosanna, hosanna," soon became the hateful mob crying, "Crucify, crucify." This sick cycle continues in today's celebrity culture where we build people up to tear people down and then build someone else up to repeat the cycle. Therefore, we should be wary of those who sing our praises too loudly because the idolize-demonize cycle is very real and painful.

8. The law of economy

When my wife, Grace, and I were newly married, she had a small import car, and I had a large truck. Her car got miles to the gallon. My truck got gallons to the mile. When we would go on road trips as a broke college couple, we would take her car rather than mine because of the better gas mileage.

Relationships are like vehicles. Some relationships get good gas mileage. These relationships don't drain our energy and tend to keep moving forward without a lot of drama or difficulty. Other relationships, however, get lousy gas mileage. These relationships take a lot of time, energy, and money, and don't seem to make much progress.

People always wanted to take Jesus' time to argue, debate, and criticize. These people did not want to learn; they wanted to fight. They did not want to be changed by Jesus; they wanted to use Jesus. These people wanted to have the same argument over and over, and Jesus ignored these kinds of people. Occasionally He would devote a bit of time to rebuke them but did not waste His time on people who were not a good investment of His life energy. The same is true for each of us. Some people are amazingly good investments of time and energy. Others, however, are exhausting and never gain much if any relational momentum.

OVERT AND COVERT

One of the most challenging things in life is learning to read people. We've all had people who completely surprised us. Negatively there are people we thought we could trust who turned out to be selfish betrayers and pretend friends. Positively there are people we did not feel particularly close to at first but who ended up being loyal, faithful, and helpful in our times of greatest need.

The truth is, only God knows the deep things in a person. On a few occasions the Bible tells us that as people we only see the outward, but God sees the inward. God alone knows the motives of the heart, thoughts of the mind, and intents of the soul.

In Jesus' life there were people constantly seeking to get closer to Him and enjoy a more intimate relationship with Him. Consider for a moment that while on the earth Jesus chose not to be present at all times and in all places. Jesus chose to not know what everyone was saying, doing, and plotting. Instead, Jesus chose to experience relationships as we do. The Holy Spirit, however, was fully aware of what everyone was saying, doing, and plotting. As a result, Jesus needed the Holy Spirit to navigate complex relationships just as you do.

Jesus was not paranoid, trusting no one. Neither was He naive, trusting everyone. Instead, Jesus was wise and discerning. His wise discernment was possible by the Holy Spirit who knew everything about everyone. For this reason, even though Judas and Peter failed, Jesus restored Peter to friendship and ministry but sent Judas away. Thanks to the Holy Spirit, Jesus knew what was in each man's heart and knew who to walk with and who to walk away from.

The difference between Judas and Peter is the difference between covert and overt. Judas was covert. His sinful scheming and plotting were secretive, hidden, and deceptive. For the entirety of his three years with Jesus, he stole money and plotted against Jesus. Outwardly one would never know this. He listened to the same sermons, went on the same mission trips, prayed in the same group, sang the same worship songs, and witnessed the same miracles as the other disciples. But he hid who he really was from everyone except Jesus who alone knew his heart.

> Jesus was not paranoid, trusting no one. Neither was He naive, trusting everyone. Instead, Jesus was wise and discerning.

Lots of people are like Judas—they can steal money from their bosses, cheat on their spouses, use church membership solely as a means to appear pious in public, and have no heart for the Lord.

Covert people are incredibly difficult to have a relationship with because, unless the Holy Spirit reveals to you who they truly are, you never know them, and they only use you.

Peter, however, was overt. He could not keep his mouth shut, and as a result, you always knew what he was thinking, feeling, and doing. He would boss Jesus around, grab a sword and cut someone's ear off, and seemed utterly incapable of hiding his inner life.

Some people are like Peter. They want to get it all out, put all their cards on the table, and just tell you up front who they are, what they think, and what they are doing. Overt people can be blindsided by covert people. They simply cannot understand how someone could lie, hide, cheat, steal, and conceal who they truly are throughout life. Covert people often take advantage of overt people since overt people assume they agree unless they say otherwise and have no idea there is a problem unless something is said.

THE COUNSELOR YOU NEED
FOR YOUR RELATIONSHIPS

During a very difficult season of our lives when we did not know who we could trust, Grace and I started meeting with a wise and godly counselor who was part certified clinician, part Spirit-filled pastor, and part loving grandpa. In that challenging season we thank God we had such wise counsel helping us process relationships, teaching us who to walk with closely and who to run from quickly.

The Holy Spirit is also a counselor. Jesus promised in John 14:26 that "the Counselor, the Holy Spirit—the Father will send Him in My name—will teach you all things" (HCSB). Most counseling appointments with pastors and therapists are about relationships—who to trust and who not to trust, how to proceed on a path forward and how to part ways forever. As a practical point, it seems that this discernment of the Holy Spirit is often referred to as your "gut." Oftentimes you cannot put your finger on the exact reason why someone seems unsafe, and perhaps you feel bad even thinking ill of someone, but the Holy Spirit often works through your gut. This gut instinct of the Spirit is often God's way of helping you have caution concerning other people.

Have you prayerfully considered your relationships? Are there any that you need to modify or end? Has the Holy Spirit been giving you a gut feeling about someone that you need to heed? Do you have any pattern of making foolish relational decisions because you have not been Spirit-led in your relationships? How is your relationship with the Holy Spirit, and how can the Holy Spirit help you have wisdom and health in your other relationships?

Once you understand the relational discernment brought by the Holy Spirit, you can grow in wisdom and know how to handle foolish and evil people. This starts by treating different people differently, as we will examine in the next chapter.

Chapter 8

FACING FOOLISH AND EVIL PEOPLE WITH THE SPIRIT'S WISDOM

T IS CURIOUS how people can grow up in the same home, share the same life, have the same experiences, and respond entirely differently.

Thomas, Susan, and Harold all grew up in a working-class home. Their father was an angry man who had allowed bitterness to infect his inner life as well as his outer life. He was angry at the way his parents raised him, the way his company treated him, and that God hadn't given him the life he had hoped to have.

On the worst days this dad would have too much to drink. When he did, his volume level, anger, and intensity increased. Like a grenade with the pin pulled, he exploded over the slightest issue with anyone in the family. He would stand up, become aggressive, and start cursing and yelling. His wife and kids would run from the room because sometimes he would hit his children.

As the three children grew up, they each responded very differently.

Thomas tragically became just like his dad. When he married and had kids of his own, he sadly carried the sins of his father into his family. People feared him, but no one respected him.

Growing up, Harold decided he would be the funny one and try and make jokes and lighten the mood when his dad would start to rage. He never really learned to deal with problems, but instead turned everything into a joke and made light of serious things. As an adult, Harold avoided tests, trials, and doing hard things, and instead just acted foolishly. Always the life of the party, he could not hold a job or have a serious conversation and became the stereotypical happy drunk who ignored reality. Harold became foolish. Lots of people liked him, but no one respected him.

Susan did not want to marry a man like her dad or raise children in a home like theirs. At school she met a kindhearted girl. They began eating lunch together and building a friendship. Curious about her family, Susan started asking about their home life. The girl explained that her family members were Christians who prayed together, served together, and had a lot of fun as a close-knit family. So as a teenager Susan started hanging out at her friend's house a lot, and before long they were picking her up on Sundays to attend church with them. Then Susan met other kids her age and families who invited her into their homes for meals and fun events. As Susan observed other families, the unhealthiness of her own family grew obvious. Over time she learned to forgive her father as God had forgiven her, and she decided to attend college and get a counseling degree. Today she is a mother with a healthy family and a licensed Christian counselor who helps abused children. Susan is wise, and those who know her respect her wisdom.

> Your experiences in life do *not* determine who you become. Instead, *how you choose to respond* to your experiences determines who you become.

From this family, we learn that your experiences in life do *not* determine who you become. Instead, *how you choose to respond* to your experiences determines who you become. When an awful experience occurs, one person uses it as an excuse to be a horrible person for the rest of her life. Another person uses the same experience as a catalyst for her greatest personal growth and health. Others might decide what happens to you, but you decide who you become.

As our kids grow up, we tell them to treat everyone the same. Perhaps that's not a good thing. To be sure, everyone bears the image of God, and in that regard they are equally valuable. But not every person is equally safe, healthy, or trustworthy. The truth is, we need to treat different people differently. People decide how we treat them by how they behave.

In the book *Necessary Endings* Henry Cloud does a great job dealing with how to decide when it's time to move on from a role, responsibility, or relationship. Grace and I got to thank Dr. Cloud personally for this book, and we encourage you to get his book if you are facing an important decision about staying where you are or moving on. We found chapter 7 particularly helpful as he delineates three kinds of people commonly grouped in Proverbs and other wisdom literature: wise, foolish, and evil people. In this next section I'll give you a bit of a summary along with my thoughts on Dr. Cloud's useful categories.

WISE PEOPLE

Wise people are not the most intelligent or educated, but they are humble, godly, teachable, open, and responsible. These people meet reality and life's demands by changing their actions and attitudes as needed to align with what is true and good. They welcome correction, invite others to teach them, and you can build a growing relationship with them by being honest.

Wise people also have empathy for others and consider more than just their own desires and feelings in a situation. Because of these character traits, there is always hope for a wise person to grow. The time you spend with them, instruction you give to them, and investment you make in them is worthwhile because they personally mature and your relationship grows and flourishes. Proverbs 9:8–9 means this by saying, "Correct the wise, and they will love you. Instruct the wise, and they will be even wiser. Teach the righteous, and they will learn even more" (NLT).

The way to respond to a wise person is with *more*—more time, more discussion, and more information—because they are a good investment of time and energy. You can trust a wise person and enjoy a personal relationship them. A wise person lives by the power of the Holy Spirit, which I'll explain next.

ARE YOU WISE?

We all have had the painful experience of someone wrongly judging us or not understanding us, and as a result, our relationship with them suffers or is severed. Additionally we all have had the painful experience of thinking we knew someone and trusting them, only to find—much to our misery—that they were not the person we thought they were.

Jesus came to earth in large part for the sake of relationship, but even devout religious leaders were foolish or evil in dealing with Him. In John 7 they sought to kill Jesus rather than have a relationship with Him because they wrongly judged Him. Jesus then rebuked their poor relational wisdom, saying, "Look beneath the surface so you can judge correctly" (v. 24, NLT).

In relationships we rely on predictable patterns of behavior when deciding who we trust and who we don't. This method causes problems because we judge by what we can see outwardly, and to truly know someone and judge correctly, Jesus said we must "look beneath the surface" of that person to their inner world that only the Spirit sees.

> Jesus came to earth in large part for the sake of relationship.

Following this statement, John 7 records that a great debate arose over whether Jesus was a good man or a bad man. Some said He was demon-possessed, others said He was Spirit-filled. Then we read, "Jesus stood and said in a loud voice, 'Let anyone who is thirsty come to me and drink. Whoever believes in me, as Scripture has said, rivers of living water will flow from within them.' By this he meant the Spirit, whom those who believed in him were later to receive. Up to that time the Spirit had not been given, since Jesus had not yet been glorified" (vv. 37–39, NIV).

Jesus' point is simple: without the Holy Spirit it is impossible for any of us to know anyone else's true nature on the inside. But with the Spirit we can look beneath the surface of what we see in the visible world (the clothes they wear, words they say, or actions they choose) and see a person's true self in the invisible world (the state of their soul, condition of their heart, or motive of their mind).

Jesus had wisdom for His relationships because the Holy Spirit helped Him look beneath the surface in order to judge people correctly. Isaiah 11:2 promised this trait of Jesus, "The Spirit of the LORD shall rest upon him, the Spirit of wisdom and understanding, the Spirit of counsel and might, the Spirit of knowledge and the fear of the LORD."

To properly deal with people and have any healthy relationships, you must have the discerning wisdom of the Holy Spirit. The Holy Spirit and wisdom are often closely connected in the Bible because the Holy Spirit is the source of wisdom. Job 32:8 links the Spirit to discerning wisdom, saying, "But it is the spirit in man, the breath of the Almighty, that makes him understand." In Ephesians 1:17 Paul prays that believers receive "the Spirit of wisdom."

Elsewhere in the Bible many believers in addition to Jesus are said to live by discerning wisdom through the Spirit. These include the following:

- "Joshua...was full of the spirit of wisdom" (Deut. 34:9).

- The Bible says of Othniel, Caleb's younger brother, "The Spirit of the LORD was upon him, and he judged" (Judg. 3:9–10).

- Unbelievers said of Daniel, "In whom is the spirit of the holy gods...Understanding and wisdom like the wisdom of the gods were found in him.... The spirit of the gods is in you, and that light and understanding and excellent wisdom are found in you" (Dan. 5:11, 14).

- Early Christian leaders were "full of the Spirit and of wisdom" (Acts 6:3).

- Stephen possessed both "wisdom and the Spirit" (Acts 6:10).

The Spirit of God knows people better than anyone, and He will help you have healthy relationships. God wants you to be wise and seek wisdom so that you can know how to handle foolish and evil people.

FOOLISH PEOPLE

Foolish people are not necessarily less intelligent or less educated. However, they are unteachable, defensive, unyielding, arrogant, irresponsible, and prone to make excuses for themselves and wrongly blame others when things go poorly. Sadly, if we are honest, everyone is foolish in areas and seasons of our life. None of us is immune to folly.

But people who are primarily foolish have an ongoing pattern of folly that infects and affects most if not all of their lives. Rather than changing, they want everyone and everything to change to accommodate them. Efforts to correct and instruct foolish people result in a fight or flight response where they fight back or run away. They have low empathy and tend to see themselves as both morally superior to others and a constant victim.

When dealing with a foolish person, you tend to have the same conversation over and over, and to them it sounds like nagging. The more you address the areas a foolish person keeps making the same error, the more conflict and disagreement ensues, and the relationship deteriorates.

The way to respond to a foolish person is with *less*—less time arguing, less frequently having the same conversation, less being on the defensive trying to get them to come around and take responsibility for their own life. This response sharpens through consequences and boundaries. Proverbs 1:7 provides a reason when it says "fools despise wisdom and discipline." Because a foolish person will not change but instead plows ahead in the same direction of destruction, the best thing to do is to impose consequences and limit the ability they have to harm themselves and others.

A foolish person pushes their responsibilities and the consequences of their folly onto responsible people, and the best thing to do is push the responsibilities and consequences back onto them. Hopefully, this preserves your life energy, protects you and others from them, and causes them enough grief to be motivated to make life changes. Proverbs 26:3 says, "Guide a horse with a whip, a donkey with a bridle, and a fool with a rod to his back!" (NLT). And Proverbs 10:13 says, "Those lacking sense will be beaten with a rod" (NLT).

A foolish person lives by the power of the sinful flesh (our sinful human nature). A foolish person will waste what you give them because they do not embrace it. They are like a bucket in which the bottom has rusted out; anything you pour into it just spills onto the ground. You need to limit your relationship with a foolish person by establishing clear boundaries and consequences. Peter started out as Jesus' most foolish disciple. Jesus helped Peter move from foolish to wise by rebuking him and inviting him to change. Jesus knew Peter was foolish and asked Peter to walk with Him toward wisdom.

EVIL PEOPLE

Some people have a hard time thinking that a professing Christian can be evil, but the Bible is painfully pointed. For example, in Acts 5:3 Peter says of one church member, "Ananias, why has Satan filled your heart to lie to the Holy Spirit…?"

Evil people do not cause harm unintentionally as fools do. Instead, evil people intentionally plot harm, scheme to bring pain and destruction, and feel vindicated in doing so because of their hurt, self-righteousness, or corrupt nature. They find satisfaction in causing others pain, loss, shame, humiliation, and fear. They feed off the notoriety of toppling others, are often motivated by jealousy and envy, empowered by the harming of others, and self-righteous—even mistakenly believing they are doing God's will—when bringing devastation, destruction, and death.

The way to respond to an evil person is with *nothing*—the exact opposite of our response to a wise person. Draw near to a wise person and run from an evil person. Give more information to a wise person, and no information to an evil person. Deal directly with a wise person, and let the cops and lawyers deal with the evil person.

A wise person can be influenced toward godliness, and a fool can perhaps be brought toward wisdom after they have sat in their mess for a while. But the evil person has to be considered hopeless apart from a dramatic intervention from God—one that does *not* involve you, because there is little to nothing you can do. An evil person might not be beyond *God's* ability to help, but they are probably beyond *your* ability.

At this point you separate, protect yourself, and establish a definite ending to the relationship with no contact or information going forward. Proverbs addresses this situation in several passages.

- Proverbs 1:15–18 says, "My child, don't go along with them! Stay far away from their paths. They rush to commit evil deeds. They hurry to commit murder. If a bird sees a trap being set, it knows to stay away. But these people set an ambush for themselves; they are trying to get themselves killed" (NLT).

- Proverbs 2:12–15 says, "Wisdom will save you from evil people, from those whose words are twisted. These men turn from the right way to walk down dark paths. They take pleasure in doing wrong, and they enjoy the twisted ways of evil. Their actions are crooked, and their ways are wrong" (NLT).

- Proverbs 24:1–2 says, "Don't envy evil people or desire their company. For their hearts plot violence, and their words always stir up trouble" (NLT).

Evil people live by the power of demonic forces to harass and harm. Because of their demonic empowerment, they are far more powerful when seeking to cause harm than they otherwise are in normal life. Evil people who move into ministry leadership become wolves who strike the shepherd in an effort to scatter the sheep. Evil people require a professional relationship with someone trained to deal wisely with their issues.

Judas was Jesus' evil disciple. For three years he plotted against Jesus and stole from Jesus. Jesus did not try to save Judas from himself because He knew that Judas was evil and ultimately, possessed by Satan. He simply told him at the time of betrayal in Matthew 26:50, "Friend, do what you came to do." Jesus treated Judas like a friend to the end, but Judas never changed. Instead, he betrayed Jesus and hung himself. Jesus knew Judas was evil and let him go.

Six Kinds of Relationships

The first key to healthy relationships is to accept that not everyone is Spirit-filled, wise, responsible, teachable, or a good investment of time and energy. We must determine which category we are in and invite wise people who love us enough to tell us the truth to help us see ourselves more clearly. Then they can rightly discern the categories of people in our other relationships.

Every one of us has at least some areas of our lives that are foolish, if not even evil. This explains why, for example, someone can be amazing at managing money and awful at maintaining relationships, or vice versa. We are all works in progress, and where we are foolish or trending toward evil, we need to find folks who are wise to help us move toward wisdom.

When it comes to relationships between two people, there are six kinds of relationships they can potentially have. Therefore, understanding each category and seeking to be wise in all relationships is crucial for a healthy life.

Wise + foolish = parental relationship

Irresponsible people seek out overly responsible people and dump their responsibilities on them. You know you have picked up a relationship like this when you are doing for someone things they should be doing for themselves.

A wise person seems competent since they are responsible and get things done with what appears to be ease. So a foolish person thinks it will be easier to get the wise person to do things for them instead of doing things for themselves. This only perpetuates their foolishness and irresponsibility, and it creates a parental relationship when the wise one acts like the parent, and the foolish one acts like the child. This explains why some adults still have parents paying their bills and picking up their messes.

This also explains why a wife might get frustrated when her husband acts like one of the kids. She feels like a mom to her husband, which eventually causes her to lose any attraction to him or respect for him. The worst I've personally seen was a home in which the wife and mother put together a chore chart for the kids and included dad on the chore chart. If he completed his tasks, Dad got an allowance like the kids. But if he did not do his duties, like the kids, he did not get a gold star on his chart, was denied dessert, and could not stay up past bedtime as a punishment.

Jesus was always wise when dealing with foolish people. He did not enable them by allowing them to continue in their irresponsibility. Instead, He called them to repentance, which is God's way of inviting us to walk away from our way of life and walk with Jesus in wisdom. When Jesus says "follow Me," He invites us to grow in wisdom one step at a time.

The Holy Spirit can help you with this type of relationship in the same way He helped Jesus. When Jesus encountered the woman at the well in John 4, she had come seeking well water to nourish her body but discovered living water to nourish her soul. Jesus sat down with her, and they had a conversation about her pattern of unhealthy relationships that included five husbands and some guy she was living with. Possibly an abuse victim, this woman's life was lonely and sad. Jesus told her that the only way she could become emotionally healthy and have healthy relationships was if the Holy Spirit brought His spring of fresh spiritual water to reside in the center of her soul much like the well that resided at the center of her town. The Holy Spirit, Jesus was saying, would wash away her filth, bring life where there was death, and cool refreshing for a life that felt like clay baking in the sun.

The woman was converted, left her pail at the well, and ran into town as a missionary to other foolish people who needed Jesus to give them the Holy Spirit so they could be changed by God. To be wise like Jesus when dealing with foolish people, make sure to point them to the well of the Holy Spirit to quench their emotional thirst.

Wise + evil = distant relationship

When an evil person seeks to build a close relationship with a wise person, the wise person maintains the distance. An evil person is like a predator always on the lookout for their next prey. Evil people do not love people; they use people for such things as sex, money, power, or fame. Evil people can be domineering, difficult, and demanding. As a result, they work through coercion, pushiness, and threat of punishment. When you let an evil person have access to your life, you place yourself in harm's way.

Over and over in the Bible we read about evil people repeatedly seeking to get close to Jesus so that they could hurt Him. John 10:39 records one of their many attempts saying, "Again they sought to arrest him, but he escaped from their hands." Aided by the discernment of the Holy Spirit, Jesus kept His distance from evil people, and we should do the same.

Foolish + foolish = codependent relationship

When two foolish people come together in a close relationship, they multiply their folly. This happens a lot. Foolish people tend to find one another, do life together, and are maddening and frustrating because it seems like the fools are winning.

There is simply no way to escape every foolish person. Neighbors, classmates, coworkers, and family members are in our lives, and some are foolish. Our goal must be twofold: (1) to allow the Holy Spirit to make us increasingly wise in every relationship and (2) to help others to pursue wisdom.

Jesus operated like this, and the religious leaders who were non-relational did not understand His relationships. Jesus was friends with foolish people and even attended their parties but only to help make them wise. He never acted foolishly or sinfully.

There are never-ending opportunities for us to engage with foolish people, and each one comes with the inherent danger of drawing us toward folly rather than the other person toward wisdom. We must rely on the Holy Spirit as Jesus did if we are to avoid becoming foolish ourselves, and instead speak the Spirit's wisdom that has the power to draw them out of their foolishness.

If you have been foolish and find yourself in a codependent relationship with another foolish person, the first and best step to getting out is to seek the Holy Spirit's wisdom. The Bible promises that anyone who asks for wisdom will receive it (James 1:5). The next step will likely be to separate yourself from that relationship for a time to make sure you are not drawn back into their folly.

In addition to the Holy Spirit's help, always seek godly advice from wise people to help you deal with fools. They can tell you whether your friendships and relationships with others are wise or not. If you are friends with foolish people, follow Jesus' example and never participate in their foolishness. If they continue in their foolishness, then you must be wise enough to trust God to take care of the fools.

Foolish + evil = abusive relationship

Foolish people are often gullible and vulnerable. Because they do not deal with reality or have much of a plan for their lives, they are easy prey for evil people. If we think of wise people as shepherds and foolish people as sheep, then evil people are wolves. Wolves love to eat sheep. When an evil person can get into a romantic or business relationship with a foolish person, they do great damage. Evil people use and abuse foolish people. Sadly, foolish people allow this kind of abusive relationship to continue for far too long and pay a steep price.

Sadly, as the father of two lovely daughters who are now at the age that their peers are dating, it devastates me to see foolish young women in romantic relationships with evil men. The world is filled with these kinds of abusive relationships that break the health of people while also breaking the heart of God.

I will never forget a devastating counseling session I had with a man and his daughter many years ago. Her upbringing made her naïve, and she did not understand the danger that some guys pose. She began dating a bad guy, and her father said and did nothing. The bad guy began abusing her in multiple ways, and she told her father. He did nothing.

This abusive dating relationship continued for many years and caused great damage to the young woman. Eventually she managed to get away from the bad guy despite him stalking and threatening her. As she grew older and became a parent, the failure of her father became clear.

We sat down so that she could explain to her father how he had contributed to her suffering. As she wept uncontrollably telling her tragic testimony, her dad got defensive. Then he said something like, "I don't know why she's upset with me. *I did not do anything.*"

"*That* was your sin," I said.

As the father of five children I call the Fab Five, I tend to think like a dad on most any issue. For starters, those of us who are given the great honor of raising children need to teach them that there are wise, foolish, and evil people. These categories are found throughout the Book of Proverbs, a book that tells us it is written to help parents raise children. One of the most important things we learn growing up is how to be a good friend and how to pick good friends. Our children need to know that there are evil people and that God does not want them to be evil or closely involved with evil people. Our children need to know that there are foolish people and that God does not want them to be foolish or closely involved with foolish people. If we fail at this parental duty, then we ourselves are being foolish and possibly even evil.

Evil + evil = dangerous relationship

When two evil people come together, they are like two barrels on a gun. If you get in front of them, you are likely to get shot. These might be married couples, business partners, or two hurt people who form an unholy alliance around their common enemy.

The Bible often speaks of evil people working together in a demonic partnership. We can see this in the cases of Jannes and Jambres who opposed Moses, the married couple Ananias and Sapphira who lied to the Holy Spirit and Peter to steal from God, as well as Hymenaeus and Alexander who attacked and undermined the ministry of Paul until he handed them over to Satan.

Sometimes evil people have been hurt, and rather than forgiving and healing, they choose the path of bitterness and destruction. As a result, they feel vindicated and justified to hurt people because they were hurt by people, and torment others because they are tormented by the devil. United by their common goal, when two evil people come together, they make it their life's mission to do the same thing as the devil—steal, kill, and destroy.

Jesus was invited by evil himself to bow down and worship him in exchange for the passions, pleasures, and powers of the entire earth. Like I discussed in chapter 5, all that Satan asked was that Jesus join him in a relationship where they would do evil together. Jesus turned down that offer, but Satan continues to invite others to take the deal. Sometimes the most religious people take up that offer and do evil like the religious leaders who conspired together to kill Jesus.

Wise + wise = healthy relationship

When two wise people walk humbly together, they make the good times twice as good and the bad times half as bad, as the old saying goes. This kind of healthy relationship causes both people to be blessed and benefit. Proverbs 13:20 speaks of this kind of relationship saying, "Whoever walks with the wise becomes wise."

In one of the most difficult seasons of my life and ministry God gave wise counsel to me through one of my pastors. Anticipating a tsunami on the horizon, looking me in the eye with great seriousness he said, "Foolishness and evil are about to come upon you. You cannot stop others from putting it on you. But the Lord can remove

> When two wise people walk humbly together, they make the good times twice as good and the bad times half as bad, as the old saying goes.

it from you so long as you do not let it get in you. Do not let it in you or it will ruin you!"

I'm certainly no Jesus, but I looked to Him as my example in this situation. A lot of foolishness and evil was put upon Jesus—shame, condemnation, hatred, betrayal, attacks, lies, and abuse. But Jesus never let what was *on* Him get *in* Him to poison His heart, mind, and soul. My pastor's words were wise: you cannot control what people put *on* you, but you can control what you allow *in* you.

Looking back on that experience makes me realize how incredibly valuable my relationships with wise people are. The Holy Spirit often works through wise people. I don't think I would have made it without them.

Do you have relationships with wise people? If not, seek the Holy Spirit's guidance, begin to surround yourself with wise people, and build relationships with them. Listen to their wisdom and apply it to your life. It will make you wise and might even save your life.

Filled with the Spirit, Jesus had health and healthy relationships with all types of people—demonic people, critics, enemies, strangers, family members, married couples, single people, troubled people, leaders, and the broken. How about you? Are you more wise, foolish, or evil in your current relationships? Are you actively inviting the Spirit to help you know yourself and others accurately so that you can be health relationally? Which of the six kinds of relationships do you most commonly find yourself in?

Relationships are rough. If we are honest, it is our relationships that cause much if not most of our suffering. Jesus' relationships also contributed to His suffering, which we will examine in the next chapter.

Chapter 9

BE PERFECTED THROUGH SUFFERING

I N MY FAMILY one of our favorite people is a little girl with bows in her hair, braces on her legs, and a walker that holds her up. Her little body struggles to be healthy, but her soul is perhaps the healthiest I have ever seen. She has a huge smile, lovely personality, and kind word for everyone she meets. Every time I read Jesus' words that those with pure hearts will be blessed, this little girl comes to mind.

This lovely little lady has spent much of her dozen years of life in the hospital undergoing various surgeries. On one occasion I was honored to be at her bedside as she came out of surgery and began to awaken. Her lovely blonde hair was shaved, and in its place were numerous large stitches from yet another surgery.

With parched lips and droopy eyes due to the medication, she looked at me and smiled. Holding back tears, I asked her how she was doing. She said, "I'm fine, but Mister Mark, how are you? I'm more worried about you."

This little girl has been through more suffering than any child I know, yet she is perhaps the godliest, maturest, and most Christlike child I have ever met. In various conversations we have had, she has explained to me how her suffering has helped her more fully appreciate Jesus' suffering and increased her love and compassion for others who are suffering. At times the profound insights she shares make it obvious that God's Spirit is present and powerful in her suffering, giving her wisdom that defies the number of candles on her birthday cake.

OUR GOD SUFFERS

Only a few pages into the Bible after sin enters the world we read in Genesis 6:5–6, "The LORD observed the extent of human wickedness on the earth, and he saw that everything they thought or imagined was consistently and totally evil. So the LORD was sorry he had ever made them and put them on the earth. It broke his heart" (NLT).

We have heard that sin breaks God's laws. Great theologians trained as lawyers, such as Luther and Calvin, focused on the laws of Moses and rightly saw sin as the breaking of God's laws. However, we tragically learn that sin also breaks God's heart.

Who has broken your heart? What has broken your heart? Have you considered that you and your life have broken God's heart? Let that sink in. Your sinning causes God's suffering.

The rest of the Bible reads pretty much like a horror story if you read it from God's perspective. Examples include redneck Noah who had the first camping binge where he passed out naked in a tent; Abraham who gave away his lovely wife Sarah—not once, but twice—and had a kid with the girlfriend his wife picked,

> We have heard that sin breaks God's laws....However, we tragically learn that sin also breaks God's heart.

which lead to a geopolitical crisis between their descendants ever since; his grandson Jacob who was a trickster and played favorites with his sons; and Judah who was a perverted patriarch (check out Genesis 38 if you don't know the story) and ancestor of Jesus Christ.

These are just the lowlights in the first book of the Bible that Sunday school teachers read quickly, hoping no one raises a hand and asks a question. Before the first book of the Bible is over, we have the first murder between the first brothers, followed by adultery, incest, violence, prostitution, thievery, and the rape of a young woman with her angry brothers murdering an entire town in response while their passive dad says and does nothing.

In Exodus we learn that Moses was a murderer and coward, and as we read the rest of the Bible we find that the great King David was also an adulterer and murderer, and that his son Solomon, who built the temple, had no less than seven hundred wives, three hundred concubines, and a heart that turned to worship false demon gods, even making pagan shrines where his wives could offer sacrifices that possibly even included child sacrifices. With this history in mind, Ecclesiastes 7:10 takes on a whole new meaning when it says, "Don't long for 'the good old days.' This is not wise" (NLT).

When you read the Bible, it's hard to believe in evolution. Instead, you're more likely to believe in devolution. We didn't start out like animals, but we're becoming animals.

Have you ever had a shirt with a stain so deep you could not get it out? Somehow the stain became so ingrained that it literally turned into part of the shirt.

Sin is like that. It has completely infected and affected the totality of our being. The story of the Bible is that everyone is sinful and that God is patient, loving, and gracious, and He forgives from a broken heart for no reason other than He alone is good. So good, in fact, that He adds humanity to His divinity when the Creator enters His creation as the God-man Jesus Christ.

The Bible repeatedly stresses the fact that Jesus, unlike the rest of us, was without sin.

Perfect.

Faultless.

Spotless.

Blameless.

Nonetheless, people hated Him, berated Him, and exhausted Him.

As we read the four Gospels in the New Testament, we discover that only two of the biographies even mention Jesus' birth that we celebrate every Christmas, but that each biography of Jesus devotes at least a third of their content to one particular week in the life of

Jesus—the final week when He died and rose again. John's Gospel spends nearly half its content on this final week.

Before we examine the suffering of Jesus, I ask you to reflect on one scripture. In the rest of this chapter my goal is to paint a picture of Jesus' suffering that culminated at the cross. But framing this picture to give it context is something written by Jesus' lead disciple, Peter, who learned about suffering by watching his Savior suffer.

> The story of the Bible is that everyone is sinful and that God is patient, loving, and gracious, and He forgives from a broken heart for no reason other than He alone is good.

Speaking of Jesus' suffering and your suffering, 1 Peter 4:12–14 says, "Beloved, do not be surprised at the fiery trial when it comes.... But rejoice insofar as you share Christ's sufferings, that you may also rejoice and be glad when his glory is revealed....You are blessed, because the Spirit of glory and of God rests upon you." Bible commentator Karen Jobes said the following about this scripture:

Those who suffer for Christ...are blessed. The blessing is not in the suffering itself but because the presence of the Spirit of glory and of God is present....The blessing comes not because of an opportunity for self-improvement but because of the presence of God....All too often, when believers suffer and face hard times, they question where God is. Have they displeased God? Has God left them to their own resources? Is their suffering a sign of God's disfavor or even his anger?...Peter's teaching corrects his reader's understanding of their experience. First, suffering that comes because one is living for Christ should not be a surprise; Jesus' suffering normalized (and dignified) it. And second, the Spirit of glory and of God rests upon the believer who suffers rather than sins. For it is only by the power of the Spirit that one finds the resolve and strength to live an uncompromising life in a society that is hostile to one's fundamental convictions and values. One's willingness to suffer rather than compromise indicates the inner transformation of the sanctifying work of the Spirit....God has not abandoned the Christian who suffers; to the contrary, God is powerfully present in the experience of suffering for Christ. The phrase "the Spirit of glory and of God rests upon you"...is probably an allusion to Isa. 11:2....Peter claims that the same Spirit of God predicted to rest upon the Messiah also rests on the believer who is willing to suffer for Jesus Christ. Peter consoles his readers that because the same Spirit of glory and of God rests upon them, their current suffering is as Christ's was, a prelude to the glory to follow.[1]

Jesus suffered and yet He was blessed because the Holy Spirit rested upon Him in glory during His suffering. You can suffer and be blessed because the Holy Spirit will come to rest on you in a unique and glorious way when you suffer.

By the time Jesus reaches His final week, He has already been run out of His hometown as a prophet without honor. Jesus ominously begins talking openly about His impending death. Jesus sits down with His Jewish disciples to eat the traditional Passover meal that God's people have been eating ever since their deliverance from bondage and slavery in Egypt as recorded in Exodus.

Today we call this meal the "Last Supper,"and it has been memorialized in the painting by Leonardo da Vinci. Passover is about forgiveness and deliverance. Passover memorialized the night in Egypt when in faith God's people painted the doorposts to their home with the blood of a lamb. The lamb had to be unblemished, showing its purity, and slaughtered as a substitute in the place of the sinner. They painted the doorposts with the blood as an act of faith, showing that the household believed they were sinners deserving death but that through the death of a substitute without spot or blemish they received forgiveness and God's wrath passed over them. Conversely those who were not covered by the blood of the lamb saw death come to their home. This ritual foreshadowed the coming of Jesus in John 1:29 when John the Baptizer said, "Look! The Lamb of God who takes away the sin of the world!" (NLT). Reflecting back, Paul would later write in 1 Corinthians 5:7, "Christ, our Passover Lamb, has been sacrificed for us" (NLT).

Sitting at the Passover, Jesus broke with fifteen centuries of tradition. The Scriptures to be read and words to be spoken had remained virtually unchanged from generation to generation. However, everything was about to change at the cross of Jesus. Luke 22:19–20 (NLT) says that while eating the Passover,

> [Jesus] took some bread and gave thanks to God for it. Then he broke it in pieces and gave it to the disciples, saying, "This is my body, which is given for you. Do this in remembrance of me." After supper he took another cup of wine and said, "This cup is the new covenant between God and his people—an agreement confirmed with my blood, which is poured out as a sacrifice for you."

As Jesus was eating, His suffering was beginning. What kinds of suffering have you endured? We're going to look at several types of suffering, and as we do, keep in mind that Jesus endured every category of suffering and has compassion for you.

Spiritual suffering: satanic attack

Satan, who showed up to eat with our first parents, also showed up as Jesus and His disciples were eating the Passover. Satan entered Judas Iscariot, who had opened himself up so completely to demonic influence that he became possessed. Like a crooked Vegas dealer who pockets the pot, Judas was a pretend friend of Jesus who had been stealing money from Jesus' ministry for some time. By the time they sat down to eat, Judas had already agreed to hand Jesus over for thirty pieces of silver just as the prophet Zechariah had promised hundreds of years prior (Zech. 11:12–13).

Has Satan attacked you through an agent of demonic destruction? He attacked Jesus too.

Mental suffering: stress

Knowing His time was short, Jesus went to the Garden of Gethsemane to pray to the Father. Alone in the darkness of night, Jesus knew that His crucifixion was impending. He was so distressed by what awaited Him that the Bible records Him sweating like drops of blood. Jesus was literally at the limit to what the mind and body can endure, and this was only the beginning of the bleeding. Hebrews 5:7 summarizes this moment saying, "While Jesus was here on earth, he offered prayers and pleadings, with a loud cry and tears" (NLT). Doubled over, screaming, weeping, agonizing, and bleeding from the stress, Mark's Gospel tells us Jesus was "deeply troubled and distressed" (Mark 14:33, NLT). Luke 22:43 says that Jesus was so weary that "an angel from heaven appeared and strengthened him" (NLT).

Have you ever been so stressed that your heart raced, mind blurred, hands shook, and breath trembled while your tears flowed in the middle night because you could not sleep, knowing what your future held? Jesus has too.

Emotional suffering: anguish

You can sense the anguish as Jesus prays in Luke 22:42: "Father, if you are willing, please take this cup of suffering away from me" (NLT). Jesus is dreading what is coming. This cup is an awful, horrible, dreadful cup. The prophets speak of this cup as drinking the full strength of the wrath of God (Ezek. 23:33; Isa. 51:17; Jer. 25:15). The Bible uses some twenty words to speak of God's wrath more than six hundred times. The wrath of God is the undiluted, undiverted, and undefiled justice of God poured out upon a sinful soul. Knowing He is going to drink this cup for us, Jesus struggles until finally surrendering to the Father's plan, saying in Luke 22:42, "I want your will to be done, not mine" (NLT).

Have you struggled to accept God's path for you because it is certain to have pain and shame? Jesus has too.

Financial suffering: poverty

In His greatest crisis Jesus did not have the resources to meet any of His practical needs. His ministry was seemingly not well funded—they owned no buildings, depended upon the kindness of others for such things as housing and food when traveling, and Jesus Himself did not have the money to pay His taxes. To make matters worse, Judas the CFO had been stealing ministry money for a few years. Jesus had no defense attorney as He was taken away in the middle of the night for a sham trial. He had no security detail to guard Him, nor did He have a counselor or therapist for soul care and emotional support.

How about you? Do you struggle financially and lack the resources to make life a lot healthier and easier? Jesus did too.

Relational suffering: abandonment and betrayal

In the Garden of Gethsemane, Jesus asked His disciples, the friends He had invested in for three years, to do Him one favor and stay awake to pray for Him. What did His "friends" do? They fell asleep. Not once, but twice. They abandoned Jesus in His hour of greatest need.

To make matters worse, this was not the last time they would abandon Him. Within hours, to save his own neck, Peter would go so far as to deny three times that he even knew Jesus. We usually think about how this denial made Peter feel, never considering how it added to Jesus' suffering to know one of His closest friends would reject their relationship three times.

Ultimately Jesus suffered the epitome of a faithless friend as Judas' plan of betrayal unfolded. For three years Jesus loved, served, taught, fed, and cared for Judas. Jesus even washed Judas' feet, which was the job the lowliest slave was supposed to do for the most honored guest. Stop and think about this. God washed the feet of a guy He had created, a guy He knew to be stealing money from the ministry.

Jesus never failed Judas, never harmed Judas, and never betrayed Judas. Yet Judas showed up in the garden with soldiers and betrayed Jesus with a kiss—the kiss of death.

Have you been abandoned by friends in your hour of need or betrayed by those you trusted the most? Jesus has too.

Public suffering: slander

Jesus was wrongly arrested and forced to walk for miles under cover of darkness in violation of His legal rights. His trial was a sham. There was no investigation because the entire point was an execution. One after another, false witnesses brought forth false charges. The plan seemed to be "throw enough mud and eventually some is bound to stick." Their testimony contradicted one another because, unlike the truth that always sings in harmony, discordant liars never make a good choir. Yet, no one cared because this was murder by a mob and not a trial for the truth.

Have liars destroyed your reputation? Jesus' reputation was destroyed too.

Physical suffering: beatings

Angry, cowardly men surrounded Jesus once He was in custody. They covered His eyes and proceeded to beat Him mercilessly. Mob mentality was in full swing as man after man took turn after turn landing punch after punch.

Beaten, hungry, dehydrated, and exhausted after a stressful and sleepless night, Jesus was then stripped nearly naked, and the Bible simply states that He was scourged. Scourging was so barbarous and brutal that it killed many people before they could even make it to the cross.

Jesus' hands were affixed over His head so that His back and legs were laid out for a soldier's whip to shred His body. The soldier used a specific whip called the cat-o'-nine-tails—a handle from which proceeded several long leather straps with heavy balls made of metal or stone intended to tenderize the human flesh in preparation for the hooks that would then sink deeply into the body. Once the hooks sunk into the flesh, the soldier would then rip the flesh off the body of the prisoner—sometimes so violently that a rib would come flying off. The trauma went deep into the vital organs, often causing internal bleeding.

Anticipating this horrible beating, some seven hundred years prior Isaiah 52:14 prophesied, "His face was so disfigured he seemed hardly human, and from his appearance, one would scarcely know he was a man" (NLT).

Has your body been beaten by an enemy, rapist, violent father, angry boyfriend, or cruel bully? Jesus' body was too.

Personal suffering: shame

In mockery of Jesus' title as King of the Jews, soldiers pressed a crown of thorns into Jesus' head while people laughed. Then they forced Jesus to carry His cross through the streets of town on His bloodied shoulders and back. The cross, or possibly only the crossbar, was likely a roughly hewn piece of splintered timber weighing upwards of a hundred pounds. Dripping blood, sweat, and tears, Jesus was shamefully forced to carry His cross through town.

I've walked the path Jesus did, and it is a narrow path filled with people shopping. In today's world it would be like being forced to carry your cross through a mall during the busiest shopping season, weeping and bleeding while children stare in horror. Jesus was so beaten and His body so broken that He fell under the weight of the cross. So the Romans chose Simon of Cyrene to help carry Jesus' cross the rest of the way. Once He finally arrived at His place of execution, soldiers pulled out Jesus' beard (a shameful disrespect in that culture), spat on Him, and mocked Him while His family and friends looked on—including His horrified mother. Those of us from the Western world can miss the shame for the family in all of this. Much of the Eastern world is built largely on saving face and not causing shame for oneself or one's family.

Have you been publicly shamed? Jesus has too.

All of Jesus' suffering culminated at the cross. Before we examine His final and greatest suffering, we need to consider the Spirit. How could Jesus possibly face His suffering? How can you possibly face your suffering?

Speaking of Jesus' suffering on the cross, Hebrews 9:11–14 says, "When Christ appeared as a high priest...he entered once for all into the holy places, not by means of the blood of goats and calves but by means of his own blood, thus securing an eternal redemption....How much more will the blood of Christ, who through the eternal Spirit offered himself without blemish to God, purify our conscience from dead works to serve the living God."

In the old covenant the holiest place on earth was the temple. It was there that the Holy Spirit dwelt and the priest would come to offer a sacrifice on behalf of sinners. Jesus' body was the very temple of the Spirit, and it was "through the eternal Spirit" that He was empowered to serve as both priest and sacrifice, offering Himself in the place of sinners. The church father and famous preacher John Chrysostom said that just as there was a flame that burned day and night in the temple as commanded by God (Lev. 6:9), so the Holy Spirit kept the passionate devotion of Jesus Christ continually burning in His soul even as He suffered.[2]

Suffering has a way of burning out the proverbial flame in a person. As you suffer, you can grow weary, lose heart, give up on life, and give in to sin. Jesus Christ faced all of this as He headed to the cross, and it was the Holy Spirit who kept the flame alive in Him. Jesus provides you that same Spirit to keep your flame burning bright through your suffering as well. If the Holy Spirit can keep the flame of Jesus' passion alive even as He is dying, He can do the same for you no matter what you go through!

Total suffering: crucifixion

All of the suffering that Jesus experienced culminated on the cross. There, our loving Lord and dying Deliverer suffered completely and totally in every category simultaneously.

Whatever you have faced, it pales in comparison to what Jesus then endured. The ten fingers and ten toes that Mary counted on her firstborn son were nailed to a wooden cross. The carpenter's son who grew up driving nails now had large nails driven through the most sensitive nerve centers on the human body. Jesus' body would have twitched involuntarily as His throat grew hoarse from screaming in agony. His cross was then lifted up and dropped into a hole as His body shook from the pain.

Have you endured physical pain from injury, ailment, sickness, or assault? Jesus did too.

We do not worship a God who stands back at a safe distance viewing the horror story of human history, but rather a faithful High Priest who empathizes with us. He's been through what we go through, felt what we feel, and conquered what we face—including satanic attack, abandonment, betrayal, stress, struggle, poverty, slander, beating, shame, and pain. We spend our life energy seeking to run from these things, but Jesus Christ willingly ran to them. God came and basically jumped head first into a wood chipper called the cross.

The cross.

It has become a fashion symbol in our day. But in Jesus' day it was, as the old hymn rightly says, "the emblem of suffering and shame."[3]

Theologians believe that Christians adopted the cross as the visual reminder of Christ and Christianity, starting with the church father Tertullian who lived from the end of the second to the beginning of the third century AD. Around that time believers began making the sign of the cross and putting crosses on and around their homes to identify themselves with Jesus Christ.

Crucifixion was and is brutal. In recent times crucifixion continues by extremist terrorist groups such as ISIS. The BBC reports,

"Sheikh Dr. Usama Hasan, Islamic scholar and senior researcher in Islamic Studies at the Quilliam Foundation in London, says this form of punishment arises from a very literal, or fundamentalist, reading of the Koran. Verse 33 of the fifth book of the Koran says: 'Indeed, the penalty for those who wage war against Allah and His Messenger and strive upon earth [to cause] corruption is none but that they be killed or crucified or that their hands and feet be cut off from opposite sides or that they be exiled from the land. That is for them a disgrace in this world; and for them in the Hereafter is a great punishment.'"[4]

The goal of such horror is always the same—to strike terror in the hearts of others. To crucify one person publicly is to send a chilling fear into the hearts of anyone and everyone who might agree with them, align with them, or follow them. The message is clear: do not believe what they believe or you will endure what they endure. The Romans did not even crucify their own citizens—only outsiders. For the Jews, crucifixion signified God's damnation as Deuteronomy 21:22–23 (cf. Galatians 3:13) says with haunting simplicity that "anyone who is hung is cursed in the sight of God" (NLT).

It is believed that the Persians may have invented crucifixion around 500 BC, but Romans sought to perfect crucifixion. Some Roman soldiers who oversaw crucifixion seemed to delight in experimenting with new ways to inflict the most pain, making sadism a sport. The pain of crucifixion was so intense and overwhelming that the word *excruciating* literally means "from the cross."

Contributing to the pain of crucifixion was the strain it put on the victim's breathing. Sometimes a person would pass in and out of consciousness while hanging on a cross because as the body slumped, air would leave the lungs. To get air back into the lungs, the victim would need to push himself up on the nails pounded through his feet. For this reason, sometimes the legs were broken—it sped up death since the victim could not raise himself to breathe. Jesus' legs were not broken in fulfillment of prophecy (Ps. 34:19–20).

Under such torment, crucified men were known to seek

vengeance in any way they could. As crowds surrounded and mocked the victims, they would seek to spit or urinate upon the bloodthirsty mob. Others would curse out their enemies, publicly malign the character of others, or attempt to defend themselves by giving their side of the story.

All of human history had been marching to the cross of Jesus. As Jesus hung there bleeding, weeping, and dying, the visible mob of humanity, as well as the invisible legions of angels and demons, were anxiously awaiting His response. Jesus suffered nobly, humbly, and lovingly. Then He died—and needed to wait for time to vindicate Him.

The same is true for you. If history does not vindicate you, eternity will.

In the next chapter I will share more about suffering. Before you flip the page, I sincerely want to say that I am sorry for your suffering. What I'm sharing in these chapters on suffering are things I've learned as I walked through my own valley of the shadow of death. It's an honor if anything I learned through that season can be of help to you, so thank you for giving me the opportunity to walk with you through your valley of the shadow of death.

When we are suffering, we are to remember the ministry of the Holy Spirit as Hebrews 3:7–8 says, "Therefore, as the Holy Spirit says, 'Today, if you hear his voice, do not harden your hearts as in the rebellion, on the day of testing in the wilderness.'" When suffering comes, it does feel as if we are in a wilderness. Like a dry and desolate desert, there are not enough physical, spiritual, emotional, or financial resources to continue forward. You feel overwhelmed, discouraged, fearful, and even hopeless. In your worst moments the Holy Spirit cries out to you, begging you to not harden your heart toward God or rebel against God's will for your life. Our greatest need when suffering is the Spirit. He reminds us of Jesus' suffering for us and comes to help us suffer well.

With the cross on the horizon, Jesus teaches us about one of the most needed ministries of the Holy Spirit. In John 13–17 Jesus knows that His crucifixion is coming and prepares His followers for the suffering that awaits them as well in what Bible commentators like to call "the farewell discourse." Consider this for a moment: if you knew that you were dying soon, what would you tell the people you loved the most? Jesus prepared His people for their suffering as He was facing His suffering. Jesus promised in John 14:26–28 (NKJV) that He would send "the Helper, the Holy Spirit" so that you can experience a supernatural "peace" that only comes from God and "let not your heart be troubled, neither let it be afraid."

Speaking of the ministry of the Holy Spirit as our Helper, Bible teacher Charles Swindoll says, "The Greek term can also be translated 'advocate,' 'encourager,' or even 'coach.' It carries the idea of a trainer running alongside someone in a race to provide counsel, correction, hope, comfort, and positive perspective....Like a coach encouraging and challenging an athlete to reach a particular goal, He trains believers to dedicate themselves, to discard hindrances, and to become obedient like Christ. The Helper does this supernaturally."[5]

Just as the Holy Spirit walked with Jesus to the cross, coaching Him along the way, He too will walk with you through your valley of the shadow of death. This is especially comforting when we consider that suffering is a school we *all* attend—something we will learn in the next chapter.

Chapter 10

SUFFERING IS A SCHOOL WE ALL ATTEND

THE FIRST DAY of kindergarten absolutely terrified me. Feeling like my mom was abandoning me, I sat big-eyed and freaked out in my little desk, trapped between a boy who was so scared he wet his pants and a girl who brought sardines for lunch. My mom backed out of the classroom watching me beg her to take me home. As a Catholic boy, this was my purgatory.

Middle school was rough as I transferred from a Catholic school to a public school with kids who smoked and listened to gangster rap while waiting for the bus. I once saw lunatics take over an asylum on the news, and I think their kids all rode my bus.

High school was pretty good as I played sports, made friends, and deftly managed to avoid joining a gang. There, I met Grace, and the only two things I remember from high school are that *chapeau* is the French word for *hat* and that Grace was adorable.

College started out badly. I joined a fraternity until I learned that *frat boy* is apparently the Greek word for a loud, demon-possessed, wearing-no-shirt-for-no-reason alcoholic. I did not drink, but I did manage to get in a fight with a drunk guy. Guys were doing nefarious things that I did not want to be involved in, so I moved out just before my pledge class got arrested.

Shortly after that, I got saved, and Grace transferred to my college so we could be together and get married, which made college awesome. I also ate so many slices that even though I graduated in 1993, I still have the phone number to the pizza place memorized.

Going to seminary to get a master's degree while pastoring a church and raising kids was fun—even though I drove to another state one day each month in my old, rusted-out Chevy truck with no speedometer or radio.

We've all got some curious school memories. What are some of your most memorable school moments?

THE SCHOOL OF SUFFERING

We've all been to different schools where we learned different things. But every Christian attends one school in particular and learns one lesson. That school is suffering, and that lesson is how to become more perfectly like Jesus.

The Book of Hebrews says a lot about the school of suffering Jesus attended for us and attends with us. We will examine four different scriptures that appear as a theme in the first half of the great Book of Hebrews.

In Hebrews 2:10 we read this astonishing statement regarding Jesus' suffering: "It was fitting that he, for whom and by whom all things exist, in bringing many sons to glory, should make the founder of their salvation perfect through suffering."

What does it mean that Jesus was made perfect through suffering? Jesus was perfect before He came to earth and suffered. But He became perfectly perfect through the experience of suffering. One Bible commentary explains it this way:

> Christ always has been perfect in a moral sense. He *is* sinless. The word translated *perfect* here frequently recurs throughout this letter. It signifies the completion of a process…"its use here means that Jesus became *fully qualified* as pioneer of man's salvation by undergoing experience of human sufferings, inasmuch as through suffering is the way to salvation." Although Christ was morally perfect and sinless, his life and work were brought by suffering to a

form of perfection or completion which cannot have been possible without them.[1]

There are some things that you can learn by watching others experience that you cannot completely understand until you share that experience. Single people can know *about* marriage, but they understand much more once they have lived together as husband and wife for some years. A childless couple can know *about* parenting, but they understand much more once they are raising their own child. An older couple without grandkids can know *about* grandparenting, but they understand much more once they are taking their grandchild out for ice cream on the way to the park.

So it is with Jesus. From heaven He watched our suffering and knew *about* suffering. But He added the experience of His suffering. In this way His learning was perfected so that He now completely understands our suffering.

Jesus, our King, came to earth to pioneer a path for His people to march into His eternal kingdom. This plan required our King to leave His throne in glory where angels served Him and come to the earth in humility to serve us. Our humble King Jesus suffered because of our sin and died to deliver us from death.

Today our humble King has returned to His throne. Today Jesus can thoroughly empathize with you as you suffer. He has faced what you face, He has endured what you must endure, and He has defeated what is opposing you. He loves you, He helps you, and He has sent the Spirit so that you have the power to endure suffering as He did.

Continuing to speak of Jesus' suffering, Hebrews 2:17–18 says, "Therefore he had to be made like his brothers in every respect, so that he might become a merciful and faithful high priest in the service of God, to make propitiation for the sins of the people. For because he himself has suffered when tempted, he is able to help those who are being tempted."

The original target audience for the Book of Hebrews was Jewish Christians. They were familiar with the concept of a priest. Much like a bridge over a chasm that cannot otherwise be connected, the priesthood was part of the bridge that our Holy God in heaven built to have a relationship with us sinners on earth. As the embassy for heaven on earth, the Spirit of God dwelt in the holy of holies at the temple. Once a year the high priest, as the representative of the people, would enter into the presence of the Spirit of God and slaughter an innocent animal as a substitute for sinners. We call this *propitiation* because God's wrath is propitiated or appeased—it's diverted from us and imputed or placed upon the substitute.

Just like the blood on the doorposts, this sacrificial system foreshadowed the coming of Jesus. His body was the holy of holies where the Spirit dwelt. He came as our High Priest and offered Himself through His suffering as the substitute for our sin.

Having forgiven sin and defeated death, Jesus lives as our High Priest. He continues to intercede for us before God the Father. He forgives our sin and sends the Spirit to make our bodies a sort of holy of holies where God dwells on the earth, going with us wherever we go. Jesus empathizes with us when we are tempted since He too was tempted and needed the Spirit's help. He sends the same power of the Spirit that He lived by to empower our lives when we are suffering and tempted.

Reflecting back on the suffering of Jesus, Hebrews 5:7–10 says, "In the days of his flesh, Jesus offered up prayers and supplications, with loud cries and tears, to him who was able to save him from death, and he was heard because of his reverence. Although he was a son, he learned obedience through what he suffered. And being made perfect, he became the source of eternal salvation to all who obey him, being designated by God a high priest."

Suffering is one of the primary ways that we learn obedience as Jesus did. Reflecting back on the late night alone in the Garden of Gethsemane where Jesus wrestled with the Father's will for His life reminds us that He prayed, wept, and cried in absolute anguish. As the cross approached, Jesus suffered and knew His suffering had just started. This shows it's not a sin to become emotional, struggle with God's will for your life, or feel genuine concern for the suffering you face. Jesus was sinless, and He struggled with suffering. You too will struggle and get emotional when you suffer, and like Jesus, you need to take time alone to wrestle with God in prayer until you and God agree on what is next for you.

Jesus obeyed by doing this. He was honest, emotional, and relational.

What is true for Christ is true for the Christian. When you suffer, the Spirit wants you to remember the sufferings of your Savior in two ways. First, the Holy Spirit who inspired the writing of Scripture wants you to study the suffering of Jesus as you are suffering. This allows you to appreciate His suffering for you and helps you to learn how to suffer in a meaningful and purposeful way as He did.

Second, the Holy Spirit, who was with Jesus in His suffering, wants you to invite Him into your suffering in very practical ways as you process your pain and make decisions about your future. Praying, worshipping, journaling, and seeking God's presence in other ways will help your soul to grow healthy even as your physical or emotional life suffers. The Holy Spirit brought this ministry into Jesus' suffering, and Jesus sent the Spirit to bring this same ministry to you.

What suffering do you face right now? For the Christian and non-Christian, suffering is many things—an injustice, pain, frustration, terror, horror, and discouragement. For the Christian, however, suffering is also a classroom. Your suffering experience is a unique learning opportunity for you to become perfected as Jesus was. Through suffering, you will learn to (1) perfectly hate sin and the suffering it causes, (2) perfectly love Jesus and the suffering He endured for you, and (3) grow into a perfect relationship with Jesus that will endure forever once all the suffering has ceased.

Dear Christian, you do not want to suffer, but you do want to become like Jesus, and there is no other path toward perfection. One way to make the most of your suffering is by learning about lamenting.

LEARNING TO LAMENT

I remember a stormy season of life that caused me to linger in portions of the Bible I knew but had driven by without pulling over to fully take in the landscape—laments. The majority of the songs in the Book of Psalms are laments—both public and private—where God's people pour out pain and grief. The Book of Lamentations invites us alongside Jeremiah, the weeping prophet. Many Old Testament prophetic writings include stretches of personal laments.

> You do not want to suffer, but you do want to become like Jesus, and there is no other path toward perfection.

During that season I realized I'm guilty of one of Western culture's most unhelpful habits: celebrating victories publicly and mourning defeats privately, resulting in very few of us knowing how to lament. We isolate ourselves when we hurt the most, which for many hastens a slide into depression. Modern men especially strike a pose as silent, steely-eyed types, whereas Bible guys, including fierce warriors like David, knew how to lament like men. Making matters worse is the pressure on social media to continually give the impression that all is well and we are winners, which forces us all to be liars to some degree.

Here are some benefits of God-centered, tear-soaked, Spirit-filled, Bible-based, gut-level lamenting amidst your suffering.

When you lament, you allow yourself to feel.

People in pain often self-medicate with anything from drugs and alcohol to sex, gambling, food, gossip, and rage, or they disconnect from loved ones to avoid feeling emotion. But numbing yourself to the hurt means you stop feeling everything else in life. You not only continue in pain, but you become isolated from those who love you. You become emotionally unavailable to God and fellow human beings. Lamenting helps you feel life's full range of normal emotions, so you can "walk through the valley of the shadow of death" into whatever future God has for you on the other side.

When you lament, you process pain.

Life hurts, and if you don't have a way to work out your hurts through lamenting, you're left hurt, bewildered, confused, angry, or depressed. Failing to process pain only prolongs your agony. Lamenting helps you work through your heartaches as you ponder what you're going through, so your pain propels you to growth. Lamenting engages your mind to learn from your pain so that, like Jesus, you can be refined through suffering. You have to feel so you can heal.

When you lament, you grieve your involvement and shed your victim mind-set.

When you hurt, the evils and errors of others so overwhelm you that it's easy to overlook your own evils and errors. By lamenting with the Lord, you readily see yourself from God's perspective. Lamenting allows you to evaluate what you have done, where you must change, and how you can act differently in the future.

When you lament, you don't lash out in vengeance at others.

If you're anything like me, you counterpunch by nature. But retaliating either physically, verbally, or via social media is just returning evil for evil and insult for insult. Lamenting helps you work out with God the energy and frustration that naturally comes from pain.

When you lament, you empathize with others who are hurting.

When Paul says we have a ministry comforting others with the comfort we receive, he is spot on. After you have lamented your pain with the Lord and experienced healing in your soul to the depth that you no longer rant and rave, you can invite people who have experienced similar pains to share those with you.

When you lament, you feel hope for the future.

Failing to lament leaves you forever circling the drain of the past, never escaping the toxicity that surrounds. When someone dies physically, there is both an autopsy and a funeral. Lamenting allows both. By lamenting, you figure out how something living came to die. You also mourn the death of what you treasured—a relationship, marriage, job, friendship, health. Lamenting allows you to look up from your tears to see what God might have on the horizon.

When you lament, you escape anger and depression.

Some people stuck in a spiral of grief are prone to depression, with weepiness and feelings of being spent, weakened, and defeated. Others feel anger, unleashing feelings of power instead of powerlessness. In my years of pastoral ministry I have seen countless women and men who are depressed, but I more often see men masking it with anger. Lamenting allows you to avoid depression—as well as depression masked by anger.

In the Bible lamenting didn't happen in private. It was an accepted part of an individual's public life. Middle Eastern culture set a pattern of mourning that marked a period for people to express grief openly. In the West public grief is rarely acceptable.

How did Jesus deal with His suffering? By Spirit-led lamenting. Isaiah 53:3 calls Him our "suffering servant" (NASB) a "man of sorrows," and "acquainted with grief." Emotional and tear-filled New Testament scenes let us see the Lord Jesus weep over Jerusalem, mourn the death of His dear friend Lazarus, and agonize on the cross. Jesus worked through His suffering by lamenting, and He helps us do the same.

Connecting the concept of lamenting with the ministry of the Holy Spirit, Romans 8:26–27 says, "Likewise the Spirit helps us in our weakness. For we do not know what to pray for as we ought, but the Spirit himself intercedes for us with groanings too deep for words. And he who searches hearts knows what is the mind of the Spirit, because the Spirit intercedes for the saints according to the will of God." There are times when words cannot express our grief. In those moments the Holy Spirit helps us to process our pain, transfer the burden that would crush us to the Lord who alone can carry it, and grieve what we cannot fix or change.

I will never forget one of the first hospital visits I made as a young pastor. A young man stood next to the bedside of his mother who had tried to kill herself. The only thing keeping her alive was a machine, and the son, a new Christian, was called in to say goodbye before they unplugged the machine so she could die. He could not change the circumstances, so he wept, prayed, and sang in the Spirit. In other words, he lamented the pain, which allowed him to heal through the process.

YOUR GREATEST MINISTRY
COMES FROM YOUR DEEPEST PAIN

It has been rightly said that the greatest ministry comes from the deepest pain. Jesus' greatest ministry came from His deepest pain. The same is true of you and me. Your greatest ministry comes from your deepest pain. Suffering not only sanctifies you to make you like Jesus, but it also sends you out into the suffering world to minister like Jesus. Your experiences, lessons learned, and empathy gained through suffering are the very things that make you a better minister. What suffering have you endured? How has it changed you, taught you, and improved you? How can you use your suffering to serve others who are suffering?

After roughly two decades of teaching, I took a break for healing and learning during the most difficult season of life for my family and me. As Grace and I met with godly ministry couples, professional counselors, and deeply spiritual leaders to process what we had been through, every meeting was markedly different and yet incredibly helpful. Each person asked very different questions, saw things from very different angles, and provided very different biblical insights and points of view.

In each meeting I took notes to help me remember what God was doing for us through these wonderful people. Within months I had filled numerous notebooks. After I had met with multiple people and considered things from various perspectives, I started putting it together. I realized they *all* offered biblical, godly, wise, helpful, and necessary counsel. Had we been ministered to from only one perspective, there would have been much we missed and a lot misdiagnosed.

During this time out of ministry set aside to learn and grow, I noticed various Christian leaders had a paradigm by which they saw my problems and through which they offered solutions. Each had obvious biblical moorings, and it seemed that various teams, tribes, and traditions had one predominant paradigm through which they ministered to Grace and me. We found it unbelievably beneficial that instead of sitting in the "helper" seat, we were sitting in the "helped" seat.

As Christian leaders and counselors from a range of backgrounds kindly ministered to us, the variety of what they taught us thoroughly blessed us. I believe this has ignited a new understanding on how to best help people, gleaning from all that the Holy Spirit says in the Bible without being limited to one tradition and its emphasis on one paradigm for helping people. Let me spell out the approaches I saw, and you'll quickly get my point as you see both the sources and solutions for suffering.

Sin and repentance

The problem is sin, which is made known through the law; the solution is repentance, which opens the door to the power of the gospel and grace.

Idolatry and worship

The problem is that we have put someone or something in God's place as the object of hope and joy to which our heart clings; the solution is to repent of our idolatry and worship God alone.

Condemnation and forgiveness

The problem is that we feel guilty for our sins, and by failing to avail ourselves of God's forgiveness we continue to beat ourselves up and live without hope; the solution is to accept God's forgiveness and live in the grace and freedom that comes from forgiving ourselves and others.

Oppression and deliverance

The problem is that Satan and demons oppress us; the solution is that we obtain deliverance from bondage and oppression by breaking strongholds in the supernatural realm and walking in the authority of Jesus.

Slavery and freedom

The problem is that our sinful desires enslave us to someone or something that rules us; the solution is to realize God has already set us free and to live in that freedom.

Lies and truth

The problem is that people believe lies and live accordingly; the solution is applying truth from God's Word to combat lies and live in obedience.

Brokenness and healing

The problem is that people are broken emotionally, spiritually, physically, and mentally; the solution is to invite the Holy Spirit into the brokenness and bring inner healing.

Defilement and cleansing

The problem is that sin stains us, so that we see ourselves as dirty, defiled, unclean, and damaged; the solution is to understand the doctrine of expiation—that God in Christ washes us white as snow and gives us a new identity.

Folly and wisdom

The problem is that foolish decisions ruin our lives; the solution is to get wise counsel and to make practical new choices.

Sickness and wellness

The problem is mainly physical (injury, ailment, chemical or hormonal imbalance, etc.); the solution is physical healing through the hand of a doctor or miracle from God our great physician.

Injustice and justice

The problem is broken human systems; the solution is remaking social and governance structures and bringing justice for all.

These categories could justify writing an entire book in explanation, but for our purposes, a summary must suffice. Furthermore, these categories are not mutually exclusive, and multiple kinds of suffering can be happening to someone simultaneously. As we received counsel from various teams and tribes of the church, we came to appreciate each approach and grieve the pride and cynicism that often divides these biblical insights into warring camps. To be truly helpful we need to be deeply Spirit-led. The Holy Spirit knows exactly how someone is suffering and what the solution is. His help is not limited to one perspective or the other; He is able to bring complete wholeness to our suffering souls and perfect us at the same time.

Christian counseling is incomplete and often uses one solution for every problem. As an example, one female friend attended a church where the counseling paradigm focused mainly on idolatry and worship. When she kept miscarrying, she spiraled into a deep depression mourning her inability to have a baby. Rather than pointing her toward healing from her brokenness, her counselor instead suggested that maybe having a baby was an idol from which she needed to repent. Just like math class, the right answer to one problem is not the right answer for every problem.

How does this way of looking at change hit you? Can you see where you have possibly locked into one mechanism for bringing about transformation in yourself, your family, or your church? How would a more encompassing perspective alter your walk with the Lord or the way you teach or counsel others?

> Every problem you face isn't a nail, and every solution doesn't require a hammer.

Every honest pastor and Christian leader reaches a point where they realize the same truths taught in the same way bring the same incomplete results. Who in your immediate world would bring a new biblical perspective to your struggles as a follower of Jesus? There's a good chance you stand on one side of various theological, methodological, and relational divides, and the help you need is right on the other side. Ask people who aren't in your tribe for practical wisdom drawn from real ministry. Invite them to tell you their case histories of real change. Let them enthusiastically draw out their biblical emphasis and challenge yours. Why? Because every problem you face isn't a nail, and every solution doesn't require a hammer.

When you suffer, it is essential to ask the Holy Spirit to reveal to you why you are suffering and how you can be growing. Your suffering is so expensive that you should not waste it on sin, folly, or rebellion. Instead, you would be better served to invest it by reflecting on Jesus' suffering for you so that you can become more like Him.

I admit that at times I have wished there were another way. I wish we could go online and shop for character, punch in our credit card information, and have it delivered to our house along with the rest of our Amazon order. But that is not how the Christian life works. When Jesus says to pick up our cross and follow Him, He is inviting us to *suffer with* our Savior so that we can *become like* our Savior. Often our healing from suffering begins by forgiving those who hurt us, which we will explore in the next chapter.

Chapter 11

FORGIVEN PEOPLE SHOULD FORGIVE PEOPLE

P AYING BILLS IS never fun. The routine of sitting down to go through the bills and pay debts can be downright depressing. Each month we are reminded of precisely how much debt we've accrued and how much we owe.

What is your current total debt?

Now imagine how hopeless it would be if every month God also sent a bill to you listing every spiritual debt you had accrued through sin in the previous month. Imagine that your spiritual debt had been mounting over the course of your entire life, and you had never paid for any of it. Picture what it would look like if, every month for the rest of your life, bill after bill arrived, showing your mounting debt in devastating detail. Can you imagine the massive score you'd have to settle when you stood before God for sentencing to the debtors' prison of hell?

We sin by commission when we do bad things that we are not supposed to do. We sin by omission when we do not do the good things we are supposed to do. We sin in our thoughts that only God sees. We sin in our words and deeds that God and others hear and see. We also sin in our motives that only God knows as sometimes we are so sinful that we do what appears to be good things with selfish, impure motives.

Jesus Forgives Our Debt

Now consider the collective debt that all of humanity owes to God.

You know what it is like to be you and all the drama, disappointment, and devastation you have had to endure. But have you ever sat down and thought about what it must be like to be God? We tend to only see things, including the story of the Bible, from our perspective. Consider, however, what life is like for God.

While the earth's combined population total remained at a whopping two people, Satan, the lead demon, recruited them for his glory-heist plan in robbery of God. They signed the pact, sealed the deal, and placed all of humanity in league with the dragon, unleashing hell on a planet that was supposed to be a heaven.

Shortly after our first parents sinned, God graciously pursued them and promised that Jesus was coming as the dragon slayer. Eventually Jesus arrived, and people sinned against Him continually. They stalked Him, lied about Him, harassed Him, publicly maligned Him, threatened Him, arrested Him, beat Him, flogged Him, and crucified Him.

Hanging on the cross with His mama weeping below, what would He say? Would He give His side of the story and vindicate His reputation? Would He spew forth truthful but harmful facts about the secret sins of His enemies? Would He curse God the Father for His horrible fate?

What would He do? Would He call forth the angelic army to destroy His enemies? Would He call down fire from heaven like Elijah? Would the one who spoke creation into existence speak curses upon His enemies and their descendants?

Jesus did nothing. He absorbed all the pain, all the shame, and all the wrath.

Straining to breathe while blood, sweat, and tears dripped off His dying body, Jesus opened His mouth. Luke 23:34 records the first of Jesus' seven declarations from the cross, "Father, forgive them, for they do not know what they are doing" (NIV). Rather than attacking His enemies, Jesus interceded for His enemies.

Forgive? Them? The ones who thought they were doing God's will by murdering God? The ones who did not even say they were sorry or see that they were sinful?

How did they respond? The Bible says they took a sponge with wine vinegar on it, put it on a stick, and shoved it in Jesus' mouth. I never really understood this until I visited ancient sites for early Christianity in Israel, Greece, and Turkey. There I discovered from an archaeology professor that Rome issued soldiers a sponge to use as toilet paper and cleanse themselves after going to the bathroom while out on patrol or the field of battle. They would affix it to a stick to scrub their feces and then dip it in wine vinegar as an antiseptic to prevent infection. Perhaps it was precisely this kind of sponge that was shoved into Jesus' mouth to keep Him from speaking any more about forgiveness from the cross.

Possibly with the taste of a soldier's most recent bowel movement on His lips, Jesus then had a few more things to say before dying so that we could be forgiven in answer to His prayer. For three hours darkness covered the sun, just as the darkness of human sin covered the Son. In a loud voice of triumph Jesus then declared, "It is finished" (John 19:30).

Forgiven.

If you belong to Jesus or give your sin and self to Him right now, you are forgiven by God. You're forgiven for everything you have ever done or failed to do—past, present, and future.

Jesus died so that you and I could be forgiven. To ensure He was dead, they took a spear and ran it through Jesus' side. It punctured His heart. We broke God's heart. You broke God's heart, and from it poured forth water like the days of Noah as the judgment that came upon sinners now came upon their Savior.

Christians call this good news and celebrate it every year on Good Friday. Have you ever wondered how the worst treatment of the greatest person could be good news? It's good news that Jesus died in our place for our sins as our substitute. Romans 5:8 says, "But God demonstrates his own love for us in this: While we were still sinners, Christ died for us" (NIV).

Jesus died for you. Jesus died for your forgiveness. In giving His life, Jesus was forgiving your sin and giving you the ability to forgive others. Ephesians 4:30–32 is a remarkable section of Scripture. The big idea is that "God in Christ forgave you." Because God forgives you, you can follow God's example by "forgiving one another."

How is this possible? How did Jesus forgive you? How can you forgive others? Forgiveness is made possible solely by the "Holy Spirit of God." The Holy Spirit empowered Jesus to die in your place for the forgiveness of your sins. The Holy Spirit then brings you the forgiveness purchased by Jesus and enables you to forgive others as He did Jesus.

Subsequently, when we refuse to forgive someone, we "grieve the Holy Spirit of God." When we are unforgiving, the Spirit is grieving. He always stands ready to empower us to experience the forgiveness bought by Jesus and share that forgiveness with others. To reject His help is to break His heart. Had Jesus grieved the Holy Spirit rather than surrendered to the Holy Spirit no one would be forgiven.

WHAT FORGIVING IS—AND IS NOT

Simply stated, forgiveness is the canceling of a debt.

We accrue debt by (1) taking what is not ours or (2) not repaying what we owe to someone else. Forgiveness is what happens when we owe but are not required to pay because someone else has chosen to pay for us. In this way forgiveness is a gift of grace—the receiving of something we have not merited or earned in any way.

Jesus had this in mind when He taught us how to pray in Matthew 6:9–13 (emphasis added):

> Pray then like this: "Our Father in heaven, hallowed be your name. Your kingdom come, your will be done, on earth as it is in heaven. Give us this day our daily bread, *and forgive*

us our debts, as we also have forgiven our debtors. And lead
us not into temptation, but deliver us from evil.

The debt we must ask God to forgive is the debt of sin. Teaching
the same thing in Luke 11:4, Jesus uses the word *sin* interchange-
ably for *debt*, saying, "Forgive us our sins, as we forgive those who
sin against us" (NLT). Writers of the Bible linked the concepts of
sin and debt so closely that older translations of the Bible, such as
the King James Version, speak of "remission of sins," whereas more
recent Bible translations using the same original Greek texts say
"forgiveness of sins."

Colossians 2:13–14 says that God has "forgiven us all our trespasses, by canceling the record of debt that stood against us with its
legal demands. This he set aside, nailing it to the cross." We owed
a debt to God, but Jesus canceled it through His payment on the
cross. This concept forms the bedrock of Christianity—God forgives the sinner's debt through Jesus Christ's payment on the cross.

The payment for sin is death. God told this to our first parents,
Adam and Eve, before the original sin, warning with fatherly affection in Genesis 2:17, "You shall surely die." Paul is emphatically
clear that the debt for sin is death, saying in Romans 6:23, "the
wages of sin is death." We must pay this debt in one of two ways—
plan A or plan B.

In plan A sinners who do not turn to Jesus Christ to receive
forgiveness pays in this life by living apart from God and storing
up wrath against themselves. Then they die to experience the conscious eternal torments of hell with no opportunity for forgiveness
on the other side of the grave.

In plan B sinners who do turn to Jesus Christ to receive forgiveness have their debt to God canceled by virtue of the payment of
Jesus in their place on the cross. This payment is often referred to
in the Bible as a ransom. Jesus explained this, saying in Mark 10:45
that He "came not to be served but to serve, and to give his life as
a ransom for many."

Now imagine that one month you opened your bill from God to find the following message: "Your total spiritual debt, past and future, is paid in full and thereby canceled by Jesus Christ!" This massive pardon happened the day you became a Christian and Jesus' payment on the cross was credited to your account. This gracious gift is burden lifting, life changing, heart restoring, and life giving. The right response is found in Romans 4:7–8, which says, "Oh, what joy for those whose disobedience is forgiven, whose sins are put out of sight. Yes, what joy for those whose record the LORD has cleared of sin" (NLT). If you enjoy this debt repayment, the question is now whether or not you will do the same for others.

WHO OWES YOU?

- Who is in debt to you?

- What did they take?

- What do they owe you?

Is it a father who walked out when you were little and owes you a lifetime of memories from summer vacations to school visits? Is it a bully who stomped on your dignity and owes you an apology? Is it a business partner who swindled your income and owes you financially? Is it a pervert who stole your purity? Is it a boyfriend or girlfriend who broke your heart and owes you a happily-ever-after fairy tale ending? Is it a spouse who betrayed your trust through adultery and owes you fidelity?

In the same way that most people have multiple accounts at the bank, we have various accounts in our lives, such as emotional, spiritual, financial, relational, and mental. To use Jesus' teaching, when someone sins, they make a withdrawal from one of these accounts. Some people make substantial withdrawals and others take pocket change. Some people make withdrawals from one account and others from numerous accounts. In a relationship there are deposits and withdrawals, and some people bankrupt the relationship by taking more than they give.

Who has made the most substantial withdrawals from your accounts?

I am not talking about occasional little withdrawals. In an imperfect world filled with imperfect people, everyone makes minute withdrawals all the time. We say things we should not, we get busy with our own lives and miss the needs of those around us, we get worn out and aren't as considerate as we should be—you know how this works. None of us likes that family member, friend, or coworker who acts like a moody moral auditor, following us around and keeping a list of every little thing we do wrong. Colossians 3:13 says, "Make allowance for each other's faults" (NLT).

This chapter is not talking about the little things you need to get over, move past, overlook, and stop nitpicking about. I am talking about the big things, those things that you wish you could get over but just cannot because the withdrawal was so great that forgiving the debt seems just plain wrong. It might be one significant withdrawal or a small withdrawal over and over. I am talking about something being done that was just plain unnecessary—it did not need to happen. We cheapen forgiveness when we use it too often, applying to every and any annoyance or inconvenience. Like stitches on an open laceration that will get infected if not closed up, we should reserve forgiveness for the real wounds—those that cut us deep because they were so personal and painful, causing so much hurt that we cannot move on without healing up.

Knowing that this concept is so otherworldly that many would miss it, ignore it, or twist it, Paul picks up where his Lord left off. Colossians 3:13 says, "Forgive anyone who offends you. Remember, the Lord forgave you, so you must forgive others" (NLT). Ephesians 4:32 says, "Be kind to each other, tenderhearted, forgiving one another, just as God through Christ has forgiven you" (NLT).

Forgiven people are supposed to be forgiving people. That's the big biblical breakthrough. It's hypocrisy to be forgiven and not be forgiving.

- Are you forgiven?
- Are you forgiving?
- Is there anyone who you have not completely forgiven?

Whose face or name comes to mind? If there were one person you could send to hell right now who would it be? If anyone came to mind, you have not forgiven them.

UNDERSTANDING FORGIVENESS

Here are some important things to understand about forgiveness.

Forgiveness is often a private matter between you and God.
Often the other person does not even need to know about it. If you have nursed a grudge against someone for a long time and pretended you have forgiven them when in fact you have not, or if the person is unsafe and you do not want to invite them back into your life, then they don't even need to know about your forgiveness. Sometimes the person you need to forgive is dead, in which case there's no earthly way for them to know about your forgiveness.

Forgiveness is both a one-time event and an ongoing process.
We forgive someone in a moment, but full forgiveness sometimes requires time to process the pain. Furthermore, sometimes we learn more details that bring up the issue again, or the person we forgave commits the offense yet again. In Matthew 18:21–22 Peter asks Jesus how many times we should forgive someone. People apparently debated this in that day, with the most liberally loving people saying that seven times was the maximum anyone could be expected to forgive someone else. Jesus said the limit was seventy times seven—or in other words, limitless.

Forgiveness is the opposite of vengeance.

Romans 12:19 says, "Beloved, do not avenge yourselves, but rather give place to wrath; for it is written, 'Vengeance is Mine, I will repay,' says the Lord" (NKJV). To seek vengeance is to climb down to the level of your offender—and further from God—to punish them by making them pay in some way. To forgive is to rise, moving away from your offender and closer to God and letting God handle them.

The lie of vengeance is that it rights a wrong. The past cannot be undone, and all vengeance does is escalate so that we inflict and endure more and more damage. For this reason, an ancient Chinese proverb says, "He who seeks revenge should dig two graves." Forgiveness is the opposite of denial, bitterness, vengeance, nursing a grudge, and continuing to see yourself as a wounded and hurt victim with no future hope because of past pain.

Forgiveness does not require an apology.

Sometimes a wrongdoer couldn't care less. Sometimes two people never agree. Sometimes one person is just plain evil. Sometimes it will be years and years before a person comes around to repent of their wrongdoing. Forgiving someone before they apologize allows you to heal up and move forward in your life rather than staying bound in the painful prison that holding on to your hurt creates.

> Forgiveness is free, but trust is earned. Forgiveness is for all people; trust is for safe people.

Forgiveness is not enabling foolishness, irresponsibility, or sin.

You can forgive someone and at the same time stop giving them money, being their designated driver, and shoveling up the mess around the circus that is their life.

Forgiveness is not trust or reconciliation.

Forgiveness is free, but trust is earned. Forgiveness is for all people; trust is for safe people. Just because you forgive someone does not mean that you have to trust them or have a close relationship with them now or in the future. You can if you want to, but you do not have to. Furthermore, if a crime is being committed, you can forgive and call the police to help avoid injury to others. This differs from vengeance because the heart motive is not to harm your offender but to prevent them from harming others.

Your forgiveness is not God's forgiveness.

When you forgive, you choose not to sit in the judgment seat and convene court over someone's life. Instead, you send the case to God's court and let Him deal with everyone and everything impartially and justly, and you accept whatever outcome God chooses for you both. You can forgive someone whether God sends them to heaven or hell.

> When you forgive someone, you are not allowing them to get away with anything, but you are allowing yourself to get away from everything.

Forgiveness is not covering a crime.

A lie creeps into your mind that if you forgive someone, you are participating in injustice by letting that person get away with something. You need to remind yourself of this truth continually—when you forgive someone, you are not allowing them to get away with anything but you are allowing yourself to get away from everything. When you forgive, you leave the field of battle where all the bleeding is happening. You stop focusing on winning and begin to focus on living. Forgiving is how you start healing.

EIGHT KINDS OF UNFORGIVING PEOPLE

After a few decades as a senior pastor, I would have to say the number one issue people struggle with is unforgiveness. Are you an unforgiving person? Do you care about someone stuck in the pit of unforgiveness? There are eight kinds of unforgiving people I have met over the years. (These are composites of people I've encountered in ministry, not descriptions of specific individuals.)

1. The archaeologist

This person always digs up the past. She will dig up anything you have recently done and throw it like a rock onto the big pile of rocks she's been digging up and gathering into a small mountain. She is like a wife who fights with her husband for an entire one-week cruise that is supposed to celebrate their fiftieth wedding anniversary, and when you ask what the problem is, she starts talking about all the things the husband did wrong on their honeymoon night and proceeds to list every single wrong thing he has said or done over the course of fifty years—in chronological order!

2. The stalker

This person is so bitter and obsessed that he fixates on his offenders. He keeps tabs on his offenders through mutual friends, drives by their houses, swings by their places of employment, digs up their public records, and follows them on social media, peering into their lives. When they suffer, he feels happy. When he sees a picture of them happy, he suffers.

3. The tragic tale teller

This person has told her story of pain so many times that she can recite it by heart to anyone at any time. The story of her life is mainly about the pain of her past and how it has robbed her of faith for her future. The tragic tale teller can be a bit of an emotional exhibitionist. She quickly opens up the most shocking and private parts of her life to people she hardly knows. This guarantees the hearer of her sad story never corrects her for unhealthy behavior because they don't want to be the next chapter in her never-ending saga. Over time her tragic tale grows larger and larger. She embellishes things that happened and adds things that did not happen. She starts to freely assign motive to the other person or persons involved and fills in the gaps of the story with her own speculation.

The better use of her energy would be to involve God in the story of her life and discover the way in which He uses something terrible to give her a transformation tale.

4. The negative anniversary funeral planner

This person has un-holidays instead of holidays. He notes the worst days in his life and plans the equivalent of a heart funeral every year. He is like a man who keeps these dates on his digital calendar and every time something bad happens he adds another date. He has the date that his girlfriend dumped him, the date his dad died, the date his boss fired him, the date he found out his wife committed adultery, and other such dates marked on his calendar. As these dates approach, he tells people in his life how awful the day is going to be and goes into a depression leading up to the negative anniversary. Why? He has not healed up from anything and just builds his life around his bitterness. When he's told by counselors that he needs to erase the negative anniversaries from his calendar, forgive, heal, and make new memories, he stops meeting with them. Sadly, he probably marks the date of that final meeting in his negative anniversary funeral planner!

5. The emotional leaker

This person is so hurt that she carries her pain right at the surface all the time. When a cup is bumped, whatever is inside spills out. It is the same with people. Whatever is in us spills out when we are bumped. The emotional leaker seems rather fine until something happens and then all the pain of the past comes spilling out. She can get very emotional very quickly because she is unhealthy.

6. The wounded digital warrior

This person lives online to patrol and troll those they are bitter against, leaving negative comments, inciting digital flame throwing, finding causes to go to war for, and creating unholy online alliances with other digital arsonists who like starting fires. Technology allows a bit of a swarming effect. One bee sting cannot really hurt a person, but a few hundred is a problem. The wounded digital warrior knows this, and he seeks to gather a swarm that will join him in flying from site to site and platform to platform, stinging and killing. Because they were hurt, they hurt. Because they were harmed, they harm. Because they are tormented, they torment.

7. The nasty nicknamer

This person no longer sees the person he is bitter against as a human being worthy of any dignity. We tend to nickname the people we love the most—and the people we hate the most. When the nasty nicknamer decides to no longer regard someone with the dignity they deserve by virtue of being a fellow image-bearer of God, he turns them into a caricatured character. He embellishes their faults and overlooks anything possibly good or redeemable about them. He sees them as unsalvageable, freezes them in his version of their worst moments in time, and forever brands them with a shameful label.

8. The bitter believer

This person blames her pain on God. If a person has a faulty view of God's sovereignty and wrongly believes everything that happens is exactly what God wants, this is somewhat easy. One sexually assaulted woman was bitter against God for many years. When I asked her why, she said, "Because God had me raped!" I just started crying. I am the daddy to two delightful daughters. I know that the Father heart of God does not make plots and plans to have His daughters defiled. God is good, not evil. God does not sin, people do.

In the Book of Ruth we meet Naomi whose name means sweet or pleasant. Her unwise husband moved their family to an ungodly nation, her sons married ungodly women, and then all the men in the family died. She says in Ruth 1:20, "Do not call me Naomi; call me Mara, for the Almighty has dealt very bitterly with me." She basically blames God for making her bitter and asks that people accept her name change to Mara, which means bitter.

The bitter believer has wrongly taken on her bitterness as her identity and sees God as the sinner who needs to repent to her. Thankfully Naomi returned to God's people and presence where eventually a son-in-law named Boaz redeemed her and God blessed her and healed her hurts. The final scenes of her life include her holding her grandson, from whom descended Jesus Christ.

THE SPIRIT OF FORGIVENESS

Because sin is so pernicious and pervasive, we cannot merely change what we do. Instead, we need God to change who we are. New Testament writers conveyed this by using words such as *new creation*, *new man*, and *born again* to explain the profound change that occurs when someone becomes a Christian. As God the Holy Spirit enters a person and begins to transform them to be increasingly more like Jesus from the inside out, God's glory shines forth more and more. They experience an ongoing, profound, lifelong change in their thoughts, feelings, choices, actions, speech, and deepest longings.

As a new person with a new identity based on a new nature, you also have a new power. No longer are you left to rely solely on your own abilities, you now have God the Holy Spirit indwelling and empowering you.

> Because sin is so pernicious and pervasive, we cannot merely change what we do. Instead, we need God to change who we are.

My family and I live in the desert. When we hike the mountains, the surrounding hills are at first dry, barren, and without trees or greenery. But everything is different—alive, vibrant, growing, and flourishing—near the flowing desert rivers. In the winter the source of the river's water is far away, high up in the mountains where snow collects all winter long. As the snow melts in the spring, the water flows down, bringing life with it.

Forgiveness is like that river. Forgiveness does not start with us but instead starts high up in the heart of God. Our heavenly Father, who forgives us from His heart, places His Spirit in our hearts so that His forgiveness does not merely flow down *to* us but also *through* us, bringing life to others in the streams of our lives.

Paul explains this when he says in Ephesians 4:23–24, "Let the Spirit renew your thoughts and attitudes. Put on your new nature, created to be like God—truly righteous and holy" (NLT). As a new person with a new nature seen by God as holy, you can have new thoughts about people and attitudes toward them—if you flow with the Spirit rather than fighting against the Spirit. He goes on to say, "And do not bring sorrow to God's Holy Spirit by the way you live.... Get rid of all bitterness, rage, anger, harsh words, and slander, as well as all types of evil behavior. Instead, be kind to each other, tenderhearted, forgiving one another, just as God through Christ has forgiven you" (vv. 30–32, NLT).

According to God, forgiveness flows from Him to us by the Spirit. It's an anointing that is not meant for any one of us to enjoy alone but to share with others. God the Spirit is grieved when forgiveness flows from God to us, and rather than allowing it to flow freely to others we dam the flow of God's gracious anointing through bitter unforgiveness. By being a forgiven person who chooses to flow with the Spirit of God and live a lifestyle of forgiving others, we open ourselves to experience the fullness of what God can accomplish both in us and through us. Jesus spoke of this in John 7:38–39, "Anyone who believes in me may come and drink! For the Scriptures declare, 'Rivers of living water will flow from his heart.' (When he said 'living water,' he was speaking of the Spirit)" (NLT).

As you read this, you may be struggling to forgive a particularly horrific situation. As a senior pastor for more than twenty years, often dealing with brutal cases such as sexual abuse, let me say that I am very sorry and that God's healing power is very real.

God's grace needs to flow more powerfully to wash the evil down the stream of forgiveness and away from the victim of true evil. For this reason, the greater the offense, the greater the measure of the Spirit's anointing God gives. The Bible explains that where sin increases, grace abounds all the more (Rom. 5:20). Therefore, the evil and vile actions of others that would otherwise destroy you actually unleash more of the Holy Spirit's anointing power in your life if you flow with God in the stream of forgiveness. In that way He washes your soul clean and showers away the evil and filth put upon you. In the next chapter we will examine seven reasons to forgive.

Chapter 12

SEVEN REASONS TO FORGIVE

I PAID FOR THIS chapter in tears.

In the most difficult season of our lives I was in a brutal and broken place feeling as if I'd been shot in the soul. Even though I'm a pastor, it was Sunday and I had forgotten what day it was. I walked into the living room in my pajamas. There, our five godly kids were waiting for their pastor dad because they were determined to meet as a little church in our house. So in our pajamas, we gathered in the living room to have church as a family.

Thankfully our kids are like their mama. Grace is a resilient pastor's daughter who never misses church. If the end of the world comes on a Sunday, you will find my best friend at church taking notes, singing songs, offering prayers, and loving people. She's way cuter and tougher than any man I know. Her babies were going to have church like their mama.

That day it felt like a funeral, with everyone fighting back tears. Grace sat across from me, and I tried not to make eye contact with her because I feared I would lose it. My little flock of adorable faces looked at me, waiting for me to open my mouth, teach the Bible, and say something helpful.

I held my Bible, bowed my head to pray, and tried to gain my composure. I then lifted my head to see the devastated faces of my family, and I completely lost it. I couldn't hold back the tears. Neither could they. With a quivering voice and bowed head, I invited the Holy Spirit to give me words to love and lead my family.

I sensed this was a fork-in-the-road moment, and whatever I said would put us on a path toward life or death. I did not want to portray any anger toward God since it would breed a spirit of rebellion in our kids. I didn't want to raise kids who grew up to hate the church or question God's goodness. I didn't want to leak or vent my hurt onto our children and provoke bitterness against others. I didn't want to ignore their pain and confusion by brushing it aside. I did not want them to carry a grudge. I didn't want any of our children to become resentful of me and cause a dangerous breach. And I didn't want to pretend in our toughest season that I was the sinless Jesus and everyone else was the devil. So I imparted what the Holy Spirit brought to my mind in that moment. As we wept together, I taught my little flock about forgiveness.

Hebrews says that just one root of bitterness in one human heart is enough to take down a whole orchard, and I wanted to make sure that with the shovel of forgiveness we dug that root up from our little family orchard. The rest of this chapter is a summary and expansion of what I shared off the cuff and from my heart with my family on forgiveness. I shared it with them because I love them. I am sharing it with you because I love you. I am happy to report that it helped them, and I am praying that it will help you too.

1. Forgiveness glorifies God.

You can tell a lot about someone by how they introduce themselves. How do you introduce yourself? What's the first thing you want someone to know when they first meet you?

Did you know that God repeats a brief script over and over to introduce Himself? God gives us His introduction in the following verses, and these descriptions of God are quoted throughout the Good Book more times than any other.

> The LORD passed in front of Moses, calling out, "Yahweh!
> The LORD! The God of compassion and mercy! I am slow
> to anger and filled with unfailing love and faithfulness. I

lavish unfailing love to a thousand generations. I forgive
iniquity, rebellion, and sin. But I do not excuse the guilty."
—Exodus 34:6–7, NLT

The God of the Bible wants to be known for His compassionate
mercy, patient forbearance, and loving faithfulness that compels
Him to forgive guilty, rebellious sinners. These words begin His
introduction to the beleaguered, battered, and broken needing
the hope, help, and healing of forgiveness. However, just as not
everyone we extend a hand of friendship to will respond in kind,
God reminds us that He too has people who reject Him and His
forgiveness. They receive only justice.

In various pantheistic and panentheistic religions as well as
Buddhism, there is no personal God to offer a relationship or
forgiveness. In Eastern religions, such as Hinduism, there is no forgiveness of sin by a loving God, but rather cycles of reincarnation
when we pay off our debt of karma. According to Old Testament
Judaism there is no forgiveness of sin apart from sacrifices made
on behalf of the sinner at the temple offered by the priest—things
that have not existed since the destruction of the temple and sacri
ficial system in AD 70. In Islam forgiveness is merited by the sinner
rather than offered in pure grace because there is no concept of a
loving Father God or atoning Son.

Forgiveness is crucial, essential, and irreplaceable to the entirety
of the Christian faith. Unless we are forgiven by God through Jesus
Christ, we have no joyful relationship with God in this life or the
eternal life to come. Unless we are forgiven by others and forgive
those with whom we journey in this life, we have no joyful relationships with others. It is not a stretch to say that without forgiveness Christianity does not, cannot, and will not exist. For this
reason, the ancient Apostles' Creed teaches us to confess, "I believe
in…the forgiveness of sins."[1]

Why in the world should you forgive someone who owes you?

What possible reason could there be for such an undeserved, unusual, and unexpected response?

The glory of God.

The glory of God is a mega-theme of Scripture. The apostle Paul pretty much sums it up by saying, "Whatever you do, do it all for the glory of God" (1 Cor. 10:31, NLT).

Those familiar with confessional reformed theology know that the first question and answer of the Westminster Shorter Catechism is, "What is the chief end of man? Man's chief end is to glorify God, and to enjoy him forever."[2]

Surely this has to have some very earthy practical implications and complications. It begs the question, what does it mean to glorify God?

Making us male and female, God bestowed on us the highest dignity of any created thing—making us in His image and likeness. Very simply we were made to mirror. In our homes, purses, and cars we have mirrors. The purpose of a mirror is to image, or reflect, your likeness. The next time you look into a mirror, remember that you too are supposed to be a mirror reflecting the goodness, greatness, and glory of God to Himself and others.

Jesus alone is the perfect mirror who faultlessly reflected the glory of God the Father in all He said and did while on the earth. Anything and everything that we can know about God the Father we learn by looking at God the Son. Jesus says in John 14:9, "Anyone who has seen me has seen the Father!" (NLT). Colossians 1:15 says, "Christ is the visible image of the invisible God" (NLT). Hebrews 1:3 says, "The Son radiates God's own glory and expresses the very character of God" (NLT).

When we see Jesus forgiving people, He is reflecting the forgiving Father heart of God. When Jesus tells the guilty thief that his debt will soon be forgiven, saying in Luke 23:43, "I assure you, today you will be with me in paradise" (NLT), God is glorified because His forgiving heart is reflected in Jesus Christ for others to see. We do the same when we pick up our cross to follow Him and forgive others.

For the Christian, forgiveness has far more to do with you and God than it does with you and the person you are forgiving. Though painful and awful, when you are wounded and offended, you are also being given an opportunity to give God great glory through forgiving. This is what Jesus meant when He said that by loving your enemies and being kind and merciful to those who owe you without making them pay through vengeance you are acting like "sons of the Most High" (Luke 6:35). If you've ever heard the adage "like father, like son," you know it means as you get to know a son and his father, you can start to see the family resemblance. In the same way, as a Christian you are to resemble or glorify your Father by forgiving others as He has forgiven you. This is also what Paul means when he writes in the context of forgiveness, "Imitate God, therefore, in everything you do, because you are his dear children" (Eph. 5:1, NLT).

2. Forgiveness blesses you.

God is so good and gracious that when we forgive we not only glorify Him, but we also bless ourselves. The Bible repeatedly tells us not to be *self-consumed to the point that we ignore God's will and the welfare of others*; however, it does tell us to be *self-concerned*. For this reason, Jesus says in Matthew 22:39, "Love your neighbor as yourself." Paul also tells us in Philippians 2:4, "Don't look out only for your own interests, but take an interest in others, too" (NLT). God wants us to take care of both ourselves and others.

Dr. Fred Luskin, director and cofounder of the Stanford University Forgiveness Project, says that forgiveness has become his life's work. It's no wonder when you consider that he heads up the largest interpersonal forgiveness training research project ever conducted.[3] To help us uncover any unforgiveness in our lives, Dr. Luskin asks four questions about our painful situation and gives an assessment:

- Do you think about this painful situation more than you think about the things in your life that are good?

- When you think about this painful situation, do you become either physically uncomfortable or emotionally upset?

- When you think about this situation, do you do so with the same old repetitive thoughts?

- Do you find yourself telling the story about what happened over and over in your mind?

If you answer yes to any of these four questions, you have likely formed a grievance that is renting too much space in your mind. If you answer yes to any of these four questions, you most likely have a grievance that can be healed.[4]

Although it isn't faith-based and has no explicit reference to being forgiven by God through Jesus Christ or empowered to forgive by the Holy Spirit, Luskin's encouraging research concludes with this summary:

Fascinating research has emerged...that documents the healing power of forgiveness. In careful scientific studies, forgiveness training has been shown to reduce depression, increase hopefulness, decrease anger, improve spiritual connection, increase emotional self-confidence, and help heal relationships. Learning to forgive is good for both your mental and physical well-being and your relationships. Studies reveal:

- People who are more forgiving report fewer health problems.

- Forgiveness leads to less stress.

- Forgiveness leads to fewer physical symptoms of stress.

- Failure to forgive may be more significant than hostility as a risk factor for heart disease.

- People who blame other people for their troubles have higher incidences of illnesses such as cardio-vascular disease and cancers.

- People who imagine not forgiving someone show negative changes in blood pressure, muscle tension, and immune response.

- People who imagine forgiving their offender note immediate improvement in their cardiovascular, muscular, and nervous systems.

- Even people with devastating losses can learn to forgive and feel better psychologically and emotionally.[5]

Unforgiveness is the path to unwellness. God wants you healthy and moving forward, not sick and sliding backward. Paul, who was a murderer of a Christian leader before becoming a persecuted Christian leader, had a lot to be forgiven for as well as a list of enemies he needed to forgive. He says in Philippians 3:13, "I focus on this one thing: Forgetting the past and looking forward to what lies ahead" (NLT).

> There is a terrible myth that time heals all wounds. Time heals nothing. Time can actually make wounds worse.

There is a terrible myth that time heals all wounds. Time heals nothing. Time can actually make wounds worse. A gunshot to the body or soul will not just get better the longer you let it bleed and get infected. Only time with God the great physician heals all soul wounds. Time with God helps you do as Paul did—bury the past with Jesus and rise to march forward into a hopeful and joyful new life with Jesus.

Why would you give your best energy and your best years to the worst people and worst experiences? God wants you to bury the past with Jesus and get on with your new life in Christ.

- Emotionally, forgiveness lifts a burden from you and allows you to manage your feelings, find wholeness, and start to enjoy a healthy relationship with God and others.

- Mentally, forgiveness allows you to stop obsessing over unresolved issues and frees up your mind to start thinking about goodness and God rather than pain from the past.

- Practically, forgiveness allows you to stop trying to control everyone and put everything in order and allow others to make their own decisions and deal with the consequences.

- Relationally, forgiveness allows you to enter into new relationships with new insights to experience new intimacy with healthy, godly, safe people.

- Spiritually, forgiveness allows God to be the center of your life and not your hurt so that His life can flow into your life, bringing His health into your soul.

One bitter person I'll call Sheila, who had been brutally treated by those closest to her throughout her life, said that she felt as if her soul had a migraine. She magnified every minor conflict, disappointment, and hurt, making them incredibly painful. After she worked through a forgiveness process with the Lord, being forgiven by God for her sins and forgiving those who sinned against her, she said she felt as if her "soul migraine" was healed forever. God wants the same for you.

Who has caused you hurt and bitterness? Most likely it's the people you care about the most. Often bitter people are not even bitter against the people who have committed the worst offenses. A total stranger or distant acquaintance can do something major, but it barely affects you. But someone you care about very deeply can do a comparatively minor thing, and you feel wrecked to the core. You continue to obsess over it, grieve, and replay it in your mind many years later. I learned this lesson the hard way as a pastor.

An emotional young man once told me I had hurt him some years prior. Honestly I did not remember the event he referred to. I looked him in the eye and said, "I am very sorry. I can see that my sin against you was very painful. I am sorry that you have carried this for so long. I also ask your forgiveness and would like to pray together so that we can get this burden off of you."

We prayed together. Before he left my office, he said in passing something I will never forget: "What you said was not a big deal to me, but you are a big deal to me."

I had failed him, and he was kind enough to teach me a vital lesson. It is not the size of an offense as much as your affection for the offender that determines the degree of disappointment.

3. Forgiveness blesses others.

If you are unforgiving, you may not like that word much. Instead, you may use words such as *bitter, hurt, broken, wounded, damaged, disappointed,* or something else that says the same thing in a way that presents you as a victim with good reason for how you are feeling. I want to be tender in approaching a painful place in your soul but also ask you to honestly consider if, perhaps, you have become selfish because of your suffering. Sometimes when you are hurting you become so aware of your own problems and pain that you neglect the trials and troubles of others. Furthermore, you can overlook how you are actually hurting the people who love you and live in relationship with you by dragging them into your drama.

When we are hurting and need healing, we should invite safe

counsel from trusted friends or leaders full of godly wisdom to help us get unstuck. But often we leak and vent randomly in conversations with people who need not be involved. Even worse, we share with people who are also bitter, and together we form an unholy alliance that enables us both to remain bitter and respond unhealthily. Just as we need skilled surgeons and patient physical therapists to help our bodies heal from serious injuries, we can also get injured in our souls and need the same kind of soul care.

Bitterness can grow unseen in your heart for a long time, much like roots underground. Hebrews 12:15–16 warns, "See to it that no one fails to obtain the grace of God; that no 'root of bitterness' springs up and causes trouble, and by it many become defiled; that no one is sexually immoral or unholy." Eventually roots burst through the surface, grow into a mature plant, and begin to scatter and spread so that the plant multiplies over and over. When the root is bitterness, it chokes out the flow of grace in your relationships—starting with God—until it bursts forth in gossip and social media ranting. When this happens, you have become a sick person who is making other people sick.

The result is factious, us-against-them behavior, which leads to divided families, ministries, and communities. Eventually things get worse and worse until people see themselves as victims who have earned the right to do what they want. They behave in ways that are unholy, even throwing off restraint and becoming sexually immoral.

God hands each of us a shovel of forgiveness to dig up the root of bitterness. You need to accept God's forgiveness of your sin—including your unforgiving bitterness—and then forgive those who have sinned against you. Otherwise the bitter root will choke out all the healthy relationships in your life.

4. Forgiveness defeats the demonic.

Satan and demons are never forgiven for anything, and they in turn never forgive anyone else for anything. Forgiveness is divine.

Unforgiveness is demonic. To refuse to forgive is to open oneself to the realm of demonic activity. One bitter believer empowered by the demonic realm can unleash hell in the church. They become emboldened, powerful, and unrelenting because they are accessing a supernatural power.

The Holy Spirit revealed this fact to me during a lengthy Bible study I conducted on forgiveness and unforgiveness. Over and over the same sections of Scripture that taught this theme also mentioned Satan and demons. This tremendous insight helped me, and I pray it helps you too. Here are some examples.

- Through Jesus' cross, God has "forgiven us all our trespasses" and "disarmed the rulers and authorities" (Col. 2:13–15).

- "Anyone whom you forgive, I also forgive. Indeed, what I have forgiven, if I have forgiven anything, has been for your sake in the presence of Christ, so that wo would not be outwitted by Satan" (2 Cor. 2:10–11).

- "Give no opportunity to the devil.…Let all bitterness and wrath and anger and clamor and slander be put away from you, along with all malice. Be kind to one another, tenderhearted, forgiving one another, as God in Christ forgave you" (Eph. 4:27, 31–32).

- "If you have bitter jealousy and selfish ambition in your hearts, do not boast and be false to the truth. This is not the wisdom that comes down from above, but is earthly, unspiritual, demonic" (James 3:14–15).

Those who are forgiven by God but refuse to be forgiving of others end up in a prison of demonic torment. There, they live in the haunting anguish of the most painful days of their lives, reliving the horror over and over. In Matthew 18:21–35 Jesus tells a parable where one guy owes a lot of money—let's say it is a million dollars. Unable to pay, he goes to his lender and begs that he not be sold as a slave along with his wife and children to repay the debt. Graciously the lender forgives the man's entire debt by paying it himself. This is a picture of the gospel of forgiveness. The forgiven man then heads home to tell the good news to his family.

The scene then shifts and the forgiven man encounters another man who owes him a bit of money—let's say a thousand dollars. Rather than forgiving the man of his minor debt in the same way he had been forgiven of his million-dollar debt, we read beginning in verse 28, "And seizing him, he began to choke him, saying, 'Pay what you owe.' So his fellow servant fell down and pleaded with him, 'Have patience with me, and I will pay you.' He refused and went and put him in prison until he should pay the debt."

The witnesses to this horrific scene contact the man who forgave the massive debt. His response in verse 32 is, "'I forgave you all that debt because you pleaded with me. And should not you have had mercy on your fellow servant, as I had mercy on you?' And in anger his master delivered him to the jailers, until he should pay all his debt. So also my heavenly Father will do to every one of you, if you do not forgive your brother from your heart."

Jesus' point is that when you allow your hurt to turn into hate, you find yourself trapped in a bitter prison of demonic torment. We all know somebody who lives in such a cell, and it's sad to see. If you are the one trapped in unforgiveness, the good news is that you can be set free.

The question is, who has the key to set the bitter prisoner free? You might think your offender has the key and if they would only insert it into the lock by repenting and owning what they have done and apologizing to you, you would be free. But if so, the offender holds all the power over your life and future, and you must beg and beat them to agree and apologize so that you can exit your cell. Sadly, there is a category of "biblical" counseling that teaches you cannot forgive someone until they repent. This sentences people to a lifetime of bitterness and a life sentence of demonic torment.

Thankfully we hold the key to our deliverance in our own hands. We can place the key in the lock through receiving God's forgiveness and giving that gift to others by forgiving them, whether they ever apologize or not.

5. Forgiveness is grace to your offender.

It is often easier to receive God's gracious forgiveness than it is to give grace and forgive others. It is easier to have Jesus pay your debt than it is to pay someone else's. The truth is, if someone owes you, that debt must be paid. If you forgive them and cancel their debt, you will pay for it by allowing them to take it from your account.

Jesus asks us to do precisely this—to love our enemies as He loved us when we were His enemies. Jesus refers to this enemy love in Luke 6:27–36. Anyone who says Christianity is easy, never paid attention to these words of Jesus. Here's His punch list for us to do:

- Love your enemies.

- Bless those who curse you.

- Pray for those who hurt you.

- Endure an insult gladly.

- Let a thief keep your possessions.

- Do good things for bad people.

- Lend money with no expectation of repayment.

- Be kind to the unthankful and downright wicked.

- Be compassionate to ruthless people.

Consider for a moment that you are the enemy who has cursed, hurt, insulted, and stolen while being unthankful, wicked, and ruthless. Do Jesus' words sound like good news to you? Now consider for a moment that the shoe is on the other foot, and you are the one whose enemy cursed at you, hurt you, insulted you, and robbed you. That unthankful enemy responds to all your goodness with only wickedness and ruthlessness. Do Jesus' words still sound like good news to you?

Jesus' words are good news no matter which shoe you are wearing. If you are forgiven *by* God, then you are to be forgiving *like* God.

Now we will look at two verses of Jesus that line up like two barrels on a gun to shoot down unforgiveness. In Matthew 6:14–15 Jesus says, "If you forgive those who sin against you, your heavenly Father will forgive you. But if you refuse to forgive others, your Father will not forgive your sins" (NLT). To ensure we did not miss the point, in Mark 11:25 Jesus also says, "When you are praying, first forgive anyone you are holding a grudge against, so that your Father in heaven will forgive your sins, too" (NLT).

> If you are forgiven *by* God, then you are to be forgiving *like* God.

Forgiven people are supposed to be forgiving people. That's Jesus' big idea. It's hypocrisy to be forgiven and not be forgiving. What you have done to Jesus is worse than what they have done to you. You have no right to be forgiven and then be unforgiving. You cannot have it both ways.

Grace is a gift for you to enjoy, but also for you to share. God gave you grace even though you were His enemy, and He asks you to give His grace to your enemies. Who knows, perhaps some of them will even become your loving friends as you have become loving friends with the God who gave you grace. This is the hope you receive from Romans 2:4, which says, "God's kindness is meant to lead you to repentance."

6. Forgiveness is a witness to others.

It is particularly damaging to the cause of the gospel of Jesus Christ when bitter Christians fight in front of non-Christians because everyone loses and only Satan wins. It is very challenging to invite people to have their sins forgiven and join our family when we are unforgiving and fighting publicly. In our age of social media such evil has only gotten more awful.

One of the most inspiring forgiveness stories involved a man named Stephen in Acts chapter 7. Bitter, jealous, demonic religious leaders came to murder Stephen, but verse 55 says, "But he, full of the Holy Spirit, gazed into heaven and saw the glory of God, and Jesus standing at the right hand of God."

In a sporting event when a team is on the brink of winning a big game, all the fans jump out of their seats to cheer. When Stephen forgave his enemies, Jesus Christ jumped off of His throne to give a standing ovation and cheer. The next time you forgive someone, don't forget that Jesus is jumping up and down in the kingdom, cheering for you as you represent "Team Jesus," which is "Team Forgiveness!" Jesus cheered that Stephen was "full of the Holy Spirit" and empowered to forgive in the same way Jesus had done at His own public execution.

Dying at the hands of those he was forgiving, in Acts 7:59–60 Stephen "called out, 'Lord Jesus, receive my spirit.' And falling to his knees he cried out with a loud voice, 'Lord, do not hold this sin against them.'" As he was dying, Stephen did the same thing Jesus did, entrusting his soul to God and praying for the forgiveness of his enemies.

We then read in Acts 8:1, "And Saul approved of his execution." Who watched Stephen pray for the forgiveness of his murderers? A man who would later ask Jesus to forgive his sin and go on to be a preacher of the forgiveness of sins through Jesus Christ—the apostle Paul! Yes, the murdering Saul became the forgiven and forgiving Paul. He watched Stephen die and heard Stephen pray, and God answered that prayer and forgave that sin.

Child of God, when you are hurting, please remember that others are watching. The most awful days of your trial will become the most awesome days of your testimony.

7. Forgiveness opens you to the flow of the Holy Spirit.

Apart from Jesus Christ, the most remarkable act of forgiveness in all of Scripture might be the story of Joseph (Gen. 38–50). Like most of us, he was born into a messed-up family, and we all know that forgiving family is the hardest forgiveness of all. His father, Jacob (also called Israel), has twelve sons and one daughter with four women. Jacob makes it very obvious that Joseph is his favorite, giving him a flamboyant coat of many colors to parade around in like a peacock. While Joseph is a young man, God reveals his destiny of ruling over his family through a dream.

> The most awful days of your trial will become the most awesome days of your testimony.

The brothers become so jealous of Joseph that they consider murdering him, but instead, throw him in a pit and sell him as a slave. Joseph is taken away from home to the godless nation of Egypt with iron shackles around his hands, feet, and neck (Ps. 105:17–18). A military leader named Potiphar buys Joseph, and before long Joseph is running the entire household. Potiphar's wayward wife, however, continually seeks to seduce Joseph—but he repeatedly rejects her advances out of loyalty to her husband and the Lord.

Even though he is an innocent virgin, she falsely accuses him of rape, which sends him to prison. Before long this faithful servant is running the prison. In time the mighty Pharaoh who ruled Egypt has a dream that his spiritual advisors cannot interpret. Joseph is brought forth to reveal what God wants Pharaoh to know—seven years of abundance are coming to the nation, followed by seven years of famine. Joseph is then given the task of managing the food for the coming famine and is made the right-hand ruler of Pharaoh as the second most powerful man in the most powerful and longest-standing empire in the world.

As providence would have it, Joseph's family back in the Promised Land is starving. His brothers come before him seeking food. They do not recognize Joseph because he looks and speaks Egyptian, but he recognizes them.

In conversation he learns that they lied to his father, telling him Joseph was dead, and they even got up at the funeral to pretend they mourned and missed their brother. Rather than seeking vengeance, Joseph, after losing more than twenty years of his life because of his brothers' sin, is gracious to them, giving them silver and grain.

Joseph had already forgiven his brothers years prior, but he does not yet trust them. For a few years he tests them without them knowing. Eventually Joseph sees that his brothers have changed and he can trust them and reconcile with them. The entire family moves to Egypt, followed by a heartwarming reunion between Joseph and his loving father who then gets to be a grandpa to Joseph's two sons.

After father Jacob dies, the brothers have still not learned about the blessing of forgiving. Genesis 50:15–18 says, "When Joseph's brothers saw that their father was dead, they said, 'It may be that Joseph will hate us and pay us back for all the evil that we did to him.' So they sent a message to Joseph, saying, 'Your father gave this command before he died: "Say to Joseph, 'Please forgive the transgression of your brothers and their sin, because they did evil to you.'"' And now, please forgive the transgression of the servants of the God of your father.'"

Hearing this, Joseph weeps. The brothers had been forgiven, but they never completely accepted forgiveness from God or Joseph. Are you like this? Has God or someone else forgiven you but you have not received that gift and instead wrongly live in shame or fear? Joseph was so forgiving and emotionally healthy that he wept because he wanted his brothers to be healed up and freed up through forgiveness.

Joseph then says to his brothers, "Do not fear, for am I in the place of God?" (v. 19). The truth is, in Egypt he *was* in the place of God. Pharaoh was god, and Joseph sat at his right hand, ruling and reigning over a kingdom as their version of Jesus. Joseph could have killed them, punished them, or thrown them and their families into the same prison cell where he had suffered. But he did not because he had forgiven them many times from the heart over the course of many years.

Joseph continues in verse 20 by saying, "As for you, you meant evil against me, but God meant it for good, to bring it about that many people should be kept alive, as they are today." Joseph has lived by faith in the power of forgiveness his entire adult life. He tells his brothers that they "meant evil" but that God used their evil for good and the saving of many lives. He then lovingly assures them saying, "'So do not fear; I will provide for you and your little ones.' Thus he comforted them and spoke kindly to them" (v. 21).

We can certainly see that the brothers represent us and Joseph represents Jesus. He forgives us, weeps for us, loves us, blesses us, and pays the price for our evil. Just look at all the similarities between Joseph and Jesus.

- Both Joseph and Jesus were sons loved by their earthly and heavenly fathers.

- Both were destined by the heavenly Father to save and rule.

- Both were shepherds, had family that did not believe their destiny, and were hated by jealous brothers.

- Both were sold for pieces of silver.

- Both were stripped of their clothing, had their robes dipped in blood, and were thrown into a hole.

- Both were taken to Egypt when they were young.

- Both were falsely accused and paid a brutal price for something they did not do.

- Both were separated from their fathers, yet both forgave those who sinned against them and brought salvation to many after getting out of their pit.

- They are together in the kingdom right now, preparing for the colossal homecoming reunion for the entire family of God.

How did Joseph forgive, heal, and fulfill God's destiny for his life? The same way that Jesus did and you can. By the power of the Holy Spirit. Four times in Genesis 39 we are told that Joseph lived all of his life in the presence of God. Furthermore, the godless Pharaoh who had everything but one thing—the Holy Spirit—says of Joseph in Genesis 41:38, "Can we find a man like this, in whom is the Spirit of God?" You can forgive by the power of the Holy Spirit and begin unleashing the power of God in all your life.

We've talked about Jesus. We've talked about my family. We've talked about Joseph and his family. Now let's talk about you.

Have you truly received God's forgiveness for all your sin? Is there anything from your past that continues to haunt you because you have not completely accepted and invited the Holy Spirit to help you experience the application of Jesus' death in your place? Who has hurt you the most, starting with family members? Have you taken the time to get alone with God, journal out your thoughts in a raw and real way, and invited the Holy Spirit to help you to forgive them? Is there anyone you remain bitter against, hold a grievance toward, or are plotting vengeance against? If so, you are grieving the Holy Spirit who stands ready to help you forgive.

Before you turn the page and consider life in the Spirit versus life in the flesh, I need you to take some time alone with the Spirit. Turn off your technology and tune in to His presence. Sing worship songs, pray honestly and conversationally, journal out your hurts, and invite the Spirit of God into the places that your soul needs the most healing.

Write a letter from your heart to the people you need to forgive. List in earnest what they did and what it did to you. Be real and raw so that you can forgive and be free. Then pray to forgive them and tear up your letter. The Bible says that you should not keep a record of wrongs. By making a record of wrongs, forgiving that debt, and not keeping the record, you will free up your soul to heal. Make this a sacred meeting between you and God, not to be shared with anyone else. I have had this experience many times, and every time it was good for my soul and changed my life. I want the same for you and know that the Spirit is waiting to meet with you.

Chapter 13

THE SPIRIT,
NOT THE FLESH

BEFORE MY FAMILY moved to the desert, getting family time away was difficult. The winters were long with the sun setting early, cold temperatures, driving winds, and enough rain to make you want to start building an ark.

During one winter break a friend offered to let us use their cabin near the coast. Hoping for a bit of rest, we loaded up the five kids and made the drive to the beach. The winds were howling so strongly that I feared our youngest would get blown over. We tried to walk the beach in parkas and boots, but the wind blew the sand at such a high velocity we felt like cars being sandblasted in a body shop.

We loaded the kids into the suburban and headed into town to look for something fun to do. That's when we saw a large kite store. Pulling over, the kids jumped out of the car and ran inside.

The kite store was a step back in time. The old building had obviously been there for a long time and was filled with every kind of kite imaginable. Each of the children picked out their favorite kite along with enough string to let it climb to what Paul calls the third heaven where Jesus lives.

The kites were lifeless and uninteresting until we let go of their strings. The kids started screaming with joy as each of their kites exploded into the sky. As the kites danced above, our kids danced on the ground below. The children were mesmerized as their kites soared under the power of the wind.

As the wind filled each kite, the Holy Spirit brought to my mind two scriptures. John 3:8 says, "The wind blows where it wishes, and you hear its sound, but you do not know where it comes from or where it goes. So it is with everyone who is born of the Spirit." Ephesians 5:18 says, "Be filled with the Spirit."

A person without the Spirit is like a kite without a breeze. A person filled with the Spirit is like a kite brought to life, soaring and dancing in the wind. The Christian life cannot be lived apart from the powerful filling of the Holy Spirit.

After His resurrection, the first Christians wanted to tell the world about Jesus. But He told them to wait, promising in Acts 1:8, "You will receive power when the Holy Spirit has come upon you." Jesus then returned to heaven and sent the Spirit to fill His people, and we read in Acts 2:4, "They were all filled with the Holy Spirit." Once the people were filled, Christianity soared.

The Bible is very simple. We can live our lives from one of two sources: the flesh or the Spirit. When the Bible speaks of the flesh, it speaks to that which is sinful, fallen, and contrary to God. The flesh is our shadow side, our dark side, and our personality disconnected from God and drifting toward darkness, destruction, and death.

When the Bible speaks of the Spirit, it speaks of the presence of God at work in and through you. Practically this means that if you live by the Spirit, you experience an ongoing process where your life and character become increasingly like Jesus Christ. This contrast between the flesh and Spirit, found in Galatians 5:13–6:5, helps us understand life in the Spirit.

THE FLESH WORKS IN TWO WAYS: RELIGION AND REBELLION

Jesus' brother James speaks of "pure religion," which cares for those in need. There is also impure religion corrupted by fleshly human desires and deeds. One of the most religious churches in the New Testament was Galatia. Paul wrote a letter to sharply rebuke them for their arrogance, lack of love, and godless rule making. Paul hits a fevered pitch in Galatians 5:13–15, "For you were called to freedom, brothers. Only do not use your freedom as an opportunity for the flesh, but through love serve one another. For the whole law is fulfilled in one word: 'You shall love your neighbor as yourself.' But if you bite and devour one another, watch out that you are not consumed by one another."

FEED YOUR DEEPEST
HOLY SPIRIT–GIVEN DESIRES

When I was a little boy, I loved staying at my Grandpa George's house. He was a loving, fun, and generous man. He wore overalls and boots, and so did I because I was his little buddy. I would help him with woodworking projects in the garage and run errands with him in his huge brown Buick that always had a bag of suckers in the glove box for the grandkids.

Sometimes he would tuck me in and give me a wink. That was our secret signal that once Grandma fell asleep, we would sneak out of bed to eat caramel apples and black licorice and watch old school wrestling. Grandma did not approve of our preferred pastime, so we had to do our best ninja impersonation around the house late at night.

On one particular night I ate what seemed to be my body weight in black licorice while watching wrestling with Grandpa. Before long I started to feel sick. I knew I was going to throw up, but I did not want to make noises and wake Grandma. I clenched my jaw, and...I threw up the chewed black licorice out of my nostrils.

That smell changed my life. I can mark my life into two periods. One period is before that moment when I loved black licorice. The other period is after that moment when I absolutely hated black licorice. Since that day I cannot even smell black licorice without feeling a bit queasy. In an instant my desires simply changed.

Something similar happens for Christians—once we receive

the Holy Spirit, our desires transform at the deepest level as God changes our appetites. Galatians 5:16–18 says, "Walk by the Spirit, and you will not gratify the desires of the flesh. For the desires of the flesh are against the Spirit, and the desires of the Spirit are against the flesh, for these are opposed to each other, to keep you from doing the things you want to do. But if you are led by the Spirit, you are not under the law."

A Christian's deepest desires come from the Spirit, and they lead to life; a non-Christian's deepest desires come from the flesh and lead to death. Once you become a Christian, at the deepest levels of your being where the Holy Spirit dwells, what God wants you to do is what you want to do. A Spirit-filled Christian wants to learn the Bible, wants to pray, wants to live in holiness, and wants to worship God freely. If someone is truly saved, they are changed at the level of nature and desire. This explains why a sinning Christian is a miserable Christian.

The key to Christian holiness is to nurture your deepest desires given by the Spirit, resist your weaker desires to gratify the flesh, and do what you and the Spirit agree is best. Think of it like gardening. In any garden there are wonderful plants that grow, and there are awful weeds that grow. A bad gardener simply pours fertilizer and water over the entire garden, allowing nature to take its course. When this happens, the weeds eventually choke out the plants and the garden is ruined. A good gardener pulls the weeds and seeks to ensure that sunlight, fertilizer, and water are invested in the plants and not wasted on the weeds.

Your life is a garden. You are the gardener. To be fruitful you need to pull the weeds and feed the plants. In that way Spirit-filled living is a lot like gardening.

THE WORKS OF THE FLESH

How do you know when you are living from the flesh instead of the Spirit? Thankfully much like a doctor who enters the room of a patient with a list of health indicators to check, Galatians 5:19–21 gives us a checklist by which to examine the "works of the flesh":

> Sexual immorality—this is the same root word for pornography and includes all sexuality outside of heterosexual marriage
>
> Impurity—any moral filth that separates us from God
>
> Sensuality—lack of restraint or decency
>
> Idolatry—someone or something other than God is the center of our lives
>
> Sorcery—spirituality without the Spirit, including false religions
>
> Enmity—a devotion to being a hateful person
>
> Strife—conflict, drama, often causing a scene
>
> Jealousy—entitlement, selfishness
>
> Fits of anger—emotionally untethered and unhealthy
>
> Rivalries—ladder climbing, unholy competing
>
> Dissensions—factions, single-issue voters who only care about their pet issues, cliques
>
> Divisions—two visions that lead to fighting and conflict
>
> Envy—deep seething at seeing someone else flourish
>
> Drunkenness—can be any abused substance from alcohol to drugs
>
> Orgies—partying, pornography, sexual sins of various kinds
>
> Things like these—any other ungodly thought, word, or deed

Surveying this list, it is evident that the world in which we live is one big Dumpster fire of the flesh. The flesh is running the world and creating culture. Paul's naughty list is pretty much the same as the top search words online. People have parades for things that should have funerals. Things have gotten so bad and the flesh is so prevalent that rather than repenting of their behavior, people want

God to repent of His Word and take parts out of the Bible so that they can start taking off their pants. This mess needs a Messiah.

Part of the problem is that there are some who profess to be Christians who do not possess the Spirit. One of the most insightful ways to help someone know if he is truly a Christian is to help him uncover and discover his deepest and strongest desires. When the deepest desires align with Holy Spirit and the tempting, lesser desires align with the flesh, the person is a Christian. When the deepest desires align with the flesh, the person is a non-Christian. Paul speaks of this in his own experience, saying in Romans 7:18–8:9 that he has a battle between what he wants to do and does not do, and what he does not want to do but keeps doing. You can sense his agony as he confesses that he is not living up to his deepest desires. Paul concludes that he cannot live in victory over

> A sinning Christian is a miserable Christian.

the flesh apart from the power of the Spirit and closes by saying to believers, "You, however, are not in the flesh but in the Spirit, if in fact the Spirit of God dwells in you. Anyone who does not have the Spirit of Christ does not belong to him."

Any true Christian with the Spirit who begins to live according to the flesh becomes miserable as they are living against their core nature as a born-again believer with a new Lord externally, new desires internally, and new destiny eternally. They are fighting against the new nature that God the Spirit has given them and working against spiritual gravity. A sinning Christian is a miserable Christian.

FROM DESIRE TO DEATH

After spending most of my adult life in ministry as a senior pastor, I have observed a pattern of the flesh. There is a process of disillusionment that often happens, especially in the life of a leader since they tend to have greater desires than other people due to their visionary nature. What starts as perhaps even a good and godly desire leads to death. And the bigger the vision, the bigger the pain. This cycle is doubly true of motivated young Christians filled with ambitions to change the world for Christ. A godly desire can end in disappointment and death when it progresses through the following seven steps.

1. Desire

There is a longing for something that is often godly and good. What are your most ambitious plans, biggest dreams, and highest goals? Are they godly and wise? Are they for the glory of God and good of others, or mainly your own greatness?

2. Demand

When something you desire becomes something you demand, things grow dark, and you are on the path to death. Have your desires started to make the dark turn toward a demand? Are you now finding yourself angry or depressed because your desires have not come to pass? Have you started to feel any hint of entitlement that others—such as the Lord, people, or your family—owe you what you desire to any degree?

3. Disappointment

Once your desires go unmet, disappointment sets in as you sense a loss for something you felt entitled to but did not get. Have your efforts to achieve your desire met failure and disappointment? If your dreams are big or your passion for them is intense, then the likelihood of disappointment is greater.

4. Disillusionment

The thing you wanted so badly is now not going to happen, so you become disillusioned with your life efforts, lose motivation, and feel robbed. How have you handled your disappointment in the past and the present? Have you become jaded, disillusioned, or started to lose heart? Have you begun to question why you tried to pursue your desires in the first place, started losing motivation to press forward, or even just started going through the motions and dreaming about quitting and giving up altogether?

5. Demonize

You then have to blame someone (maybe even God or an entire group of people or organization) for "robbing" you of what you had coming to you, you end up demonizing them. Have you started to refer to someone, or a group of people, by a pejorative nickname? Is there someone, or a group of people, who you are struggling to forgive as they dominate your mind and emotions? Which hurtful or even harmful thoughts haunt your mind? Have you started to blame "them" for the pain, loss, and grief in your life and allowed bitterness and hate to root in your heart?

6. Destroy

Since you feel that you have been ruined, you then seek to destroy the person, group, or organization that you think caused your disillusionment. You may even make this a moral crusade where you become the righteous victim-turned-savior who will protect others from the harm you received. People often do this in the name of some God-given ministry, which is honestly just another mob in the never-ending fools' parade of angry, self-righteous, and dangerous people. Who have you started to speak ill of and find yourself angry and emotional about in an unhealthy way? When the names of certain people come up, does your blood begin to boil, do you feel a bit sick to your stomach, and wish that they would suffer as they have caused you to suffer? Has your hurt started to turn into hate?

7. Death

This cycle, like all sin, kills relationships. It leads to the death of friendships, families, companies, organizations, and ministries. In its most demonic forms, it even harms you as you become self-destructive, not only hurting others but also yourself. Where has death come to your ministry, family, business, organization, or heart? Where has death in one area of your life started to encroach on other areas of your life? How has it started taking away your joy, caused you to withdraw from safe people who love you, and even caused you not to be emotionally present with your own family but rather distracted, discouraged, and despairing? How did you get from what you thought (and likely was) a God-given desire to death?

The flesh refuses to surrender to God's will and instead prefers death. What is your story? Have you taken the time to consider it, journal it, pray through it, rejoice in it, and lament over it? Are you ready to turn from the death of the flesh to the life of the Spirit?

THE FRUIT OF THE SPIRIT

When our children were younger, some old friends were in town and stopped by our house. They lived on a massive orchard and grew peaches that were large enough to mistake for softballs Thankfully they arrived at our home during peach season with boxes of peaches for us to enjoy. Within minutes of their arrival, our kids were eating peaches and cream, and making peach milkshakes. Our friends were fruitful and shared the bounty of their fruitfulness with us so that we too were blessed. Life in the Spirit is like that.

The Bible contrasts life in the Spirit with life in the flesh in Galatians 5:22–25 where we find this menu of the fruit of the Spirit:

- Love—God's love for us, in us, and through us

- Joy—a clear conscience that allows a life-giving relationship with God

- Peace—both with God and others

- Patience—seeking God's timing rather than our own

- Kindness—considerate and not rude

- Goodness—generosity in our words, wealth, and works

- Faithfulness—reliable, trustworthy

- Gentleness—not domineering or overbearing

- Self-control—not self-indulgent or out of control but under God's influence

The flesh is so powerful that no other power, including human willpower, can defeat it; only God's power is more powerful than the flesh. To live free of the flesh, we have to live by the power of the Spirit.

Because Jesus died, you can put your sins of the flesh to death. You do not need to deny them, hide them, excuse them, or seek to manage them. Because Jesus is alive, you can live a new life by His power.

VINES AND BRANCHES

Echoing the fruit of the Spirit, Jesus famously speaks of Himself as the vine and believers as branches (John 15:1–11). A vine is filled with the life of the branch and bears fruit as long as it remains connected to the branch that nourishes it. To be a Christian is to be connected to Jesus so the life source of the Spirit flows from Jesus to you, bringing you the same health and life. The fruit of the Spirit, which is your character, exists to nourish others much like a fruitful branch connected to a healthy tree provides nourishment to others.

There are many ways to abide in Christ and have the nourishment of the Holy Spirit flowing into your soul. But nothing—including Scripture study and wholehearted worship—replaces a vibrant prayer life.

In Luke 11:1 the disciples say to Jesus, "Lord, teach us to pray." And Jesus responds in Luke 11:13, "If you then, who are evil, know how to give good gifts to your children, how much more will the heavenly Father give the Holy Spirit to those who ask him!"

Jesus' answer to the request, "Teach us to pray," is about

receiving the gift of the Holy Spirit. The Holy Spirit actually teaches us how to pray.

In Galatians 4:6 Paul writes, "Because you are sons, God has sent the Spirit of his Son into our hearts, crying, 'Abba! Father!'" This means that when we cry out to God as our Father, it's actually the Spirit in our hearts crying out. Prior to salvation, our sinful hearts neither wanted to pray nor understood how to pray. But upon salvation, the Spirit indwelling in us begins to change our hearts, and our prayers originate with Him.

Jesus Himself prayed by the Spirit. Luke 10:21–22 says, "[Jesus] rejoiced in the Holy Spirit and said, 'I thank you, Father, Lord of heaven and earth, that you have hidden these things from the wise and understanding and revealed them to little children; yes, Father, for such was your gracious will. All things have been handed over to me by my Father, and no one knows who the Son is except the Father, or who the Father is except the Son and anyone to whom the Son chooses to reveal him.'"

> No one is greater than their prayer life.

Luke describes this prayer of Jesus as a moment where He "rejoiced in the Holy Spirit," indicating that the Son conducts His prayer to the Father in the joyful power of the Holy Spirit. This beautiful description of worshipful prayer shows us how the Spirit empowers us to pray.

No one is greater than their prayer life. No one can abide in Christ without a Spirit-filled prayer life. God does not need prayer; you do. In prayer you do not change God, but invite God to change you. There is simply no way to abide in Christ and grow in the Spirit apart from earnest, regular times in prayer.

You may, however, wonder why you still struggle with the flesh even though you are a Christian who has the Spirit. There are times, no matter how godly you are, that you "quench the Spirit" (1 Thess. 5:19). When this happens, you feed the flesh and fall into sin.

How about you? Are there any works of the flesh in your life that need to be put to death? Are you growing in your sensitivity toward and submission to the Spirit? How do you see the fruit of the Spirit increase in your life? How is your prayer life? Sometimes we struggle in prayer because it seems like it's not working.

Living by Faith

Robert was a man who dearly loved his mother. His mother was a godly woman who loved and prayed for Robert during his many years of rebellion as a prodigal son sleeping with women, drinking in excess, and racking up significant debt. Like the parable of the prodigal, Robert eventually returned to his senses, his mother, and his Lord. Robert began attending church services with his mom and growing in his Christian faith.

Suddenly Robert's mom grew very ill and was diagnosed with advanced cancer. Robert and his mom regularly attended the prayer meetings at their church, asking God for healing. There they heard testimonies of people God had healed. A pastor met with Robert and showed him from the Book of Acts how people were healed in the early church and told them that they needed to have faith so that God could heal his mother. Robert clung to the hope of his mother's healing.

Eventually Robert's mom died. The pastor then showed Robert how dead people were also raised in the Book of Acts. So he went to his mothers' graveside and pleaded with God in prayer to raise her from the dead.

Robert's mom was not healed from cancer.

Robert's mom was not raised from death.

Robert grew very discouraged and felt guilty that he did not have enough faith in God to bring life to his mother. Robert started attending another church that taught that the miraculous things in the Bible had ceased and that God no longer did those things. Robert felt that his first pastor had overpromised and underdelivered. Robert also felt that his second pastor helped ease his burden of guilt for a lack of faith, but he wondered why God would not want to at least heal some people.

Robert's experience is not unusual. Christianity is the road to heaven, and there are two stripes marking the lane boundaries on each side. In the middle most Christians don't feel comfortable saying God cannot do things like heal the sick and raise the dead. But they also do not feel comfortable saying that God often heals the sick and raises the dead.

Four truths may help shed light on this difficult aspect of Spirit-filled prayer:

1. The kingdom of God has already begun with the resurrection of Jesus but is not yet fully unveiled until the second coming of Jesus. Once Jesus returns, *all* of God's people will be healed and raised forever. Until then *some* of God's people get healed and raised.

2. The Book of Acts records what the Holy Spirit did in, through, and for the early church. Page after page records extraordinary supernatural events. You can sit down and read the entire Book of Acts in a few hours. But Acts records more than thirty years of history. When you sit down to read Acts, if you think it records a few days you could assume that the supernatural was constant. It was common but spread over decades and not days.

3. Even though Christians have the Spirit in measure, we do not have the Spirit to the same degree that Jesus did. John 3:34 says that Jesus had "the Spirit without measure." Conversely believers have the grace of God through the Spirit in a "measure" (Eph. 4:7) instead of "without measure" like Jesus. This distinction can be traced as far back as to the church father Augustine as well as Bible commentator John Calvin.[1]

One Bible commentator says, "It is true that believers receive the Spirit in abundant measure....But it is not true that the New Testament regards believers as receiving the Spirit without measure. In the first place, no one else has the Spirit in any way comparable to Jesus. And in the second, there is an implied limitation when we are told that 'to each one of us grace has been given as Christ *apportioned it*' (Eph. 4:7)."[2]

Jesus is filled with the total fullness of the Spirit, and the rest of us are filled from His fullness. Perhaps an analogy will help. I once saw an enormous water feature at a beautiful resort that was a cascading waterfall of fountains. At the top of the fountains was one giant lake that was filled with the fullness of all the water. From that lake the water flowed down into a series of fountains so that the fullness of the lake flowed down and filled the smaller fountains. Jesus is like that lake, given the fullness of the Spirit "without measure," and from Him the Spirit flows down to the fountains that are our lives so that we too are filled with a measure of His fullness.

4. Until we rise from death and our flesh is forever gone, we remain imperfect vessels for, in, and through which the Spirit of God works. Jesus, however, was a perfect vessel for the Spirit to work in and through. You are not perfect. Jesus was and is perfecting you by the Spirit.

When I think of myself, I think of my trucks. The first truck I ever owned was a 1966 Chevy that I bought from an Idaho farmer. The truck ran, but it ran rough. I was constantly working on it, and sometimes it ran all right, but other times it ran rough or not at all. Some years later I bought a new Chevy truck, and it ran perfectly.

You and I are like my old truck—we run rough. After the resurrection you and I will run like my new truck. So don't be discouraged on your bad days. Tune up what you can, thank God for the improvements He's made, and keep rolling ahead.

As you grow in your relationship with the Holy Spirit, your life begins to increasingly be lived kingdom down instead of culture up, as we will study in the next chapter.

Chapter 14

KINGDOM DOWN, NOT CULTURE UP

F OR THE CHRISTIAN, this life is as close to hell as you will ever be. For the non-Christian, this life is as close to heaven as you will ever be.

Your job will end. Your bills will end. Your sickness will end. Your tasks will end. Your stack of dishes, pile of laundry, unanswered texts and emails, social media pages, and check engine light will one day be gone forever.

Ultimately everything you know—your life, family, community, and nation—will end, and when everything else goes away, a kingdom will come down. That kingdom is the kingdom of God God's kingdom replaces every culture on the earth. God's kingdom is your eternal home if you are a child of God. Your residence may be in your city and country, but your citizenship is in that kingdom. That kingdom has a king named Jesus. In Matthew 6:10 King Jesus told us to live and pray "kingdom down" and not "culture up."

> Your kingdom come, your will be done, on earth as it is in heaven.

Today we live in the time between the times. In one sense the kingdom of God has already begun with the defeat of the devil at the cross, the resurrection victory of Jesus, the Holy Spirit coming in power to the church, and the spreading of the gospel across the nations of the earth. In another sense the kingdom of God has not fully begun, because unlike Jesus we have not yet resurrected from death and entered into our eternal and glorified state with the curse lifted and the devil and his demons finally sentenced to the eternal lake of fire.

When we boil all of life, history, and culture down to the bottom line, it's pretty simple: people either live culture up or kingdom down. Those who live culture up tend to see their cultural morality, politics, and spirituality as superior and normative. Such people then judge other people and other cultures by their culture. People from the other cultures do the same in return. The results are aptly called culture clashes, and they lead to culture wars. Culture wars are what happens when two visions collide and cultural, political, moral, spiritual, and sometimes even real war is waged with the winning culture ruling over the other. This state continues, of course, until the next subculture or counterculture rises to dethrone the majority culture.

Think of it as the kids' game king of the hill. In that game all the kids push and fight as they battle over who will stand atop the hill as the king. Eventually the biggest, strongest kid wins and stands on the hill gloating over his victory. The other kids who lost then band together as an alliance, hoping that their combined efforts can overthrow the king of the hill. Eventually they wear down the king of the hill, and someone from their group becomes the new king. Those who are not the king then repeat the process of plotting and overthrowing the current king of the hill.

Yes, all of human history is a version of a kids' game played by adults who fight to get their way with legal maneuvering, personal threatening, public attacking, and private deal-making.

If you pay any attention to what is happening culturally within your country, you quickly grow despondent. Different sides fight to get their king on the hill, and even if they make it, eventually someone else knocks their king off the hill, and the culmination of all the battling seems to get us nowhere.

Thankfully there is another option. The Bible tells us that history has a destination and it is moving toward the Lord Jesus who is returning to the earth to be our forever King of the hill.

John's Vision

The division in the world is really because of two visions. In fact, the word *division* literally means two visions. Anytime there are two visions of what should be, there is division.

The vision of those who think culture up is that if God exists He should make their vision a reality. Kingdom-down vision is that God does exist, He sees us and our world differently, and we should make His vision a reality. The Book of Revelation is not only the last book of the Bible, but it is also literally a God-given vision.

Revelation 1:9–10 reports, "I, John, your brother and partner in the tribulation and the kingdom and the patient endurance that are in Jesus, was on the island called Patmos on account of the word of God and the testimony of Jesus. I was in the Spirit on the Lord's day, and I heard behind me a loud voice like a trumpet." It had to be sad for Pastor John to be alone on Sunday, the Lord's day, and day of Jesus' resurrection. He had no flock to shepherd, no sermon to prepare, and no ministry to undertake. But in an amazing moment in human history, Jesus Christ came back down from heaven to meet with His old friend John.

> The word *division* literally means two visions. Anytime there are two visions of what should be, there is division.

Revelation is about perspective. All we can see on the news is the never-ending game of king of the hill. But when we open our Bibles we read about God's good news. The Holy Spirit raises us above it all so we can see God's bigger and better plan. God's Word gives us God's perspective just as it did John.

Perhaps an analogy made popular by Holocaust survivor Corrie ten Boom will help. She said that life is like a loom. If you hold a loom up and look at it from underneath, all you will see is a tangled mess of disparate threads and knots that appear to be a series of mistakes, errors, and a waste of time and resources. But if you change your vantage point and look down upon the loom from above, suddenly you see what the weaver saw—a very intentional and beautiful tapestry marked by incredible symmetry and mastery. God lives above the loom. We live below the loom. God has a plan to take all the frayed ends of culture, political knots, and disparate threads from nations and faithfully, patiently, and daily knit together a beautiful tapestry called the kingdom of God. What Jesus gave to John and gives to us through John's writings is a seat above the loom with Jesus, the master weaver.

In Revelation the central piece of furniture in John's prophetic vision is a throne. That throne appears about forty-five times in Revelation, which is roughly two-thirds of all mentions of a throne in the entire New Testament. In a day when people reclined on the floor, a chair of any kind was a status symbol, which is how thrones came to be associated with rulers and royalty. Jesus Christ, our King of kings, is both ruler and royalty. It is Jesus' throne that is the center of the kingdom and center of human history. No person, culture, nation, political party, gender identity, spirituality, morality, or ideology will ever sit on that throne or rule in that seat of sovereign authority. In Revelation all truth, justice, and authority proceed from that throne across the entire kingdom, which encompasses all creation. All glory, honor, and worship throughout creation proceed to that throne and the King of the hill seated upon it.

Since Jesus is your King, your ultimate allegiance must be to Him. Since the kingdom is your eternal home, your lifestyle must be patterned after the kingdom and not the culture. And since who you are in the kingdom is the real and true you, how you see yourself and conduct yourself must be in light of who you will be when God has finished His work and unveiled the perfect version of you. Where you live today is not where you will live forever. Who you are today is not who you will be forever. So rather than living in light of where you came from or who you were, kingdom life is about living in light of where you are going and who you will be!

FEAR NOT

As Christians, living kingdom down is how we live a life of faith. We trust that the same God who began a good work in us will see it through to the end—fully, totally, and eternally transforming us from one degree of glory to another! Knowing the end helps us live in the middle of history. We know the end, and Jesus wins!

Conversely, living culture up is how we live a life of fear. If we forget our eternal destination, we are prone to get lost in culture and become exhausted, frantic, and panicked. Being afraid takes many forms. There's fear of success and failure, fear of being attacked, fear of getting fired or having to "work this job with these people" forever like a life sentence at a prison, and fear of disappointing people. We feel these fears despite the fact that the number one command in the Bible, appearing roughly one hundred fifty times, is "Fear not!" God keeps talking about our fears because we keep forgetting to live by faith in His kingdom.

> Rather than living in light of where you came from or who you were, kingdom life is about living in light of where you are going and who you will be!

Counselors can tell us the countless ways we can manifest fear. Fear amps up our bodies to fight or flee, putting us on edge, disrupting our sleep and our ability to rest while awake. Fear makes our thoughts race with imaginations that run wild, and it puts us in a state of terror. Extended seasons of fear can lead to generalized anxiety, a feeling that we're under siege without reprieve, which in turn can lead to panic attacks. Fear reveals itself in our emotions as despondence, moodiness, and hypersensitivity. Fear feeds social anxiety and withdrawal. It ruins relationships by isolating us, fueling distrust, and leaving us ashamed and humiliated. Fear can also show up as selfishness, where we ignore the needs of others while expecting them to cater to our needs. Fear shows up in our overall outlook, diminishing our current joy and hope for the future.

People who self-medicate with food, alcohol, spending, sex, or drugs are likely responding to fear. Even unrestrained anger, which can make us feel powerful instead of powerless, is a response to fear.

There are simple solutions you can implement to keep fear from getting hold of you in the first place. When you feel fear rise within you, check how you're managing these areas:

- **Your mind:** How can you process a situation rather than react? What are the odds of the thing you fear coming to pass? What's the worst that can happen? How can you best spend your energy right now to head off the problem?

- **Your body:** What warning signs is your body trying to communicate to you? How are you sleeping, eating, hydrating, exercising, and breathing? Are you self-medicating with food, caffeine, alcohol, sex, drugs, etc.?

- **Your soul:** How can you disrupt your fears by journaling, praying, reading, worshipping, or lamenting? How can small daily practices keep you from building up a large deficit in your relationship with the Lord?

- **Your relationships:** Who bears the brunt of your fears? Who do you trust to come alongside you to help you move forward?

- **Your life:** How can you reduce noise by unplugging tech? How can you block out unhelpful sources of bad news, especially about events you can't control? In the midst of your demanding schedule how can you create recovery breaks?

None of these survival tactics are new. But I do know that most of us are challenged to live out these practices. If we aren't guarding ourselves in these basic areas, fear is entirely likely to gain control of us.

If you want to put an end to feeling frantic, exhausted, and overwhelmed in life, these tactics only get you halfway there. The bigger key to energy management and energy replenishment is to break free from fear-based living to live in faith-based living. Fear-based people run out of energy, while faith-based people find their energy renewed by God like manna in the morning. Faith-based people are motivated by conviction from God and not condemnation from people.

Exhaustion hits every believer, even the godliest and most gifted. Jesus got tired. Paul talked about being poured out like a drink offering (Phil. 2:17). So it isn't ungodly to be emptied out. The problem is that fear preempts the inner peace and outer rest that allows us to recover, replenish, and renew our energy.

Fear is the opposite of love, which is proactive and propels us to move closer to the Lord and people. Fear causes us to withdraw, hide, cower, and have the heart of a hermit. In 1 John 4:18 we read, "There is no fear in love, but perfect love casts out fear. For fear has to do with punishment, and whoever fears has not been perfected in love."

The only way out of the fear cycle is to know God's love and presence. Fear is a demon spirit that has to be "cast out" and replaced with the presence of the love of God through the Holy Spirit. This is why almost every time God tells us "fear not," He also says in some way, "for I am with you." Faith in God's loving presence is the answer to our languishing fear.

Some years ago our family was preparing for a family trip to Scotland. I started showing the kids photos of where we would go and what we would do. All the kids were excited except our youngest son. He kept adamantly saying that he refused to go on the trip, so I kept increasing my sales pitch. "Little buddy, you will fly on a plane. You will go in a cool old cab. You will ride a double-decker bus and tour the city. You will visit castles. You will see John

Knox's house and church—you remember the preacher who could swing a two-handed sword with one hand and pounded his pulpit so hard that splinters would fly off!"

The more I sold the trip, the more he refused to buy in.

I was baffled, bewildered, and befuddled.

Exasperated, I got down on one knee, looked him in the eye, and said something like, "But, little buddy, if you don't go with me it won't be as fun. I really wanted to take you on this adventure with me."

Immediately, his countenance transformed as he asked, "Dad, so you are going with me?"

Ugh. Dad failed to point out the obvious—I was not sending him out on his own, but I was going with him. In fact, this was a family trip, and we were all going together. As soon as he heard that major fact, what sounded like a death march turned into an epic adventure. So long as Dad was nearby, leading the way, and keeping an eye on him, my little buddy was on board.

The presence of God in your life is the Holy Spirit. The Holy Spirit is like the hand of God the Father reaching down to walk each of His sons and daughters lovingly and safely home to the kingdom of God.

Along the journey home, a life lived kingdom down instead of culture up is also not surprised to see the King show up now and then and show off His coming kingdom with a sneak preview. These occasions are times of salvation, healing, deliverance, miracles, and sacred moments when we experience the King's presence as a sneak preview of the coming kingdom.

How did John gain this perspective? Very simply, he tells us in Revelation 1:10, "I was in the Spirit." So it is with you. The only way to have God's kingdom perspective is to receive revelation from the Spirit, starting with the Scriptures, so that your faith can grow.

Living culture up is what the Bible means by being "of the world." Living culture up causes people to expect God to repent of His ways rather than people repenting of our ways. To live kingdom down is to live life in the Spirit under the rule of King Jesus as we repent of our ways and seek to see the kingdom transform the cultures of the earth.

Nearing the end of Scripture, we read of an invitation in Revelation 22:17, "The Spirit and the Bride say, 'Come.' And let the one who hears say, 'Come.' And let the one who is thirsty come; let the one who desires take the water of life without price."

Jesus is your King, and the kingdom is your home. Your life is a walk with Jesus to the Father's house by the Spirit's power. Like any walk, the key is spending time alone with the Spirit of God to constantly ask Him what His next step of obedience is for you. Do you know what your next step is?

The King and His kingdom are coming, and the Spirit of God invites you to a life-changing, soul-satisfying, mind-transforming, eternity-altering, kingdom down relationship with the Spirit-filled Jesus that lasts forever and ever. This is the life of faith lived kingdom down.

You can live by His power!

A FINAL ENCOURAGEMENT TO MINISTRY LEADERS

D EAR MINISTRY LEADER,
Thank you for your service to Jesus Christ and to people He loved so much He died for them. In this book I have admittedly sought to move the conversation regarding the Holy Spirit from the well-worn categories. I have read a stack of books about the Holy Spirit taller than me (which is not a giant feat), and nearly every one covers the same ground, falls into the same debates, and continues to beat a stable full of dead horses over and over and over.

The biggest debates around the Holy Spirit are in relation to the supernatural spiritual gifts, such as healing, prophecy, casting out demons, miracles, dreams, visions, speaking in tongues, etc. There is a spectrum of belief on these issues with one end of the spectrum basically saying no to everything and the other end of the spectrum basically saying yes to everything. The following categories are admittedly imprecise and are offered only to show a spectrum in which various teams, tribes, and traditions (including yours) fall.

1. Cessationists

As the name suggests, cessationist Christians believe that the supernatural gifts have ceased. They assert that the supernatural gifts of the Holy Spirit were used by God in the earliest days of the Christian church to affirm the authority of the early apostolic leaders and their message. However, once the books of the Bible were written, there was no longer need for these supernatural gifts as the Bible was the once for all perfect revelation from God and sufficient for all we need. They also tend to consider speaking in tongues as only a known earthly language and deny the continuationists' claim that there is an angelic heavenly prayer language also referred to as tongues. The concern for many cessationists is that when extrabiblical revelation is permitted, it sometimes if not oftentimes results in unbiblical revelation that disagrees with the Bible. Some of my friends who are high-profile cessationist pastors will privately talk about personal pain they experienced as a result of false revelations people claimed were from God. As a boy one of these international movement leaders was told by a visiting revival preacher that he would be dead by a certain age. This horrific false prophecy caused the boy great angst as he reached the age at which he was told he would be dead. Of course, he lived to be an old man in good health, and his goal is now to have the Bible faithfully preached and to prevent false revelation because it caused him so much suffering. To be fair, we have to admit that sometimes cessationism is a response to the abuse of spiritual gifts.

2. Open but cautious

Open-but-cautious Christians share many of the same concerns as cessationists. But they struggle to make a clear biblical case that all the supernatural gifts have in fact ceased. Furthermore, as they read the record of church history they quickly discover that there are reports of supernatural spiritual gifts continuing among God's people in every age and never stopping since the days of Pentecost in Acts. Feeling the tension between operating more as a cessationist, but having weak biblical and historical footing, this group of open-but-cautious Christians believes that the supernatural spiritual gifts are theoretically possibly in operation, but unlikely and infrequent with numerous counterfeits to be wary of. However, this group is often concerned about possibly missing something the Holy Spirit has for them and so they try and remain cautiously open.

3. Continuationists

Continuationist Christians believe that the supernatural spiritual gifts have continued and will continue in every age until the second coming of Jesus Christ. There is a broad range of Christians in this doctrinal position, from Catholics and Methodists to Charismatics and Pentecostals. Differences among continuationist Christians include what is meant by "the baptism of the Holy Spirit" and whether this refers to something that happens to all believers upon conversion or is a second and subsequent experience marked by speaking in tongues. Another difference would be whether or not the supernatural spiritual gifts should occur publicly in a church service or be reserved for more private occasions where non-Christians are unlikely to be present.

4. Crazies

There are always some people who claim to be Christians but have things that they declare to be visions from God, words from God, or other forms of revelation such as angelic insight that cause them to sound like the teaching equivalent of a drunk driver. Crazies can function as false teachers denying the clear teachings of Scripture, or even tragically morph into cult leaders. Sadly, they can become so proud that they believe they have authority equal to God's Word, or even exceeding God's Word with new revelation that supersedes and adds to the Scriptures.

As you can probably guess, the cessationists are rightly concerned about the crazies. Sadly, sometimes the case is made as if there are only two categories in practice—you are either a cessationist or a crazy. The cessationists then start pulling out all the spooky verses in the Bible about false teachers, the increase of demonic deception in the last days, and apostasy, while naming other pastors and authors that they are beating like a piñata on Cinco de Mayo.

In response, the crazies start pulling out all the Bible verses commanding us to not grieve, quench, or resist the Holy Spirit while also obeying the Bible's clear commands, "Do not forbid speaking in tongues" (1 Cor. 14:39) and "Do not treat prophecies with contempt" (1 Thess. 5:20, NIV). Unfortunately debates about the Holy Spirit can become a prison riot fairly quickly, complete with mattresses on fire.

One thing is sure when it comes to the ministry of the Holy Spirit: He wants us to be "eager to maintain the unity of the Spirit in the bond of peace" (Eph. 4:3). This command is perhaps more vital than ever. I have always been continuationist, but the seminary I attended is a mix of continuationist and open-but-cautious. The first church I worked at was cessationist, and most of the pastors I am walking with and learning from in this season of my life are continuationist Charismatics and Pentecostals.

In my experience we are better together, and a lot of the time we are speaking about the same thing but using different words. For example, some will talk a lot about walking in your destiny, while others will talk a lot about God predestinating—either way, the big idea is that God rules over our future and we need to walk in His will.

In the Christian faith there are borders between cities and borders between nations. City-border issues include such things as spiritual gifts along with other things such as mode of baptism, role of women in ministry, style of worship music, and age of the earth. National-border issues include such things as the Bible as God's Word, the Trinity, the full humanity and divinity of Jesus, His death on the cross for our sins, and His resurrection from death as our Savior. If we agree on the national-border issues, like the twelve tribes of Israel we need to still see ourselves as one nation even if we are in differing theological tribes.

When someone crosses a line on a national-border issue, they have abandoned the Christian faith. This is called apostasy, and the church is facing an apostasy that is well underway.

I have had a front-row seat for what I believe is the apostasy of this generation. At issue are gender identity and marriage. For my entire ministry career I have had pastor friends continually shift on this issue. There are even former ministry leaders, including pastors and board members who worked with me in the past, now vocally defending such things as transgenderism and same-sex marriage as acceptable Christian conduct. There are some who want to make these city-border issues, while others see them as national-border issues. The issues are so public that they cannot be ignored, and so central and essential to Scripture that they cannot be minimized.

The Bible is about repentance. Our culture is about tolerance. In repentance, when we disagree with God, we repent of our sinful thoughts, words, deeds, and motives to avoid His wrath. In tolerance, we feed our sinful desires and demand that God repent of His Word and both tolerate and celebrate our lifestyle or face our wrath. It is time to call a cease-fire on the war over secondary, city-border issues such as the supernatural spiritual gifts and focus on the primary, national-border issues. Distinctions among Christians should not create division between Christians.

The debate over such things as speaking in tongues is important, but not of the utmost importance. Jesus is the perfect example of living a Spirit-filled life. We do not, however, know if Jesus ever spoke in tongues. The Bible is simply silent. I take this to mean that whether you speak in tongues or not, you can live a Spirit-filled life like Jesus, marked by godly character and a love for the Word of God. Word people should also be Spirit people since the Spirit of God

> Distinctions among Christians should not create division between Christians.

inspired the Bible to be written. With the oars of Word and Spirit, God's people can row together safely in the same boat toward God's kingdom.

My goal in this book has been to focus on the ministry of the Holy Spirit in the more mundane and daily issues of life—forgiving people, being emotionally healthy, having healthy relationships, overcoming temptation, having a godly family, and living by God's power in all of life—the very things that most people are struggling with every day while overlooking the person of Jesus and presence of His power to help. Lastly, my goal in focusing on the Spirit-filled person of Jesus is to point to Him so that all Bible-believing Christians can rally together and live in unity by His power in His presence in a world where God's Word is increasingly not welcome.

NOTES

Introduction
Two Years Later...

1. Acts 1:8.

2. If you would like to hear the sermons on Luke, please visit markdriscoll.org or download the Mark Driscoll Ministries app.

3. Based on the number of words, Luke's two books are quite lengthy and comprise 27 percent of the text of the New Testament, followed closely by all of Paul's letters, which add up to 23 percent of the text. Paul wrote more books of the New Testament, but Luke produced more volume. John was the third most prolific writer, with his books totaling 20 percent of the New Testament text. ("Who Wrote Most of the New Testament?," Apologika, accessed June 5, 2018, http://apologika.blogspot.com/2014/05/who-wrote-most-of-new testament.html.)

4. William Mitchell Ramsay, *The Bearing of Recent Discovery on the Trustworthiness of the New Testament* (London: Hodder and Stoughton, 1915), 222.

Chapter 1
Spirit-Filled Jesus

1. Mark Water, *The Life of Jesus Made Easy* (Alresford, Hampshire: John Hunt Publishers Ltd, 2001), 35.

2. Water, *The Life of Jesus Made Easy*, 33.

3. As quoted in F. F. Bruce, *The New Testament Documents* (Downers Grove, IL: InterVarsity, 1981), 15.

4. William J. Federer, *America's God and Country Encyclopedia of Quotations* (St. Louis, MO: AmeriSearch, 2001), 463.

5. Kenneth L. Woodward, "2000 Years of Jesus," *Newsweek*, March 28, 1999, http://www.newsweek.com/2000-years-jesus-163776.

6. Kenneth Scott Latourette, "The Christian Understanding of History," *Grace Theological Journal* 2, no. 1 (1981).

7. Maurice Burrell, "Twentieth Century Arianism: An Examination of the Doctrine of the Person of Christ Held by Jehovah's Witnesses," *The Churchman* 80, no. 2 (1966): 134–135, http://archive.churchsociety.org/churchman/documents/Cman_080_2_Burrell.pdf.

8. Larry A. Nichols, George A. Mather, and Alvin J. Schmidt, *Encyclopedic Dictionary of Cults, Sects, and World Religions* (Grand Rapids, MI: Zondervan, 2006), 195.

9. Nichols, Mather, and Schmidt, *Encyclopedic Dictionary of Cults, Sects, and World Religions*, 195.

10. Mark Water, *Teachings of the Bible Made Simple* (Chattanooga, TN: AMG Publishers, 2002), 13.

11. For example, in 1 Timothy 1:17 Jesus is the King who has the divine attributes of eternality, immortality, invisibility, and is called "the only God." According to other scriptures, other divine attributes possessed by Jesus during His life on earth include omnipresence (Ps. 139:7–12; Matt. 28:20), creator (Isa. 37:16; 44:24; John 1:3; Col. 1:16; Heb. 1:2), savior (Joel 2:32; Rom. 10:9–13), and deity as the only God (Isa. 45:21–23; Phil. 2:10–11).

12. "What Is the Apostles' Creed?," BGEA, accessed June 6, 2018, https://billygraham.org/answer/what-is-the-apostles-creed/.

13. W. A. Wigram, *An Introduction to the History of the Assyrian Church* (London: Aeterna Press, 2015), 167.

Chapter 2
How a Spirit-Filled Family Fulfills Their Destiny

1. "All the Men of the Bible—James," Zondervan, accessed June 6, 2018, https://www.biblegateway.com/resources/all-men-bible/James.

2. J. A. Kirk, "The Meaning of Wisdom in James: Examination of a Hypothesis," *New Testament Studies* 16, no. 1 (October 1969),

24–38; William Sailer ed., *Religious and Theological Abstracts* (Myerstown, PA: Religious and Theological Abstracts, 2012).

3. In the Old Testament, Deuteronomy 34:9 says, that, "Joshua... was full of the spirit of wisdom." Looking at Daniel an ungodly leader senses something divinely distinct about him and says in Daniel 5:14, "I have heard of you that the spirit of the gods is in you, and that light and understanding and excellent wisdom are found in you." In Isaiah 11:2 it was promised that Jesus would come and "the Spirit of the LORD shall rest upon him, the Spirit of wisdom and understanding..." In the New Testament, when it came time to pick leaders in the early church, Acts 6:3 reports the apostles saying, "Brothers, pick out from among you seven men of good repute, full of the Spirit and of wisdom." Lastly, in Ephesians 1:17 Paul prays "that the God of our Lord Jesus Christ, the Father of glory, may give you the Spirit of wisdom." The Bible often speaks of the cause (Spirit) and effect (wisdom) with various authors stressing one or the other while speaking of both.

4. D. A. Carson, *The Gospel According to John* (Grand Rapids, MI: Wm. B. Eerdmans Publishing Company, 1991), 389.

5. James D. Tabor and Simcha Jacobovici, *The Jesus Discovery* (New York: Simon and Schuster Inc., 2012), 122.

CHAPTER 3
MATURE LIKE YOUR MESSIAH

1. Alfred Plummer, *A Critical and Exegetical Commentary on the Gospel According to S. Luke* (Edinburgh, London: T&T Clark International, 1913), 74.

2. A. T. Robertson, *Word Pictures in the New Testament* (Nashville, TN: Broadman Press, 1933), Lk 2:52.

3. Allen C. Myers ed., *The Eerdmans Bible Dictionary* (Grand Rapids, MI: Eerdmans, 1987), 207.

4. Abraham Kuyper, *The Work of the Holy Spirit*, trans. Henri de Vries (Grand Rapids, MI: Wm. B Eerdmans, 1975), 97.

5. Gerald F. Hawthorne, *The Presence and the Power: The Significance of the Spirit in the Life and Ministry of Jesus* (Dallas, TX: Word, 1991), 234.

CHAPTER 4
LEARN TO LOVE

1. Joel C. Elowsky, ed., *Ancient Christian Commentary on Scripture New Testament* (Downers Grove, IL: InterVarsity Press, 2007), 140.

CHAPTER 5
FIVE WEAPONS TO DEFEAT THE DEMONIC

1. Francis Foulkes, *The Epistle of Paul to the Ephesians* (Grand Rapids, MI: Wm. B. Eerdmans, 1989), 78.

2. Dan Lioy, *David C. Cook's NIV Bible Lesson Commentary 2009–2010* (Colorado Springs, CO: David C. Cook, 2009), 158.

3. C.S. Lewis, *The Screwtape Letters* (New York: HarperCollins, 2001), ix.

4. Rudolf Bultmann as quoted in J. D. G. Dunn, "Myth," eds. Joel B. Green and Scot McKnight, *Dictionary of Jesus and the Gospels* (Downers Grove, IL: InterVarsity Press, 1992), 567.

5. *Unusual Suspects* directed by Bryan Singer (Beverly Hills: MGM, 2006), DVD.

CHAPTER 6
JESUS' SECRET TO EMOTIONAL HEALTH

1. Sam Williams, "Toward a Theology of Emotion," *Southern Baptist Journal of Theology* 7, no. 4 (2003): 63.

2. F. L. Cross and E. A. Livingstone, eds., *The Oxford Dictionary of the Christian Church* (New York: Oxford University Press, 2005), 376.

3. William Barclay, ed., The Gospel of John, vol. 2, *The Daily Study Bible Series* (Philadelphia, PA: Westminster John Knox Press, 1975), 98.

4. William Hendriksen and Simon J. Kistemaker, *New Testament Commentary: Exposition of the Gospel According to Luke* (Grand Rapids: Baker Book House, 2004), 583.

5. R. C. H. Lenski, *The Interpretation of St. Luke's Gospel* (Minneapolis, MN: Augsburg Fortress, 2008), 586.

6. Williams, "Toward a Theology of Emotion," 56.

7. G. Walter Hansen, "The Emotions of Jesus," *Christianity Today* 41, no. 2 (February 3, 1997), 43–46.

8. B. B. Warfield, *The Emotional Life of Our Lord* (Amazon Digital Services LLC, 2013), Kindle.

9. Wayne A. Grudem, *Systematic Theology: An Introduction to Biblical Doctrine* (Downers Grove, IL: InterVarsity Press, 2004), 533–534.

10. Robert G. Hoeber, *Concordia Self-Study Bible*, electronic ed. (St. Louis, MO: Concordia Publishing House, 1997), Luke 22:44.

11. Elton Trueblood, *The Humor of Christ* (New York: Harper & Row, 1964), 10.

12. Trueblood, *The Humor of Christ*, 15.

13. Leland Ryken, James C. Wilhoit, and Tremper Longman III, eds., *Dictionary of Biblical Imagery*, s.v. "Jesus as Humorist," 410.

14. Trueblood, *The Humor of Christ*, 127.

15. Ryken, Wilhoit, and Longman, *Dictionary of Biblical Imagery*, s.v. "Humor—Jesus as Humorist," 410.

16. Stephen Voorwinde, *Jesus' Emotions in the Gospels* (London; New York: T&T Clark, 2011), 2.

17. Voorwinde, *Jesus' Emotions in the Gospels*, 2.

18. Voorwinde, *Jesus' Emotions in the Gospels*, 9.

19. Voorwinde, *Jesus' Emotions in the Gospels*, 59.

20. Voorwinde, *Jesus' Emotions in the Gospels*, 119; In the Greek text, according to the Gramcord program, Luke has 19,496 words, Matthew 18,363, John 15,675, and Mark 11,313. (The Gramcord Grammatical Concordance System is based on the 26th edition of

the *Nestle-Aland Novum Testamentum Graece* [Stuttgart: Deutsche Bibelgesellschaft, 1979]).

21. Voorwinde, *Jesus' Emotions in the Gospels*, 119

22. Luke has eighty-six such references, John seventy-seven, Mark fifty-one, and Matthew forty-seven.

23. Voorwinde, *Jesus' Emotions in the Gospels*, 151.

24. Leon Morris, *Luke* (Downers Grove, IL: InterVarsity Press, 1988), 204–205.

25. A. T. Robertson, *Word Pictures in the New Testament* (Nashville, TN: Broadman Press, 1933).

26. Oswald Chambers, *Biblical Ethics* (Hants UK: Marshall, Morgan & Scott, 1947).

27. Chambers, *Biblical Ethics*.

28. John Piper, *What Jesus Demands From the World* (Wheaton, IL: Crossway Books, 2006), 52–53.

CHAPTER 7
REDEEM YOUR RELATIONSHIPS

1. Les and Leslie Parrott, *Real Relationships* (Grand Rapids, MI: Zondervan, 2011).

2. Parrott, *Real Relationships*.

CHAPTER 9
BE PERFECTED THROUGH SUFFERING

1. Karen H. Jobes, *1 Peter* (Grand Rapids, MI: Baker Academic, 2005), 287–288.

2. Martin Emmrich, "'Amtscharisma': Through the Eternal Spirit (Hebrews 9:14)," ed. Craig A. Evans, *Bulletin for Biblical Research* 12, no. 1 (2002): 17–18.

3. "The Old Rugged Cross," by George Bennard, 1912. Public domain.

4. Alison Gee, "Crucifixion From Ancient Rome to Modern Syria," BBC, May 8, 2014, http://www.bbc.com/news/magazine-27245852.

5. Charles R. Swindoll, *Insights on John* (Grand Rapids, MI: Zondervan, 2010), 250.

CHAPTER 10
SUFFERING IS A SCHOOL WE ALL ATTEND

1. Raymond Brown, *The Message of Hebrews* (Downers Grove, IL: InterVarsity Press, 1988), 61–62.

CHAPTER 12
SEVEN REASONS TO FORGIVE

1. "What Is the Apostles' Creed?," BGEA.

2. "The Westminster Shorter Catechism," The Westminster Presbyterian, accessed June 8, 2018, http://www.westminsterconfession.org /confessional-standards/the-westminster-shorter-catechism.php.

3. Fred Luskin, *Forgive for Good: A Proven Prescription for Health and Happiness* (New York: HarperCollins Publishers Inc., 2002), xvi.

4. Luskin, *Forgive for Good*, 10–11.

5. Luskin, *Forgive for Good*, xv.

CHAPTER 13
THE SPIRIT, NOT THE FLESH

1. St. Augustine, *Homilies on the Gospel of John, Homilies on the First Epistle of John, and Soliloquies, The Nicene and Post-Nicene Fathers* (American repr. of the Edinburgh edn.; Grand Rapids, MI: 1956), first series, vol. VII; John Calvin, *The Gospel According to Saint John,* trans. T. H. L. Parker (Grand Rapids, MI: Eerdmans,1959, 1961).

2. Leon Morris, *The Gospel According to John* (Grand Rapids, MI: Wm. B. Eerdmans Publishing Company, 1995), 218.

A FREE GIFT FOR YOU

Our world is really distracted. There are lots of books you can choose, yet you chose to read mine. Not only did you choose to read it, but you made it all the way through, which I really appreciate.

As my way of saying thank you for choosing to read this book, I am offering you a gift:

- **SPIRIT-FILLED LIFE OF JESUS—ORIGINAL AUDIO FROM THE GOSPEL COALITION**

- **EXTENDED, FORTY-FIVE-MINUTE DISCUSSION ON THE KEY CONCEPTS FOUND IN THIS BOOK**

- **OVER ONE HUNDRED HOURS OF ALL MY SERMONS ON LUKE, WHICH WERE MY PRIMARY INSPIRATION FOR THIS BOOK**

TO CLAIM THIS FREE GIFT, PLEASE GO TO
SPIRITFILLEDJESUS.COM/GIFT

THANKS AGAIN, AND GOD BLESS YOU.

Pastor Mark

Mark Driscoll Ministries

CHARISMA
HOUSE

🐦 @PastorMark   f @PastorMark

📷 @markdriscoll